D1554937

Those Were
The Days

Those Were The Days

An unofficial history of The Beatles Apple organization 1967-2002

By Stefan Granados

This edition published in Great Britain
in 2002 by Cherry Red Books Ltd.,
Unit 17, 1st Floor, Elysium Gate West,
126–128 New King's Road,
London SW6 4LZ

Information on Beatles figures used on
front cover: www.mcfarlane.com or
www.adlerandco.com

Typeset by Axis Europe Plc.
Printed and bound in Great Britain by
Biddles Ltd., Guildford and King's Lynn.
Cover Design by Jim Phelan at Wolf Graphics Tel: 020 8299 2342

ISBN 1–901447–12–X

Contents

Introduction

Just a few minutes walk from London's bustling Piccadilly Circus lies Savile Row, a quiet street of handsome townhouses that were once home to many of England's finest tailors. While several high-end clothiers are still open for business, there is usually little activity on the street, except for the small groups of people who regularly gather in front of number 3, to gaze up at the roof and take pictures on the steps of what appears to be nothing more than a typical Georgian building.

Most of the bankers and young marketing executives who frequent the remaining Savile Row tailors have no idea why scruffy teenagers and greying, middle-aged vacationers take such an interest in the offices of the Building Society of Great Britain. Older patrons and the tailors who have worked there since the sixties, however, can remember a time when busloads of tourists regularly pulled up in front of 3 Savile Row to take photos of the Hare Krishna devotees and long-haired young men who swarmed in and out of the building at all hours of the day and night.

It has been decades since young girls clad in mini-skirts huddled at the end of the stairs of 3 Savile Row, in all sorts of weather, straining to hear the muffled sounds of guitars and drums filtering out of the basement while waiting for a chance to see an outlandishly dressed 28 year-old Paul McCartney come breezing out of the front door and disappear around the corner up Vigo Street. There is indeed little left to link the unassuming building to its past life as the home of The Beatles' Apple organization – the company that the group established in 1967 to manage their business affairs and to act as a record company and music publisher – yet 3 Savile Row continues to attract a surprisingly large number of Beatles fans and tourists from around the world, curious to see if they can discern the slightest spark of magic in the group's old London haunt of the sixties.

Those Were The Days

Today, most visitors to 3 Savile Row leave with little more than a photo and perhaps an interesting story to tell the relations back home. But others – if they open up their hearts and think back to the time when the music of The Beatles encapsulated the dreams and ideals of an entire generation – can imagine how it was when 3 Savile Road was at the very heart of swinging London, where four young musicians from Liverpool plotted to revolutionize the entertainment industry from their comfortable office on the second floor of the Apple building.

More than twenty-five years after the closure of the original London office, Apple still captures the imagination of many who fall under the powerful spell of The Beatles' music. Then, as now, Apple was generally regarded as a failure, or as an idealist sixties experiment that went horribly wrong. At best, Apple is remembered – if it is remembered at all – as the ill-fated venture that The Beatles had hoped would be a corporate manifestation of sixties youth culture. But while the band, or certainly some members and some of their associates, may have indeed flirted with such ideas for a brief moment in time, Apple was initially intended to be little more than a business office and tax shelter for the group. The fact that Apple developed into something much more colourful than originally intended only adds to its mystique and appeal.

From its inception in early 1967, Apple evolved quickly and had grown to more than sixty employees by mid-1968. Although the rapid speed at which Apple developed certainly played a part in the company's ultimate undoing, The Beatles' plans for Apple were remarkably ambitious and showed just how quickly the group could transform their whims into action. In the eight years that Apple functioned as a record label – launching the careers of stars like Mary Hopkin, James Taylor, Badfinger, Billy Preston and Hot Chocolate – Apple blossomed, withered and died, much like the free-spirited sixties pop culture that had sparked its conception. From the jubilant launch in 1968, to the subdued, almost indifferent closing of the record division in 1975, Apple's ultimate collapse symbolized not only the end of the myth of The Beatles, but also the dissolution of the ideals, forward-thinking attitudes and positive energy of an entire era.

Contrary to what many Beatles fans and pop culture aficionados may think, Apple continues to exist to this day – tucked away on a quiet side street in the heart of London. In fact, Apple never really went away. Apple has long been regarded as The Beatles' great failure; yet it was far from a failure, and it continues to make millions of pounds a year on behalf of The Beatles. Though Apple's hallways are no longer filled with excited young musicians and eager young record executives, there are always several Beatles-related projects to keep Apple's small staff busy. In many ways, Apple has finally evolved into the streamlined business office that the four Beatles had envisaged when they set up the company all those years ago.

The story of Apple is a fascinating chapter of The Beatles' history, but it is a story that is by no means simply limited to The Beatles. Between 1968 and 1970, Apple was a leading UK independent record label (actually, quasi-independent, given that Apple was distributed by EMI) and the company operated much like any other of the many long-defunct (but fondly remembered) labels such as Pye, Major Minor, Track, Strike, Page One and SNB. The mid to late sixties were a time when seven inch singles ruled the music scene and a pop group could literally walk in off the street with a primitive, home-made demo recording of a song and emerge a few hours later with a record deal. It was also an era when an independent label could get a record played on the BBC on a Friday afternoon and have a national hit by the following week. Apart from the fact that Apple was owned by the most successful pop group of the sixties, it was not all that different from other independent labels of the era, and the story of Apple captures much of that special time in English pop music.

About this book

The history of Apple was perhaps the last remaining untold Beatles story. Although former Apple staff members Derek Taylor, Richard DiLello and Peter Brown each wrote superb books about their experiences at Apple, there has never been a book that looked at Apple in its entirety – from its 1967 inception to its current incarnation. Other books, such as Peter McCabe and Robert Schoenfeld's fascinating *Apple To The Core* dealt with only a small part of the Apple story. This book attempts to chronicle the Apple story through the words of the musicians, recording engineers and business people who served The Beatles as Apple employees.

Creating the definitive Apple chronicle some thirty years after the fact inevitably posed significant difficulties. Several key players in the Apple story – including John Lennon, George Harrison, Bernard Brown, Derek Taylor, Pete Ham and Tom Evans of Badfinger, Mal Evans, Ron Kass, George Alexander of Grapefruit, Rick Frank of

Elephant's Memory, and others – have died. While many other former Apple artists and staff are thankfully still alive and well and graciously agreed to be interviewed for this book, the passage of thirty years has, not surprisingly, dulled the memories of some of the participants.

So, while most of the individuals interviewed for this book can still vividly recall many of the colourful events that distinguished their respective associations with Apple, exact dates and certain details of these events may have slipped beyond the grasp of memory. I have strived to collect as much new information from interviewees as possible for this book. However, there were occasions when quotes from previously published interviews given by these people during the sixties and seventies were far more detailed and evocative of the era than the quotes taken from the recent (1996-2001) interviews that I conducted. In such cases, I often elected to use the previously printed material, rather than new quotes that did not do justice to the Apple story.

A special note of caution must also be made about the financial figures quoted in this book. Given that Apple is a privately owned company, it is not – nor has it ever been – required to publicly disclose any of its financial records. Compounding the problem of the lack of available published financial records are differences in exchange rates over the past three decades which make it hard (if not impossible) to convert accurately sales figures and royalty rates from the sixties into current pounds or dollars. Because of these factors, financial details are not likely to be exact figures and they are given for illustrative purposes only.

Ultimately, it is only The Beatles' accountants who know exactly how much Apple paid for the Savile Row building, or how much Apple artist Doris Troy was given as a weekly wage. And given the state of Apple's bookkeeping in the sixties, it is questionable if even they would be able to arrive accurately at such figures. The numbers quoted in this book were typically arrived at through comparing several different reliable sources, and in general appear to be reasonable estimates that are probably quite close to the actual amounts.

Finally, Apple itself was a potential obstacle to the creation and completion of this book. After being warned by many music journalists, music industry colleagues and almost every person interviewed for the book to stay clear of Apple, lest they try to stop the project with threatened litigation or a "gag order" on former employees and artists, I took the advice offered, and therefore declined to extend an interview request to Neil Aspinall or to the surviving Beatles. If Neil Aspinall or Paul McCartney or Ringo Starr are offended by not being invited to contribute to this work, I would offer my sincere apologies and ask them to contact the publisher so they can contribute to the next edition.

Finally, in the interest of avoiding libel suits (and sullying the memories of people who are no longer around to defend themselves) I have intentionally left out incidents that I considered to be dubious, mean-spirited or simply not relevant to the central Apple story. I have also attempted to keep my editorial voice and interpretation of events to a minimum, preferring to rely on the testament of those involved to tell the story of Apple.

This book hopefully reflects the Apple that was known by its former employees and by the artists who made the music that has endured for so many years. That is the spirit in which this book was written.

Those Were The Days

1
1967 - The Nems Years

Life in post-war England was relatively simple back in 1962. For aspiring professional entertainers like The Beatles – a four-man rock and roll band from Liverpool – a career in music promised little more than weekly engagements at local dances and youth clubs, and if they were lucky, perhaps a chance to cut a record that might get one or two spins on Radio Luxembourg or the BBC. Of course, fate held something quite different in store for The Beatles. Six months after their debut single *Love Me Do* became a minor hit, The Beatles sparked off a tidal wave of fan hysteria the intensity of which had never before been seen in popular music. During the halcyon days of 1963 and 1964, Beatlemania swept unchecked across the world. Show business, popular music and the world itself were changed forever.

Guiding The Beatles throughout the turbulent Beatlemania era was their manager, Brian Epstein. From 1962 to 1967, The Beatles were managed exclusively by Epstein and his artist management firm, Nems Ltd – an organization that Epstein himself had set up shortly after meeting The Beatles in 1962. Coming from an affluent Liverpool family, the mild-mannered Epstein was quite unlike the typical "pop" managers of the era. Prior to becoming the group's manager, Epstein's music industry experience had been limited to running the record department of his parents' Liverpool department store. But given that he was one of the few people in Liverpool to have actually conducted business with the London-based record companies, Epstein's decision to venture into artist management was not as far-fetched as it might have seemed at the outset. The Beatles were certainly impressed with Epstein's modest music industry connections and with his genuine enthusiasm for the band, so they signed a five-year management contract with him in January 1962. From that point onwards, all of the money generated by The Beatles was funnelled directly through Nems. In exchange, the four Beatles were each given a salary and had their living expenses paid by the company.

Initially, Epstein's management duties focused on securing a record contract for the group, polishing their professional presentation and overseeing the group's live bookings. But once the full force of Beatlemania took hold in 1963, The Beatles became increasingly reliant on Epstein and Nems to take care of almost every aspect of their personal and professional lives.

Receiving a 25% share of The Beatles' gross income, Epstein was certainly very well compensated for his efforts. But Epstein served the band with a remarkable sense of care and devotion and it was obvious that he regarded The Beatles as much more than just a once-in-a-life-time business opportunity. In the early days of Beatlemania, Epstein's name was synonymous with The Beatles. Due in large part to the remarkable success of the group, Epstein was able to build Nems into a high-powered management company that would become the dominant force behind the Liverpool music scene.

Having seen what Epstein had done for The Beatles, almost all of the performers in Liverpool rushed to align themselves with Nems. From 1963 onwards, Nems Enterprises managed the careers of artists such as Cilla Black, Gerry and The Pacemakers, The Fourmost and Billy J. Kramer, as well as several lesser-known Liverpool groups.

Under Epstein's skilful direction, Nems developed a diverse and initially highly successful client roster, but it was clear to all of the other Nems artists that The Beatles were Epstein's one true passion. Whether charged with finding a house for one of The Beatles, negotiating television appearances or quietly settling such personal matters as threatened paternity suits, Epstein handled his duties in an efficient, dignified manner and all four Beatles considered him to be not only a manager, but a friend. When it came to The Beatles, no matter was too trivial to be given Epstein's full attention.

In retrospect, Epstein's only real professional shortcoming was his marked lack of business acumen. Still, while much of The Beatles' success can, and should, be attributed to their immense talent, it was Epstein's music industry contacts and his careful handling of the group's image and presentation that transformed The Beatles from a rough, leather-clad rock and roll band from "up North" into a polished, international show business phenomenon.

Today, Epstein's significant contributions to launching The Beatles' career are often overshadowed by the embarrassingly poor business deals that he negotiated on behalf of the group. The original recording agreement Epstein signed with EMI in 1962 was a one-year contract that gave EMI the option of extending The Beatles' contract for three successive years. In return, the band would get one penny of recording royalties for each single sold and precious little more for each album sold in the UK. For any Beatles recordings licensed to record companies outside of the UK, the group would receive only half of the UK royalty rate. Epstein would somewhat rectify matters when it was time to renegotiate The Beatles' EMI contract in January 1967. In exchange for re-signing to EMI until 1976, The Beatles would receive 10% of the wholesale price of a British album and 17.5% of the wholesale price of each album sold in America.

2

1967 - The Nems Years

In Epstein's defence, the deals he negotiated for the group were fairly common by music industry standards in 1962. He would fare far worse with the non-music deals that he set up for the group. Epstein's most celebrated fiasco was the 10% royalty rate he negotiated for the American rights to manufacture and sell such seemingly trivial Beatles merchandise as wigs, shampoo, trading cards and the countless other items that flooded into American discount stores during 1964 and 1965. When Epstein entered into these deals in 1964, the 30 year-old ex-furniture and record salesman from Liverpool was no match for the quick-talking New York City businessmen who appeared to be offering him thousands of dollars in exchange for the simple use of The Beatles' name on what he perceived to be insignificant teen-oriented products. Due to the limited scope of his business experience, Epstein practically gave away the rights to The Beatles' American merchandising – a move that would ultimately cost The Beatles millions of dollars of revenue.

To be fair to Epstein, few music industry professionals at that time – let alone a music industry novice like Epstein – ever imagined just how much money music merchandising could generate. To Epstein, any revenue from the sale of such ancillary "Beatles products" was just "found money" to supplement The Beatles' live and recording income.

Never considered to be a great negotiator, Epstein's true strengths were his well-developed organizational abilities, his unflinching honesty and his conservative, reliable stewardship of The Beatles' finances. With Epstein overseeing the group's affairs, the four Beatles enjoyed a relatively carefree existence when it came to financial matters. If they wanted any item – be it a car, a house, or new clothes – they simply charged it to Nems and the bill would be paid with no questions asked. With Nems so thoroughly involved with managing their finances, the four Beatles made very few personal investments during the peak years of Beatlemania. The investment activities of the individual Beatles were limited to Ringo Starr's interest in a high-end construction company and Paul McCartney's decision (unbeknownst to the other three Beatles) to buy additional shares in Northern Songs, the music publishing company that held the rights to The Beatles' songs. In general, The Beatles seemed content to simply let Nems take care of business.

In addition to the money earned from live performances and record and music publishing royalties, The Beatles had several other sources of revenue prior to 1967. Their most significant collective investment was Subafilms, the Nems-run film company that controlled the group's share of The Beatles' film projects, responsible for producing Beatles promotional films (in the days before video) for television.

As well as owning Subafilms, all four Beatles held shares in Northern Songs Music Publishing, the company that held the publishing rights to The Beatles' songs. Although Northern Songs founder Dick James retained a majority interest in the company, The Beatles and Nems each held significant portions of Northern Songs. In addition to their Northern Songs stock, Lennon and McCartney were also co-owners of a company formed on 4 February 1965 named Maclen Music Ltd. Theoretically, Maclen licensed the rights to publish Lennon and McCartney songs to Dick James' Northern Songs with Maclen collecting 50% of the publishing royalties due to Lennon and McCartney from Northern Songs. The remaining 50% of the publishing revenue went to Northern Songs.

Dick James had been unusually fair to The Beatles (by industry standards of the day) when he set up Northern Songs in February 1963. Recommended to Brian Epstein by Beatles producer George Martin, James had a tremendous amount of respect for The Beatles and their music. Though The Beatles were little more than a talented group with one minor hit (*Love Me Do*) to their credit when James first met them in early 1963, James, a failed pop singer and then struggling music publisher, knew that the songs of Lennon and McCartney had the potential to become major hits.

In exchange for the publishing rights to The Beatles' second single, *Please Please Me*, James used his music industry connections to secure The Beatles a coveted spot on the BBC television programme *Thank Your Lucky Stars*. Impressed by his ability to get The Beatles on television, Epstein decided that The Beatles would sign with Dick James Music.

In a highly unusual move in an era in which songwriters would often sign away their songwriting royalties for an advance of twenty pounds or less, James set up a subsidiary company, Northern Songs, for the sole purpose of publishing the songs of Lennon and McCartney. As part of the deal James offered the group, the two songwriting Beatles and Nems were given shares in Northern Songs that represented almost 50% of the company's worth. By 1967, Northern Songs had been re-structured and had gone public, so in addition to having received significant cash payments between 1964 and 1966 for a portion of their equity in the company, Lennon and McCartney each still owned roughly 15% of Northern Songs' stock. George Harrison and Ringo Starr owned 1.6 % of Northern Songs stock between them.

But outside of investments like Subafilms and Northern Songs, all four Beatles seemed to be perfectly willing to let their royalties pile up in their Nems account and draw a weekly wage. It would not be until the mid-sixties that The Beatles, George Harrison and Paul McCartney in particular, began taking an increased interest in the group's business affairs.

In the innocent era during which The Beatles had emerged, it was generally accepted that artists were responsible for creating the music and that professional managers took care of business. Out of all of the English groups who sold millions of records during the "British Invasion" only Dave Clark of the Dave Clark Five had the foresight, and skill, to take full control of his group's business affairs. (In addition to negotiating a royalty rate with EMI that far exceeded that of The Beatles, Clark retained the rights to all of his band's master tapes and music publishing. He would also later buy the rights to the celebrated British pop music television show *Ready Steady Go*, giving him exclusive rights to live TV performances by The Beatles and almost every other top band of the mid-sixties.)

Even when Harrison and McCartney started to take a greater interest in the group's financial affairs, there was actually very little that one or even two Beatles could do to influence matters. Since the earliest days of the group, the band made all of their decisions by consensus. Given the success of this democratic system, each of the four Beatles were somewhat reticent to appear too domineering in the eyes of the others. In the interest of preserving harmony within the group, it was often simply easier to let Epstein or another outsider take care of business matters.

Compared to many of their contemporaries, The Beatles were unusually democratic for a pop group. The way they conducted their business was largely governed by the strong personal ties between the four members of the band. Having been bound together through the non-stop recording and touring schedule that they maintained for close to five years, by 1967 The Beatles enjoyed a near family-like relationship and were quite accustomed to doing almost everything together.

Each Beatle explored individual pursuits after the group ceased touring in 1966. These included such non-Beatles projects as John Lennon's acting role in the film *How I Won The War* and Paul McCartney composing the music for the film *The Family Way*. However, these projects were not regarded as serious efforts to establish careers outside of the group and none of the side projects seemed to detract from the band's intense camaraderie. When the group settled back into Abbey Road Studios in late 1966 to begin work on "Sgt. Pepper" they were still an incredibly tight-knit unit. In early 1967, the group even looked into buying a Greek island where they could live

5

and work together. They went as far as to visit Greece and select a remote Greek island to purchase before they characteristically lost interest and dropped the whole project.

Curiously, while each Beatle had at one time or another stated that The Beatles as a group would not go on for ever, none of them appeared to envisage the possibility that there could ever come a time when they would no longer be on speaking terms. It was in this spirit that they entered into their next venture, the jointly owned business that would become Apple.

In late 1966, The Beatles and their financial advisors had started to explore options for setting up a new Beatles corporation that would consolidate the groups' business affairs and enable them to lessen the impact of the notoriously harsh tax system that existed in Britain at that time. (When Apple was formed, the group's income was being taxed at a rate of around 90%.) Additionally, the band had been informed by its tax advisors that they would have to collectively pay three million pounds in tax unless they offset their tax liability by investing in a business. It is important to note that Apple was not set up to replace Epstein and Nems. It was created as a tax shelter to complement, rather than replace, the existing business structure.

The first step towards creating this new business structure was to form a new partnership called Beatles and Co. in April 1967. To all intents and purposes, Beatles and Co. was an updated version of The Beatles' original partnership, Beatles Ltd. Under the new arrangement, however, each Beatle would own 5% of Beatles and Co. and a new corporation owned collectively by the four Beatles (which would soon be known as Apple) would be given control of the remaining 80% of Beatles and Co. With the exception of individual songwriting royalties, which would still be paid directly to the writer or writers of a particular song, all of the money earned by The Beatles as a group would go directly to Beatles and Co. and would thus be taxed at a far lower corporate tax rate.

The Beatles appeared to be so anxious to begin reaping the tax rewards offered by this plan that they entered into their new partnership agreement having given little thought to the possible future implications of their actions. John Lennon – who was taking copious amounts of LSD throughout the period that Apple was being set up – would later claim that he was so high during this time of his life that he didn't remember signing any new partnership agreement at all.

Peter Brown, a fellow Liverpudlian who had worked for The Beatles and Nems since 1962, explains the origins of Apple: "When Apple was formed, which was before Brian died... it wasn't called

Apple, but the structure of the buyout was there. The reason The Beatles sold 80% of themselves to this entity, which would become Apple, and to change Beatles Ltd. to Beatles and Co. was to save taxes. The reason that the 80% sale was triggered was because of the accumulated royalties at EMI that they were due to receive and the fact that if the royalties had been paid to them as individuals, it would have been taxed at 85% or something like that. So this structure was set up by Clive Epstein [Brian Epstein's brother] as a tax structure. At one point it was suggested that this be a real estate company: that was the original idea for lack of anything else. They couldn't figure out what to do with all this capital. All of this was set up while Brian was alive. After Brian died, my recollection is that they then decided to take this entity and create what they did, which was Apple."

It was hardly coincidental that the formation of Apple coincided with a period of marked turmoil within the Nems organization. Due in part to Epstein's personal problems that sprung from his increasingly complex gay lifestyle and escalating drug use, there were times when Epstein seemed to be losing control of Nems. To Epstein's dismay, by 1967 The Beatles had also become aware of how Nems' handling of the band's American merchandising had cost the group millions of dollars of income. The Beatles also resented the fact that many lesser groups had secured far more lucrative record contracts than Epstein had secured for The Beatles.

Yet despite their displeasure with the deals that Epstein had negotiated and the deteriorating situation at Nems, The Beatles never publicly announced any intention to leave Epstein when his management contract expired in August 1967. None of the band's associates from that time believe that they would have ever left Epstein and Nems. Rather than take out their financial frustrations directly on Epstein, the group seemed to simply want to preserve the considerable sums of money that they were earning.

The new corporation would be the first step in preserving some of their hard-earned income. By mid-1967, The Beatles had established a basic corporate structure and now needed to find a business in which to invest their capital if they were going to receive any tax benefit. Given that they were among the best-known, most-respected young multi-millionaires in the world, The Beatles felt the need to invest in a business that would simultaneously complement their image and provide a good measure of financial security.

Given such an ambiguous mandate, The Beatles were decidedly unsure about what form Apple should take. By mid-year, Apple had evolved into little more than a handful of sketchy ideas and what was essentially a holding company for The Beatles partnership. But as 1967 wore on and The Beatles moved into one of the most adventurous stages of their development (both personally and musically) the group began to envisage Apple as becoming something much more ambitious than a simple tax shelter.

A good deal of the energy and enthusiasm that fuelled Apple's early development was drawn directly from the flowering youth culture and the exciting art and music scenes that had enveloped London towards the end of 1966. By the summer of 1967 – the much heralded "Summer of Love" – London (along with San Francisco) found itself at the epicentre of a burgeoning youth movement.

As the warm summer weather and increasingly carefree social climate infused the youth of Britain with a wonderful sense of energy and optimism, the BBC and pirate radio stations made sure that the entire nation was awash with the remarkable sounds of The Beatles' "Sgt. Pepper" album and of new records by such colourfully named groups as The Pink Floyd and The Jimi Hendrix Experience. The Beatles were quite taken with swinging London and it was not unusual to find one or more Beatles checking out "happenings" or performances by one of the many new bands.

It was not only music that was capturing the imagination of England's youth and the interest of the world's media. In almost every corner of London, new boutiques, art galleries and specialist bookshops were springing up and the best and the brightest young minds in England were attempting to reshape a few select London neighbourhoods in their own image. Comprising the first generation of English youth who were too young to feel the full impact of the Second World War, these fashionable teenagers and twenty-somethings felt free to pursue their interest in music, art and leisure and they did so with great zest. The introduction of drugs to the scene only served to bolster the generally giddy spirit of the time.

Poised at the absolute centre of all this activity was Paul McCartney. With his upmarket St. Johns Wood home in London, a beautiful sophisticated actress girlfriend, stylish clothes and immense musical talent, McCartney was among the best-known exponents of swinging London.

While the other three Beatles languished in the outskirts of London with their wives and young children, McCartney would attend beat poetry readings, check out the new bands, go to the theatre, listen to avant-garde composers such as Karl Stockhausen and even make experimental films. McCartney was fully consumed by the wave of creativity that had swept over London and he genuinely felt that The

Beatles could – and should – use their wealth and influence to help nurture this exciting new scene.

One of the early ideas for The Beatles' new corporation was to set up a chain of record shops across England, the idea being that The Beatles would be able to amass sizeable property holdings under the pretext of purchasing shop space. It was an interesting idea, but it never got beyond the initial planning stages. With little progress having been made on establishing some sort of property-driven company, The Beatles – at the urging of Paul McCartney – decided that their first commercial venture would be a music publishing company.

Given the low start-up costs and The Beatles' collective expertise in songwriting, establishing a music publishing company was certainly a logical option to pursue. As the driving force behind the formation of a "Beatles company" it was McCartney who finally came up with an ideal name for the company – "Apple". As long-serving Apple Managing Director Neil Aspinall recalled in an Apple press handout: "Paul came up with the idea of calling it Apple, which he got from René Magritte. I don't know if he was a Belgian or Dutch artist... he drew a lot of green apples or painted a lot of green apples [the painting in question was Magritte's *Le Jeu de Mourre*]. I know Paul bought some of his paintings in 1966 or early 1967. I think that's where Paul got the idea for the name from." Even though it was initially not clear what form Apple would ultimately take, when the "Sgt. Pepper" album was released in June 1967, The Beatles had already mysteriously thanked "The Apple" on the back cover of the album.

Whatever tentative plans The Beatles may have had for Apple that summer, however, were certainly altered when Brian Epstein was found dead in his London home on Sunday 27 August 1967. Only 32 years old at the time of his death, Epstein had apparently accidentally overdosed on prescription sleeping pills. The Beatles, who were all in Bangor, Wales attending a lecture on transcendental meditation, were naturally devastated by the news. When reached in Bangor, The Beatles appeared before the news cameras to offer a statement, looking shocked and confused. John Lennon would later admit that it was at that moment that he first felt that The Beatles were finished.

Epstein's death was a pivotal event in the development of Apple. Despite The Beatles' loyalty to Nems and the Epstein family, now that Brian Epstein was no longer running the company, it was soon apparent that The Beatles' relationship with Nems would change. In the weeks following Epstein's death, The Beatles appeared willing to remain with Nems, yet they also indicated that they were now looking to gain more direct control of their personal business.

One of the most contentious issues between The Beatles and Nems after Epstein died arose when they learned that a brash Australian named Robert Stigwood was angling to take control of Nems. It later transpired that Epstein – unbeknownst to The Beatles – had indeed made plans to sell Nems to Stigwood. Prior to Epstein's death, The Beatles had assumed that Stigwood was simply another Nems employee and they were most annoyed that Stigwood felt that he could simply pick up where Epstein left off as manager of The Beatles.

Epstein had made Stigwood co-managing director of Nems in January 1967, allegedly with the intention of later starting a new management company for The Beatles and Cilla Black, and then selling the remaining Nems assets to Stigwood. However, within months of Stigwood joining Nems, considerable tension had developed between Epstein and Stigwood. Although Stigwood was responsible for bringing the Bee Gees and Cream to Nems, Epstein and Stigwood apparently had very different opinions as to how Nems should be run. Epstein was reportedly very concerned by Stigwood's excessive spending and by the summer of 1967 he was said to be trying to find a way to ease Stigwood out of Nems.

The problem was that Epstein had extended an offer to Stigwood and Stigwood's business partner, David Shaw, which would allow them to purchase a controlling interest in Nems for £500,000. The standing offer was valid until September 1967, and when Epstein unexpectedly died in August, Stigwood and Shaw announced their intention to exercise their option. Stigwood's plans for acquiring Nems were thwarted only after The Beatles, who had previously been unaware of Epstein's plan to sell Nems to Stigwood, informed Stigwood that there was absolutely no way that they would accept him as their manager.

Stigwood, who had little interest in Nems if it did not include The Beatles, abandoned his plans to purchase the company. Instead, he left Nems altogether, taking with him the Bee Gees and Cream and starting his own company, RSO.

With Stigwood out of the picture, Brian Epstein's younger brother Clive assumed control of Nems. For several months after Epstein died, The Beatles' relationship with Nems changed very little. Despite Brian Epstein's death, Nems would continue to oversee The Beatles' day-to-day affairs. In fact, it seems that The Beatles even contemplated taking a more active role in Nems and using the company as an outlet for discovering and nurturing new artists, which is exactly what they eventually did with Apple.

Ringo Starr admitted in a 1970 interview with *Melody Maker*:

"We tried to form Apple with Clive Epstein but he wouldn't have it... he didn't believe in us I suppose... he didn't think we could do it. He thought we were four wild men and we were going to spend all his money and make him broke. But that was the original idea of Apple – to form it with Nems... we thought now Brian's gone, let's really amalgamate and get this thing going, let's make records and get people on our label and things like that. So we formed Apple and they formed Nems, which is doing exactly the same thing as we [Apple] are doing. It was a family tie and we thought it would be a good idea to keep it in, and then we saw how the land lay and we tried to get out."

Peter Brown, the Nems employee who inherited the lion's share of the responsibility for looking after The Beatles after Epstein's death, does not think that the idea of The Beatles using Nems to discover and develop talent was a likely proposition. "I don't remember that and I'm sure that if that was so I would remember because there wouldn't have been anything like that being discussed without me knowing," recalls Brown, adding, "It would have been so foreign to Clive Epstein that I don't think that it would have been workable."

Whatever the situation may have been, The Beatles appeared to be willing to stick with Nems for the time being. At the same time, they were also anxious to start handling some of their own business and creative affairs. Only weeks after Epstein's death, the first Apple project was already well under way. Apple's first venture would be the production of a new Beatles movie called *Magical Mystery Tour* which was filmed and edited in various English locations from September to November 1967. Cooked up by Paul McCartney on a long flight back from America, *Magical Mystery Tour* was intended to be a spontaneous, hip, art movie that would capture the free-spirited vibe of the summer of 1967.

Since Apple had yet to develop any formal staff structure, Beatles road manager Neil Aspinall and Paul McCartney assumed most of the responsibility for coordinating the various aspects of the film's production. The resulting chaos – which ranged from the "Magical Mystery Tour" bus and film crew venturing down small roads in rural England only to encounter a bridge that was too low for the bus to pass under, to not having enough hotel rooms for the entire cast – surely must have made The Beatles miss the brisk efficiency of the Nems organization.

For the first few months of Apple's existence, it did not even have an office – most Apple business was conducted from the Nems building. It was not until the autumn of 1967 that Apple finally opened a London office. Since The Beatles already owned a four-storey building at 94 Baker Street, that had been purchased as an investment property by their accountants, they decided that Baker Street was as good a location as any for Apple. They set up an office for Apple Music Publishing in the Baker Street building in September.

Excited by the novelty of being businessmen and anticipating Apple to develop further business interests, The Beatles appointed their road manager, Neil Aspinall, to be Managing Director of the budding Apple organization. Aspinall recalled in an interview with *Mojo*, "A lot of people were nominated or put themselves forward to run it... but there didn't seem to be any unanimous choice. So I said to them, foolishly I guess, 'Look, I'll do it until you find somebody that you want to do it.'"

Fortunately for The Beatles, Aspinall was not a typical beat group road manager. He was generally qualified to do far more than book hotels, load vans and set up musical instruments on a stage. Prior to becoming a full-time Beatles employee in 1962, Aspinall had contemplated a business career and had been close to completing a correspondence degree in accounting before his work with The Beatles took him away from his studies. But it was Aspinall's loyalty to The Beatles, rather than his innate business sense, that made him the natural choice to be Managing Director of Apple. After Brian Epstein died in August 1967, Aspinall and fellow road manager Mal Evans were the only non-Beatles left in The Beatles' inner circle and the group placed a high premium on trust and loyalty. The individual Beatles had complete trust in Neil Aspinall and the surviving members continue to do so to this day.

Unlike Aspinall, loyal Beatles road manager Mal Evans would not fit as snugly into the Apple concept. Though he would ultimately be given a free hand to scout talent and dabble in record production for Apple, it was agreed that Evans would probably be best suited to remain as a road manager for The Beatles.

With Aspinall's time fully consumed by the combined tasks of setting up Apple Corps and looking after The Beatles, the responsibility of running Apple Music Publishing was given to Terry Doran, a fellow Liverpudlian and friend of the group who had been a business associate of Brian Epstein. Prior to being named head of Apple Music Publishing, the colourful Doran had run a car dealership that he co-owned with Epstein. Doran is the first to admit that his experience in auto sales was not particularly applicable to music publishing. However, to The Beatles of 1967, enthusiasm and a social familiarity were sometimes worth far more than practical experience in a given field. To assist Terry Doran at Apple Publishing, Carol Paddon and Dee

Meehan were hired as secretaries and Apple's first three employees were charged with setting up an office at 94 Baker Street.

Doran may have had absolutely no experience in music publishing, but he seemed to make the transition well. Even before Apple had officially opened for business, he had made contact with several promising songwriters. Prior to formally launching Apple Publishing, Apple – operating out of a small office shared with Radio Luxembourg in Curzon Street – had already signed publishing contracts for several one-off singles, including a single by a group called Sands. Sands were signed to Robert Stigwood's Reaction label, and the Apple-published B-side of their debut *Mrs. Gillespie's Refrigerator* was *Listen To The Sky* – now considered to be one of the great songs of the psychedelic era. Another early signing was a Liverpool band that Brian Epstein had re-named "Focal Point". The group had come to Apple's attention through a meeting with Paul McCartney, although it was only after Doran played the band's demo tape to John Lennon and Brian Epstein that the band were given a publishing contract with Apple. *Sycamore Sid*, the B-side of their 1968 debut single, *Love You Forever*, is also now regarded as a classic psychedelic recording.

The first songwriter Doran signed to a long-term contract with Apple Music Publishing was a young man from Scotland named George Alexander. Alexander's real name was Alex Young, and he was the eldest brother of a family that also included George Young of the Australian band, The Easybeats (the Young family had emigrated to Australia in the early sixties) and Malcolm and Angus Young, who would go on to form the rock group AC/DC in the seventies.

Shortly after signing to Apple, Alexander formed a group with three former members of the London-based band, Tony Rivers and the Castaways – a harmony pop band that was often likened to a British Beach Boys. Drummer Geoff Swettenham, his brother Peter and guitarist John Perry were anxious to perform more "substantial" music than they were making with Tony Rivers. Swettenham remembers that the group actually came together in a toilet: "John Perry bumped into Terry Doran at the Speakeasy Club one night and he was just talking to him as they stood next to each other in the loo and Terry mentioned that he wanted to get a band together for this guy he signed to Apple Publishing," recalls Swettenham. "John said he was trying to form a band. So Terry said, 'Great, we'll get together,' so we went over to Apple the next day and met George."

John Perry has a slightly different recollection of the events of that evening. Perry remembers how he had gone into town with one of his band mates from the Castaways. "One of the guys in the band – Kenny

Rowe – liked to go clubbing and we'd all hop into his mini and go into town," he recalls. "I was bumping into all these people and I met Terry Doran one night in the Speakeasy and we just got chatting about this and that. I didn't know who the hell he was. Then he bought me a drink and that turned into a conversation. We chatted at the bar and I said, 'Well, who do you work for?' and he said, 'Apple Publishing'. Well of course, at the time, Apple Publishing, no one knew what that was... it sounded like a fruit company or something. All the companies at the time sounded like firms of solicitors, like Campbell and Connelly and things like that.

"But I left it for a couple of months, as a matter of fact, and then I rang him up since nothing else was going on, so I thought, well let's go see this guy. I went up to see him and played him some of my songs. He didn't like my songs that much, but he said, 'Well, we got this writer, George Alexander,' and then he played me a few of his songs and I liked them. Then he was like, 'Well, we'd like George to join the band.' I had never met him or anything, but he had already done quite a lot of stuff in Germany, with this group, The Big Six. He was a bit further down the road than us... we were all youngsters, or teenagers, and he was clearly not a teenager. I never knew what his birthday was, but I got the impression that he was possibly even five to ten years older than us. He just seemed older. I was one of those ones with a young shiny face, George's face was lived in – let's put it that way. He didn't look like pop star material to me, but Terry seemed quite keen on it. From my perspective, that was possibly our first mistake and we should have kept him as a songwriter."

As Geoff Swettenham noted, a meeting was set up for Perry and the Swettenham brothers to meet George Alexander. The initial meeting was followed by several rehearsal sessions, after which the quartet decided that they would continue working together as a band.

Doran assumed the role of manager of Apple's first "discovery" and Apple even took it upon themselves to find a suitable name for the group. It was John Lennon who dubbed the quartet "Grapefruit" – a name that was shared by a small book of poetry he was reading, written by a Japanese-American artist named Yoko Ono.

Since Apple had yet to launch a record division, Grapefruit were signed to the EMI subsidiary, Stateside Records in the UK and to Equinox Records – a subsidiary of ABC Records – in America. After a few weeks of intensive rehearsals, Grapefruit were sent into a studio with American producer Terry Melcher to record their debut single. The first session was held on 24 November 1967. John Perry remembers: "Our very first session was in the basement of IBC studios in

Portland Place. Terry Melcher was in the box, we were all set up in this huge studio space, and on the right hand side the stairs came down into the studio. And on one side of the studio there was Paul McCartney and John Lennon and Mal Evans, just this plethora of pop legends hanging out and smoking Woodbines, expecting something from us!" Perry remembers that all four members of the group were extremely nervous to be performing for two of The Beatles, but they managed to get some music down on tape. The resulting single, *Dear Delilah*, was a fine, if somewhat ominous, piece of psychedelic-tinged pop that was quite accomplished for a group that had been together for less than a month.

Once Grapefruit's single was properly recorded and the group deemed ready to make their public debut, Apple Music Publishing used all of the promotional tools it could muster to help publicize *Dear Delilah*. Perhaps hoping to sell records through the power of association, Apple paid for press advertisements that showed a photo of Grapefruit seated at a table, surrounded by The Beatles, Rolling Stone Brian Jones, Donovan and Cilla Black. Given the catchy nature of the song and the generous publicity that the group received for being "The Beatles' first discovery", *Dear Delilah* became a minor hit, eventually reaching number 21 in the UK charts in February 1968.

While Grapefruit's debut generated a good deal of press attention and some respectable reviews and sales, their second single, *Elevator*, failed to make the charts. Paul McCartney had even directed a promotional film that was shot in Hyde Park on 26 March, yet nothing Apple did could help secure a follow-up hit for Grapefruit.

Given the group's lack of success, Geoff Swettenham is still quite amazed by the amount of money and attention that Apple lavished on Grapefruit. "Apple paid for our house and gave us a retainer every week," he remembers. "They kept us alive basically. They got us a great flat just off of Baker Street... except for George, who got his own flat because he was married with a kid, but the three of us lived there and Apple paid for everything."

John Perry agrees with Swettenham, adding that, "Nems basically put us on a retainer and also gave us a car and accounts in various restaurants and clubs, so we could just sign for stuff. It was help yourself really, it was kind of wacky, but we didn't abuse that, we were very naive to be honest. We were told to go to Martin Wesson at Nems – who was the accountant – and we were told to go tell him how much we wanted. Nems also paid for our flats. George was married and had one or two kids and he lived near to Baker Street on Marylebone Road. The rest of us lived on the other side of Baker Street in Montagu Mews

North. Lennon lived in Montagu Mews. I actually rang him up once while I was on an acid trip and I asked him, 'John, what happens? What do I do? Its freaking me out,' and he said, 'Meditate man, mediate.'"

Apple, having naively assumed that Grapefruit's music and the promotional clout of The Beatles would propel Grapefruit into the charts, were dismayed to discover that managing a successful pop group was not as simple as it seemed. In fact, the British music press quickly turned on Grapefruit. Despite the fact that Grapefruit wrote most of their songs and performed on their own records, the group were dismissed as Beatles clones, or worse still, as a manufactured pop group along the lines of The Monkees. The band would release several more singles and an excellent debut album later in 1968, but they would be unable to shake the "imitation Beatles" tag for the remainder of their career.

Twenty three year-old Liverpool native Jackie Lomax was another early signing to Apple Music Publishing. Unlike Grapefruit, Lomax was already a seasoned music business veteran by the time he made his way to Apple's Baker Street office. Between 1961 and 1966, Lomax had been the bassist of a hard-edged R&B group called The Undertakers and he knew The Beatles from when both groups played the Liverpool club circuit. In 1964, The Undertakers, along with The Pete Best Band (a Liverpool group that featured former Beatles drummer Pete Best), had been lured to the United States by a record producer who desperately wanted to cash in on the British invasion. Expecting to find fame and fortune in America, The Undertakers instead found themselves stranded in New York City, unable to play shows due to visa problems and living on the floor of a dingy recording studio. After recording only one single, The Undertakers broke up in 1966. Lomax remained in New York City where he supported himself by playing clubs in Greenwich Village.

A chance encounter in New York City with old Liverpool acquaintance Cilla Black resulted in Lomax returning to England to work with Brian Epstein. Under Epstein's guidance, Lomax recorded an (unreleased) album and two unsuccessful singles for CBS Records. Lomax was astute enough to realize that he had no future with Nems after Epstein's death, so he decided to contact The Beatles to see if they would be interested in financing a group that he wanted to start with Chris Curtis, the former drummer of The Searchers. According to Lomax, John Lennon talked him out of forming a group with Curtis, telling Lomax that he would be better off as a solo artist and suggesting that Lomax should go to Baker Street and talk to Terry Doran.

The fact that Lomax was from Liverpool and had been recommended to Apple Music Publishing by John Lennon was enough to ensure that he was given an immediate contract with Apple Publishing.

Even though Terry Doran now proclaims that he "wasn't much good at music publishing" he did manage to sign some excellent song-writers to Apple. In addition to George Alexander and Jackie Lomax, Doran also signed the Scottish songwriting duo of Benny Gallagher and Graham Lyle to Apple Publishing in 1967. Gallagher and Lyle had come to London in 1966 in an attempt to make a career for themselves as songwriters, but instead soon found themselves working in non-musical, nine to five jobs. In *Blue Suede Brogans*, Lyle remembers that their fortunes changed when, "We were told by a friend that The Beatles were opening a company and he suggested that we go along and play them a few songs. The guy, Terry Doran, liked them right away. He was an old rocker really, and the hippie thing was a bit con-fusing for him, but he was a lovely guy and in charge of Apple. He said, 'We're not exactly open yet, but we will be in the next two months and I want to sign you.' We thought, 'we've heard that before', but right enough, two months later, we got our first paid songwriting job. They paid us twenty-five pounds a week each, which was more than we were getting in our jobs and it was terrific. We had to deliver product though. I know everybody says Apple was total chaos, but at the end of the week we had to come in and show them songs. It was great for us."

Serving a dual role of music publishing office and general meeting place, Apple Music Publishing's Baker Street office quickly became the centre of all Apple activity. On the occasions that Neil Aspinall and The Beatles commandeered the office so that they could sit together and map out the future of Apple, Lomax, Alexander and the Gallagher and Lyle team kept busy recording demo tapes on a Revox two-track tape recorder that was set up on the empty floor above Apple Publishing. Lomax remembers that the Revox was in constant use and he recalls going to Apple's Baker Street office almost every day, where he would work on demo tapes of his latest compositions. When a song was finished, he would take the tape downstairs to Terry Doran, who would listen to it, fill out the necessary paperwork and give Lomax twenty pounds for each completed song.

Given that Apple Records was only in the earliest of planning stages, Lomax had absolutely no idea what Apple Publishing intended to do with all the songs that he and the other Apple writers were com-posing. From what he could gather, Doran and the rest of Apple's small staff put little effort into getting other artists to record his songs.

But contrary to Lomax's perception that Apple Publishing was doing little to promote the work of their songwriters, Apple Publishing was actually working quite hard to secure cover versions of Apple published songs. Several English bands – including Moving Finger, and Ways and Means – recorded songs written by George Alexander, and Ways and Means almost had a hit with Alexander's *Breaking Up A Dream*, a song that Grapefruit had recorded for a BBC radio session.

During his first few months of managing Apple Publishing, Terry Doran had managed to find some promising writers, but he knew that he needed to find qualified help if he was going to make Apple Publishing a success. In January 1968, he hired Mike Berry – a former assistant at Sparta Music Publishing – to help scout new talent and secure cover versions of Apple Publishing copyrights.

Berry was energetic and hard working, and his presence at Apple helped make the publishing division a far more professional operation than it had previously been. The first songwriter that Berry signed to Apple Publishing was Dave Lambert, a future member of The Strawbs, who in 1968 was the lead singer and guitarist of a North London trio called Fire. Once the group had the support of Apple, they were quickly signed to Decca Records, who released Fire's debut single, *Father's Name Is Dad*, in March 1968. Berry did not hesitate to throw all of Apple's resources behind the group, getting The Fool (a trendy group of Dutch designers who had done extensive work for Nems and The Beatles) to design stage clothes for Fire. Berry allegedly even had the Apple Press office call BBC DJ Kenny Everett and suggest that if Everett did not play Fire's single, John Lennon would never speak to him again.

Ironically, the single's success was ultimately stunted by the initial radio play that Apple had helped garner for the group. A week after the single was issued, Paul McCartney heard *Father's Name Is Dad*, a stomping mod-influenced rock song, on the BBC and decided that the song was not commercial enough to become a hit. He allegedly instructed Apple Publishing to have the single recalled so that Fire could re-record the song with additional vocals and revamped guitar parts. Even though the new version of the song was soon back in the shops, any momentum that the single had was lost and *Father's Name Is Dad* failed to make the charts.

Despite the failure of *Father's Name Is Dad*, Decca was still interested in a second single from Fire. Curiously, when Lambert presented a batch of his promising new songs to Apple, Berry proclaimed that none of the songs were suitable for release and that he himself had composed a new song, *Round The Gum Tree*, to be the group's second

Decca single. Although the members of Fire were reportedly incensed by Berry forcing them to record his song, Dave Lambert was ultimately persuaded to sing on the record. The group lost their composure, however, when they were informed that the record's B-side would be *Toothie Ruthie*, a song written by Fire's managers, Derek Savage and John Turner. They refused to have anything to do with the song and it was ultimately recorded with Savage and Turner providing the lead vocals.

While Berry's attempt to supplement his Apple salary with songwriting royalties was ethically questionable and certainly not in the spirit of Apple (although he did assign the publishing of *Round The Gum Tree* to Apple), the bubble gum style of *Round The Gum Tree* did have some commercial merit and it ended up being a regional hit when it was recorded by a group called The Real McCoy later that year. Disillusioned by the whole experience, Fire spent the remainder of the year getting out of contracts with their managers, Decca and Apple, and they eventually went on to release an album on another record label.

Even though McCartney, and to a lesser extent Lennon and Harrison, took an interest in Apple Publishing groups like Grapefruit and Fire, for the most part, Terry Doran and Mike Berry ran Apple Publishing with little interference from either Neil Aspinall or The Beatles. In the closing days of 1967, Aspinall's primary concern was to sort out The Beatles' tangled business affairs, a task that had taken on additional urgency in the wake of Brian Epstein's death.

Setting up a Beatles office proved to be more difficult than anyone had anticipated. In a 1996 interview with *Mojo*, Aspinall recalled: "We didn't have a single piece of paper. No contracts. The lawyer, the accountants and Brian, whoever, had that. Maybe The Beatles had been given copies of various contracts, I don't know. I know that when Apple started I didn't have a single piece of paper. I didn't know what the contract was with EMI, or with the film people or the publishers or anything at all. So it was a case of building up the filing system, finding out what was going on while we were trying to continue doing something."

Aspinall's job was certainly not made any easier by The Beatles' lack of a unified vision for Apple. Aspinall had barely set up a tangible structure for Apple when The Beatles finally agreed to go ahead with their plan to use their new company to support and promote the work of exciting young artists whom the group admired. Perhaps swept up in the exuberant spirit of the summer of love, The Beatles now saw Apple as a company that could draw on almost every aspect of popular culture and champion new talent in such diverse fields as literature, music, films, art, television and even electronics.

Even before Apple was formed, The Beatles had lavished a great deal of attention and money on a venture that would ultimately evolve into Apple Electronics. John Alexis Mardas (dubbed "Magic Alex" by John Lennon) was a young Greek television repairman who had somehow managed to capture The Beatles' fancy with his ability to be a highly entertaining companion, his flamboyant sense of style and his crude prototypes of clever electronic gadgets (despite them having no real practical value).

Mardas had been introduced to The Beatles in the summer of 1967 by mutual friend John Dunbar, the owner of the Indica, a small, hip London art gallery. Fascinated by Mardas' electronic toys, The Beatles decided to go into business with him, financing a company called Fiftyshapes Ltd. Later, when The Beatles decided to make Apple an all-inclusive entertainment organization, Fiftyshapes Ltd. was renamed Apple Electronics and brought into the Apple fold. Until Apple could find a suitable permanent location for the Apple Electronics Laboratory, Apple Electronics set up a temporary office in the Baker Street building.

Throughout the final months of 1967, The Beatles' ambitions for Apple seemed to grow and change course almost every day. From the cosy Apple Publishing office above bustling Baker Street, various combinations of Beatles spent hours hatching far-reaching plans to develop a myriad of interlocking Beatles companies. One idea that they were particularly keen on was that of opening a retail store on the ground floor of the Baker Street building.

Ultimately known as "The Apple Boutique", The Beatles' store was to be a venture that they hoped would revolutionize the retail industry and serve as a prototype for a chain of stores to be opened across the world. The fact that Baker Street was not a well-known shopping area did not deter The Beatles from using their property as a platform for diving headfirst into retail sales.

The Beatles held lofty aspirations for their boutique, envisaging the shop as a place for "beautiful people to buy beautiful things". The reality was that the Apple Boutique was basically a "head shop", selling psychedelic trinkets and clothes, records, inflatable plastic furniture, books and jewellery. The boutique did manage to attract a regular flow of tourists, lunchtime browsers and shoplifters, but it proved much harder to lure paying customers into the store.

The task of managing the Apple Boutique had been given to John Lennon's childhood friend, Pete Shotton. Like Terry Doran at Apple

Publishing, Shotton was probably not the best person to be put in charge of a new Apple business. Prior to coming to London to run the Apple Boutique, Shotton had been successfully running a supermarket that John Lennon had bought for him to manage in 1965. Although Shotton had no experience of running a clothing boutique, the fact that he had run some sort of store, combined with the fact that Lennon, Harrison and McCartney had known Shotton since they were teenagers, made the amiable Shotton the right person for the job as far as The Beatles were concerned.

The hiring of individuals like Terry Doran and Pete Shotton also illustrated how The Beatles hoped that the open-minded business structure at Apple would provide an opportunity for young, not necessarily traditional businessmen to distinguish themselves in the world of commerce. Still excited by the novelty of being businessmen, The Beatles wanted to give friends from the same working class Liverpool background as themselves a chance to show the world that business was not the exclusive domain of the upper class, private school educated section of British society.

With great fanfare, Apple announced to the press that the Apple Boutique would open for business in November 1967. Predictably, due to several unforeseen delays, it was not until the evening of 7 December 1967 that the Apple Boutique finally opened its doors. To celebrate, Apple staged a gala grand opening where George Harrison and John Lennon mingled with invited guests who were feted with apple juice and green Granny Smith apples.

The Apple Boutique officially opened for business the following morning and the general public seemed to be genuinely fascinated by The Beatles' new shop. Even in a relatively progressive city like London, never before had such a strange collection of merchandise been collected under one roof.

The shop's stock was largely made up of vivid psychedelic outfits and posters created by The Fool. The boutique was also intended to serve as a retail outlet for the gadgets created by Apple Electronics. These creations included a transistor radio that could be used to broadcast music directly from a record player and a small box with randomly blinking lights that was dubbed "The Nothing Box". Tellingly, by the time the boutique opened, the only contribution that Apple Electronics had made to the boutique was to install the lighting in the shop. Magic Alex had also promised The Beatles a giant artificial sun to illuminate the opening of the Apple Boutique, although he was apparently unable to create anything that resembled that description.

The Fool had first come to The Beatles' attention through the

design work they had done for the Savile Theatre, a London performance venue under the wing of Brian Epstein. Greatly impressed with
The Fool's sophisticated psychedelic style, The Beatles hired the group
to work on a variety of projects, which included painting a piano and
a gypsy caravan for John Lennon, decorating the interior of George
Harrison's bungalow and creating the outfit that Ringo Starr wore in
the *Our World* broadcast performance of *All You Need Is Love.*

When The Beatles decided to open the Apple Boutique, The Fool
were naturally asked to become the shop's in-house designers. In addition to conjuring up an unusually garish line of clothes, they were
given the task of decorating both the interior and the exterior of the
boutique. With an unrestricted budget and a brief to make The Beatles'
boutique stand out on the relatively staid street of shops and private
homes, The Fool designed a massive three-story psychedelic mural to
grace the side of the building.

The resulting mural – a brightly coloured Indian-styled goddess
that took up the entire side of the building – was nothing if not striking. But while The Beatles were quite pleased with the painting, other
businesses in the area were less-than-enamoured by The Fool's creation. Bowing to pressure from the local council and the surrounding
business community, Apple was soon forced to paint the wall white
with a simple "Apple" scripted in the middle.

But having to paint over of The Fool's mural was the least of
Apple's problems. Despite the steady flow of curious tourists and students who made their way to the shop, the Apple Boutique made little
money. It seems that in addition to having to contend with uninhibited
staff helping themselves to cash from the till, the boutique's stock was
not as enticing to the public as The Beatles had anticipated. Outfits like
designer Harold Tillman's see-through chiffon tuxedo that had seemed
very hip in the psychedelic summer of 1967 looked quite out of place
on the cold streets of London during the winter of 1967-68, and, for the
most part, remained unsold.

In his fascinating memoir *The Love You Make*, Peter Brown
remembers the Apple Boutique as a very unusual place of business.
"Customers seemed to be there only to shoplift or to stare at Jenny
Boyd [George Harrison's sister-in-law] who was working there as a
salesperson along with a self-styled mystic named Caleb. Caleb slept
underneath a showcase on one of his many breaks. The store was also
sometimes tended by a fat lady who dressed in authentic gypsy cos-
tumes."

Reflecting further, Peter Brown admits that, "The Apple Boutique
was a bit of a rip off. It was a case of The Beatles trying to be too cool

for their own good. It was a beautiful shop. The merchandise looked great. I don't think it was very good quality, but you weren't looking for something to last forever, you were looking to look great next Saturday. Looking back, I suppose it's no worse than the rag industry today, where designers do what they can to take the capital they are given and run with it. But The Fool were really pretty hypocritical. They were pretending to be these cool, lovely people when they were in fact a bit less than scrupulous in the way they did things. The Fool would totally run rings around poor Pete Shotton. There was always this problem of them saying, 'Don't say that to me because we're too cool for it,' and he would be confronted with this problem of trying to be a businessman while trying to be cool at the same time."

Brown also insists that, contrary to popular belief, The Beatles were quite aware that the Apple Boutique was rapidly getting out of control. In January 1968, Pete Shotton was replaced by a more experienced retailer named John Lyndon. Realizing what he was up against, Lyndon immediately instituted more responsible business practices for the shop and made a valiant attempt to reign in The Fool's excessive expenditure. Despite Lyndon's efforts, it was estimated that the shop went on to eventually lose close to $400,000. On top of the money that was lost at the shop, it is alleged that the Apple organization would also have to write-off the cost of a Jaguar sports car that Apple had purchased for Pete Shotton but which it had never reclaimed after Shotton left the company.

To complement the Apple Boutique, Apple Retail set up a second operation called Apple Tailoring (Civil and Theatrical) in a shop at 161 King's Road. Established on 2 February 1968 and officially opened on 23 May, the shop was a partnership with John Crittle, the highly respected designer, who was a Director of the enterprise along with Apple's Neil Aspinall and Apple accountant Stephen Maltz.

By the end of 1967 Apple had developed into an interesting little company. Given that The Beatles had started the year with only a vague concept for starting a business to minimize their tax exposure, the fact that they managed to set up two fully functioning companies by the end of the year suggested that they had big plans for Apple in 1968.

2
1968 - A Is For Apple

Having laid the foundation for Apple during 1967, The Beatles and Neil Aspinall began the New Year with a flurry of Apple related activity. In January 1968, Beatles Ltd. changed its name to Apple Corps. Ltd. and registered the Apple trademark in forty-seven countries. Plans were also made to expand the music publishing and retail operations. But most of the planning in the early weeks of 1968 centered around The Beatles' desire to transform Apple into an artist-friendly, forward-thinking entertainment company that would encompass everything from records and films to electronics and television. If Apple were to become such a multi-faceted company, however, they would need more space than they had in the small Baker Street office that housed Apple Publishing. In order to accommodate the staff that would be required to carry out The Beatles' ambitious plans, Apple took out a one-year lease on offices in an eight-storey building at 95 Wigmore Street. The modern office was available for immediate occupancy and the rapidly expanding Apple organization moved into the fifth floor of the building on 22 January 1968.

Having found a proper office, Apple next needed to settle on a suitable corporate logo. The task of designing Apple's logo was given to Gene Mahon, a genial Irishman who had previously served as art director on the photo shoot for the back cover of the "Sgt. Pepper" album. Prior to recruiting Mahon to design the definitive "Apple" logo, Apple had been using several illustrated apples as well as a photo of an odd-looking apple that had been provided by American designer Tom Wilkes.

In February 1968, while The Beatles were in India basking in the winter sun and gentle wisdom of the Maharishi, Neil Aspinall invited Mahon to meet him at Wigmore Street to discuss the possibility of Mahon designing a logo for Apple. After Aspinall had explained that they were looking for a photograph of an apple to put on the record label, Mahon came up with the inspired idea of having a full apple on the label of one side of the record, and a photo of the same apple sliced in half on the other side. Mahon suggested that all the song titles and record credits could be printed on the sliced half of the label and the first side of the record would be a whole apple with no writing on it whatsoever.

Aspinall liked the idea and instructed Mahon to provide Apple with some photos. Working with photographer Paul Castell, Mahon shot pictures of a host of red, green and yellow apples on a variety of different backgrounds and submitted them to Apple for consideration. The photo proofs were then reviewed by Aspinall and the four Beatles and a decision was made to use a photo of a green Granny Smith apple. Once the final apple image was selected, the trendy English illustrator Alan Aldridge was hired to script the copyright information that needed to appear on the labels of records released in the UK. Unfortunately, due to trade requirements of the day that stipulated that the contents of a record must be printed on both sides of the record, Mahon's original idea of having an unadorned full apple on one side of the label had to be abandoned. Apple Records had nevertheless acquired a very attractive, distinctive logo and they were now one step closer to being able to release music on an Apple Records label.

Though most of Apple's activity had shifted to the Wigmore Street office in early 1968, Apple Publishing remained at Baker Street and continued to actively seek new songwriters. To help out in the publishing office, a young man named Jack Oliver was hired along with Mike Berry in January 1968. Oliver remembers: "I was at art school in London, and then I left art school to take a job at a design company, and then I got involved with the music business. I had a job at Chappell Music Publishing, and I was also in a group called The Chocolate Watchband. We recorded a few singles together but nothing happened. We didn't even know there was an American band called The Chocolate Watch Band until I came across a CD the other day... I knew we hadn't made a CD. But anyway, we had this band – because everyone in London in those days had a band – and we recorded for Decca and then decided to call it a day. There was a guy, Terry Oakes, who I had worked with at Chappell, and I said to him, 'Look, we're going to fold the group, do you know of any jobs around?' and he said, 'Well, there's a new company opening up, maybe they want someone.' So he gave me the guy's name and number and it was Terry Doran, who was running Apple Publishing at the time.

"So I went for this interview with him, and it was quite interesting," remembers Oliver. "I went into this office on Baker Street and it was this completely white office, everything in the office was white and there were these two white leather Chesterfield sofas. Everything was white except for this maniac Terry Doran, who had this big 'fro and all these psychedelic clothes... it was really funny. I still didn't know who it was. He said, 'I don't really need anyone but, I'll talk to you anyway,' so we spoke a bit and I told him, 'Well it looks to me like you need an assistant,' and he said, 'Well, alright, you can start tomorrow.' So I started the next day, it must have been January 1968 and he said,

"Oh, we're going to Midem tomorrow, do you want to go? 'So I said yeah, sure'. I went and we had a suite at the Carlton, and I was in this suite... I still didn't really know what was going on... and then from out of one of the rooms walks Paul McCartney. So then I knew, and I thought to myself this is going to be a good gig. So I spent the rest of the week with Paul McCartney, basically just posing around Cannes. We worked hard there, and we did a lot of stuff. Mike Berry came in just after me. I don't think we had anyone else signed to publishing other than Jackie Lomax and George Alexander. To be honest, I wasn't in publishing that long. As soon as I got there, I was involved in Mary Hopkin's management more than anything, because Mike Berry and Terry Doran were doing the publishing. Mike Berry had come over from Sparta Music Publishing, so he knew what he was doing. I think Mike was the one that was running around trying to sign other groups and pitch the songs... I was only with Terry for a couple of months at most and then I went over to Derek Taylor's office. Publishing stayed in Baker Street and I went over to Savile Row with Derek Taylor. I was in the press office for a while working for Derek."

With new staff being added on almost a weekly basis, Apple developed at a very rapid pace. By February, Apple had been structured into five divisions. In addition to The Beatles, there was Merchandising (Retail and Wholesale), Music (Records and Publishing), Apple Electronics and Apple Films. Apple also announced plans for further divisions, including Apple Publicity, Apple Management and The Apple Foundation for the Arts.

None of the additional Apple divisions appeared to develop further than the corporate registration stage. Apple Publicity was presumably to be part of the record division, although Apple was never involved with publicizing any non-Apple artists. Apple Management was another division that failed to develop. Apple Publishing's Terry Doran did manage Grapefruit and briefly managed Apple artist Mary Hopkin, but there never was any formal Apple Management structure. As for The Apple Foundation for the Arts, it was really nothing more than an idealistic plan.

While it may have been the least tangible part of the Apple organization, The Apple Foundation for the Arts was the division that seemed to attract the greatest interest from the general public. Soon after The Beatles floated their vague idea to assist deserving artists through The Apple Foundation for the Arts, Apple's Wigmore Street office was besieged with would-be poets, film makers, authors, musicians and event organizers, each trying to secure funding for their revolutionary ventures.

1968 - A Is For Apple

The Beatles would later claim that being besieged by countless people looking for hand-outs was one of the worst aspects of Apple. In retrospect, however, The Beatles really had nobody to blame but themselves for attracting the waves of dreamers and schemers that descended upon Apple's new office. Even though The Beatles genuinely wanted Apple to find and nurture new talent in a variety of media, they completely failed to articulate their objectives in a manner that would dissuade less-than-gifted aspiring artists from camping out in Apple's waiting room in a desperate attempt to gain an audience with one of Apple's four "enlightened" Directors. In *Fifty Years Adrift*, Derek Taylor recalled that George Harrison was the first Beatle to notice that Apple was under siege, telling Taylor that he hated Apple and especially how Apple was attracting so many people looking for a hand-outs of one sort or another. Taylor recalled that Harrison was particularly annoyed by Indians, who, having noted Harrison's fondness for Indian culture, appealed to Apple to help subsidize their education, or other personal needs.

In conjunction with the hordes of artists and opportunists who arrived daily at Apple, it was during Apple's early days at Wigmore Street that the staff first noticed the presence of a group of fans who would later become affectionately known as the "Apple scruffs". The scruffs, a group of young women who shared an intense devotion to The Beatles, were some of the most dedicated Beatles fans ever. Positioning themselves outside of the Apple offices and the recording studios where The Beatles worked, they would remain at their collective vigil all year round and in every kind of weather, just for the chance of seeing a Beatle or getting an autograph.

The arrival of the scruffs certainly added yet another splash of colour to the proceedings at Apple. Every day throughout the spring of 1968, there would always be something interesting happening at 95 Wigmore Street. As the scruffs milled around the entrance that led up to the Apple office, upstairs, Apple receptionist Debbie Wellum struggled to keep a semblance of order in the often crowded reception area. Somewhat sheltered from the chaos of the reception area in the large communal room at the back of the office, Neil Aspinall and various Beatles spent many hours making plans and assembling the management team they needed to make Apple an international presence in the entertainment industry.

To head up Apple's music division, The Beatles selected a 33 year-old American named Ron Kass to be President of Apple Records. Prior to being hired by Apple, Kass had been in charge of UK operations for Liberty Records. The selection of Ron Kass was particularly significant because Kass was the first person to be appointed to the senior management team of Apple who had not had a previous association with The Beatles.

"Ron Kass was a very, very experienced international record executive," enthuses Peter Brown. "We got him from Liberty Records, which in those days was a very big thing. He was running it in Europe and he was very successful at it. He was a very experienced man. And he did a very good job at Apple. We weren't necessarily looking for an American to run the label, but we ended up with an American who knew the American record industry, but was also experienced in Europe. So in Ron we had someone who was experienced in Europe and America, which was unique, because in those days, record industry executives didn't travel that much like today where you have Americans in London and Londoners in America. Apple was really one of the first international record labels as far as its international reach and view."

With Ron Kass given the job of running Apple Records, Paul McCartney appointed 23 year-old Peter Asher to be Apple's A&R Director. Asher would be Apple's only official A&R man and he would be responsible for finding and developing talent for Apple. Unlike other Beatles associates such as Terry Doran and Pete Shotton who came to Apple with no music industry experience, Asher, the younger brother of Jane (McCartney's fiancée), did have considerable music industry experience, albeit on the other side of the microphone. As one half of the pop duo Peter and Gordon, Asher had tasted international success in the mid-sixties with such McCartney penned songs as *World Without Love* and *I Don't Want To See You Again*. While Asher may have had no formal production experience, he had spent the five preceding years touring the world and making records, and he had developed very strong opinions of how a record company should work with artists and how records should be made.

Asher recalls that it seemed very natural for him to end up at Apple: "Paul was a friend of mine and I spent a lot of time hanging out with him at his house when he had the original idea for Apple. I was in on a lot of the planning, or maybe even more dreaming than planning, of having a record label. Paul was the most actively involved with the record label. They had this thing that they wanted to bring in an American business guy... which ended up being Ron Kass. Paul asked if I would be interested in producing some records for Apple. He liked some of the stuff I had been doing. I had produced a couple of records so I said, 'Sure,' and later on he said, 'Well, why don't you run the label. We're going to get an American business guy to be the boss but you can run the artist aspect of it.'

"At that point, none of us really knew what we were doing," Asher stresses. "We were filled with a general sense of optimism and thought how hard could this be? – I had already decided that I had pretty much had it with performing. Gordon and I were fading out and weren't working together much. I had enjoyed being in the studio more so I had produced a couple of records – one of which Paul had played on [a single by former Manfred Mann Band vocalist Paul Jones that featured McCartney, Jeff Beck, and ex-Yardbird Paul Samwell Smith backing Jones on two songs – *And The Sun Will Shine* and *The Dog Presides*] so I had a feeling that what I wanted to do was more in the production area. So when Paul talked about it, he had his ideas for the label, I made some suggestions and as the company developed, that's when he said, 'Say, why don't you come and do it?'"

Having lined up Kass and Asher to run the record division, The Beatles were able to devote time to developing other Apple projects. To take charge of the film division, they named 45 year-old Dennis O'Dell as Director of Apple Films. O'Dell had previously worked with The Beatles on *A Hard Days Night* and he was highly regarded in the film industry and within The Beatles' circle. In addition to O'Dell, Apple brought in 44 year-old Brian Lewis to assist in the Film Department and to be Apple's contracts expert.

With Dennis O'Dell needing to devote his full attention to the films that Apple was hoping to make, the day-to-day activities associated with Apple Films were delegated to former Nems employee Tony Bramwell.

Like many of Apple's early employees, Bramwell was one of the original Nems staff that had come down to London from Liverpool in 1964. Bramwell had first crossed paths with The Beatles when he was a schoolboy in Liverpool. "When I was a kid, I used to carry Gerry [Gerry and the Pacemakers] Mardsen's guitar to gigs for him so I could get in free," he remembers. "So when Gerry went off to Hamburg and The Beatles came back from Hamburg, I started doing the same thing for George... George was actually a childhood friend of mine... he used to borrow my records and never return them. So when they [The Beatles] were playing, I went on the bus to see them, and George was on the same bus... and I asked him if I could carry his guitar. So, I started to travel around with them until about the time of *Love Me Do* and then they asked me to help out with the equipment full time, which I did until around November 1963... around the time of *I Want To Hold Your Hand*, when they needed a driver. I was too young for a licence, so they got Mal. So I carried on working in the Nems office and handling the presentation side of it... the stage shows, the tours for all the

Nems acts. Then I ran the Savile Theatre until Brian's death. I was also very involved with Subafilms... we did all The Beatles' video clips.

"After Brian died, there was a day when we all moved out of Nems and went to Apple. I was hired to work for Apple Films. I was at Apple Films for about a year until we started up Apple Records. The problem with Apple Films was that United Artists, who had the rights to finance and distribute Apple Films, didn't think it was such a great idea... so that was a bit of a disaster. We actually bought the rights to *Lord Of The Rings* which The Beatles would have starred in... we were in pre-production. We actually did basic location shooting for a film called *Walkabout*. We sent a couple of guys down to Australia to shoot locations. We ended up selling the rights to *Walkabout* to Nicholas Roeg – and it was very successful. So, since nothing was happening with Apple Films, when Apple Records was getting ready to release 'the first four' they came to me and said they needed someone to do the promotion. 'Will you do the promotion?' I said, 'Sure.'"

To complete the raid of Nems personnel, Peter Brown was brought over to act as Apple's Administrative Director and to sit on Apple's Board of Directors. Although Peter Brown would work out of Apple's offices and had the appearance of being an Apple executive, Brown was actually employed by Beatles and Co, the corporate manifestation of The Beatles partnership.

After Brian Epstein's death, The Beatles increasingly turned to the embryonic Apple organization to provide them with the same sort of personal and professional services that were previously handled by Nems. Although the limited business activities of The Beatles could usually be taken care of by Apple, within Apple there developed a distinct need for someone to look after The Beatles' personal affairs.

The most obvious person to assume this responsibility was Peter Brown. After Brian Epstein died it was Brown who assumed many of Epstein's duties at Nems, both as social and personal coordinator for the individual Beatles. Bill Oakes, Peter Brown's personal assistant from 1969-1970 believes that The Beatles viewed Brown as "the spirit of Brian Epstein... he was Epstein's assistant, his lover, whatever... he was the person who discovered Epstein's body and he was keeper of the Epstein flame."

"What happened was that when Brian died, Peter simply went and sat in Brian's chair – it's as simple as that," explains Oakes. "I don't think anyone ever appointed him manager. When Stigwood made his run for Nems and then split off with the Bee Gees, The Beatles started Apple. Peter Brown certainly had nothing to do with the business set-up of Apple, because he was not a businessman... he was the front man, The Beatles' spokesman, he was the man who got on with marrying them off and who John sings about in *The Ballad Of John And Yoko*. Peter Brown was very involved with The Beatles' personal lives, all of their wives would go to lunch with him, he was like a walker, had a big expense account, and he carried on for all intents and purposes as if he was king of the roost. I mean The Beatles' room in Apple's Savile Row office... his room... it was never the office, it was 'Peter Brown's room' which was The Beatles' room. There was a red light system outside of the office and when the red light was on it meant that there was a Beatle in residence and that you couldn't come in, unless it was me or Peter... so we would put on the red light even if there wasn't a Beatle in there."

All four Beatles were reasonably comfortable entrusting their personal business to Peter Brown, but it was Paul McCartney who had the closest relationship with Brown. Unlike McCartney, George Harrison was not particularly fond of Brown, nor was Brown especially close to Harrison. Although Harrison went along with having Brown installed as The Beatles' "personal manager" Harrison wanted to ensure that there would also be a few people that he personally respected and enjoyed working with on Apple's staff.

It was Harrison who was most responsible for bringing former Beatles press officer Derek Taylor to Apple. At the time he joined Apple in 1968, Taylor, a Liverpudlian, already had a long history with The Beatles. Having come to the band's attention after writing several glowing reviews of the group for the Northern edition of *The Daily Express*, Taylor was hired by Brian Epstein to ghostwrite Epstein's 1964 "autobiography", *A Cellar Full Of Noise*, and to ghostwrite a column by George Harrison that appeared in one of the weekly British music magazines. Taylor would work as The Beatles' press officer for most of 1964, before moving to America in 1965 after falling out with Epstein. Setting up an office in Los Angeles, Taylor quickly became a very successful independent publicist for groups such as The Byrds, Paul Revere and The Raiders, The Beach Boys and several other artists. Taylor was also one of the principal organizers of the now-fabled 1967 Monterey Pop Festival.

In *Fifty Years Adrift*, Taylor recalled how the four Beatles called him at his California home to offer him the job of head of Apple Records: "At 8 o'clock one morning I had a phone call... it was all four of them, rowdy and friendly and sober and calling, I assume, on whim. I was still in bed but wide awake very quickly. 'Come back to England and run Apple,' one of them said. What did that mean? 'Run Apple Records,' said John. 'This is George's idea. I've asked Mal but you can do it anyway with Mal.' 'Bollocks to yer,' said Paul, 'he asked Peter Asher.' 'You can come and drive the big green jobs anyway,' said George... 'The best thing would be to talk about it.' Taylor agreed, and within days of the conversation, he was already making plans to move his family back to England.

Settling his wife Joan and their five children into a lovely home in the countryside of Surrey, Taylor reported to work at Apple on 8 April 1968. Despite having just moved his entire family across the Atlantic Ocean, Taylor stepped into Apple's Wigmore Street office that day with absolutely no idea of what he would be doing for The Beatles' new company. Although Taylor still hoped that he might be put in charge of Apple Records, neither Taylor, Peter Asher, or Mal Evans were asked to run Apple Records. When it was clear that he would not be given the job of running the label, Taylor discussed being given the title of "Office Eccentric" with Paul McCartney. Quite to Taylor's surprise, McCartney agreed to his quixotic request and instructed Taylor to have an appropriate sign made for his office door. Sadly, like so many of the ideas that were bounced around Apple's Wigmore Street office during that time, nothing more ever came of the idea of having an "Office Eccentric."

Taylor was ultimately coaxed into being Apple's Press Officer and he immediately became a staunch and devoted champion of Apple's idealistic goals. To assist him with his press duties, Taylor hired Richard DiLello, a 23 year-old American from New York City who had found himself in London after making a hippie pilgrimage to North Africa. Needing to assign DiLello a formal title so that the young American could register to work in England, Taylor dubbed the afro-sporting DiLello the "house hippie" and put him to work sorting out a massive pile of Beatles press cuttings.

Considering that Taylor was one of the premier publicists in the music industry, the salary Apple gave him – £115 pounds a week – was rather average, even by 1968 standards. Despite the widely-held public perception that anyone associated with The Beatles or Apple were earning fabulous salaries, only Peter Brown and Ron Kass received any special compensation. "The most I ever made was £30 a week," laughs Bill Oakes "They were cheap bastards... I was always short of money, and I was always getting stuck with the bill because my friends thought, 'He works for "them" – he's got money.' Peter Brown had a marvelous deal... he made around £100 a week, but he had everything paid for... his mews apartment, his restaurant bills, his groceries... Jimmy, the Apple doorman, used to get Peter Brown's groceries." In addition to paying for Peter Brown's apartment, Apple also rented a

London townhouse for Ron Kass.

Despite the modest pay offered by Apple, there was no shortage of people who wanted to work for the new company. With the constant influx of new employees, the Wigmore Street office soon became far too small to contain the ever-expanding Apple Music organization. On top of having to contend with the increasingly cramped working conditions, Apple's staff also found themselves having to work in a building that was not particularly suited to a music-oriented business. On 10 July, Apple accountant Stephen Maltz circulated a memo informing Apple employees that the management of the Wigmore Street building had decreed that Apple's staff were not allowed to play music in the office during business hours due to several complaints from other tenants in the building. Since there was no way that a record company could operate without being able to play music, a search was quickly under way for a new office.

Securing a suitable office was only one of a dozen important tasks that Apple's management needed to resolve. Apple's primary concern during the spring of 1968 was to finalise an international distribution arrangement for the Apple Records label. Starting in February, Ron Kass and Neil Aspinall began making frequent flights to the United States to engage in talks with five major American labels. Although The Beatles were under contract to EMI, The Beatles were free to align Apple with any label they wanted.

With all of the pieces of Apple falling into place, Paul McCartney, John Lennon and the heads of several Apple divisions flew to New York City on 12 May 1968, where the two Beatles were scheduled to discuss Apple on *The Johnny Carson Show*.

Facing off against Joe Garagiola, a middle-aged former baseball star who was filling in as a guest host for Johnny Carson, and the unsettling Tallulah Bankhead, an ageing actress who was also a guest on the show, a nervous looking Lennon and McCartney presented their vague concept of a company that would utilize the collective influence, talent and money of The Beatles to help discover and nurture deserving artists and serve as a model of "Western communism".

During their stay in America, the Apple team also held a press conference in New York City, where The Beatles and Derek Taylor further enlightened the world about their exciting new company. During the 14 May press conference, John Lennon took the lead, explaining to the assembled press: "It's a business concerning records, films and electronics... and as a sideline, whatever it's called, manufacturing. We want to set up a system whereby people who just want to make a film about anything don't have to go down on their knees in somebody's office... probably yours." Apple's last order of business during the whirlwind trip would be to hold an Apple business meeting on a Chinese junk that had been rented to sail around Manhattan.

Several weeks after the New York press junket, Paul McCartney, Derek Taylor, Ron Kass, recently-appointed Apple Records promotion man Tony Bramwell, and Ivan Vaughan (a childhood friend of John Lennon who was now on the Apple payroll as a consultant working on The Beatles' idea of starting an Apple school) returned to America to attend a Capitol Records convention in Hollywood. They brought with them a copy of one of the few films ever made by Apple Films to show to the Capitol executives.

Featuring a searing, Eric Clapton-led instrumental track from George Harrison's still unreleased "Wonderwall" album called *Skiing* as its soundtrack, the five minute promo film gave a brief summary of Apple and featured clips of Mary Hopkin performing a song in Paul McCartney's backyard as well as a bizarre greeting from Magic Alex filmed in the Apple Electronics Lab.

Although the film division had not been given any special consideration in the promo film, Apple Films was reportedly gearing up for two major projects in the spring of 1968. One of Apple Films' initial projects was to produce a film adaptation of John Lennon's *Spaniard In The Works* and *In His Own Write* books, as well as a Beatles version of *Lord Of The Rings*.

By May, Apple Films had abandoned plans to film *Lord Of The Rings* and the film adaptation of the Lennon books, and instead had settled on two entirely new projects. The first film was to be an adaptation of a short story by Julio Cortazar called *The Jam*, filming for which was scheduled to begin in England in July. Apple Films also announced that a film called *Walkabout*, written by Edward Bond, was scheduled to begin filming in Australia in November 1968.

Apple Films was also marginally involved with the upcoming Beatles' film, *Yellow Submarine*. The animated film – which revolved around a story line loosely based on characters and subjects lifted from Beatles songs – had been in development since 1966. At that time, The Beatles were under contract to deliver a third film to United Artists, the first having been *A Hard Days Night* and the second, *Help!*. By 1966, however, The Beatles were losing their enthusiasm for making feature films, and when film producer Al Bordax – who had previously produced a Beatles cartoon series shown on American TV throughout 1965 – proposed creating an animated film featuring The Beatles, the group readily agreed to his proposal, reasoning that it would allow them to fulfill their contractual obligations to United Artists without having to go through the trouble of acting.

Production of the film began in 1967 and it quickly took on a very "trippy" psychedelic feel, complete with bright colours and "far-out" otherworldly visual images. Once Beatles songs such as *It's All Too Much* and *Lucy In The Sky With Diamonds* were inserted into the soundtrack, the film became a true psychedelic landmark and it remains a fascinating encapsulation of the psychedelic era.

Although *Yellow Submarine* would ultimately be labelled and promoted as an "Apple Presentation", neither Apple Films nor The Beatles had much to do with the film. Even The Beatles' voices were supplied by actors. The band's sole contribution was limited to a few minutes at the end of the film, when the four Beatles appeared on-screen to warn of approaching "blue meanies" and to preside over a jolly sing-along sequence for Paul McCartney's *All Together Now*.

Ironically, the four Beatles were quite taken with the charm and imagination of the finished film and they later were said to have regretted not being more actively involved with the film's creation. While The Beatles may have had little to do with the actual development of *Yellow Submarine*, all four would take an active part in promoting the film. It was premiered at the London Pavilion theatre on 17 July and all of The Beatles, plus select Apple artists including Mary Hopkin and James Taylor, attended the premiere.

Unlike *Magical Mystery Tour*, which had been savaged by the majority of British media critics, *Yellow Submarine* received generally positive reviews. For reasons that were (and are still) not clear, the film was given only limited distribution in the UK and it was not a major financial success. In the United States, however, the film received glowing reviews and enjoyed a strong box office performance.

Given the multiple ongoing projects that Apple had undertaken, outsiders perceived the company to be teeming with activity. Much of that perception, however, had to do with the media's insatiable appetite for Beatles-related news items. For the first year or so of Apple's existence, it would prove to be an almost bottomless well of newsworthy items. To ensure that Apple would be able to fully publicize its music and films ventures, Derek Taylor hired 33 year-old Jeremy Banks in June 1968. Assisting Taylor with publicity matters and acting as Apple's photographic coordinator, Banks was responsible for selling photos of The Beatles and other Apple-related projects to the media.

With the Wigmore Street and Baker Street offices overflowing with recently hired staff, Apple finally solved its space problems by buying two properties in mid-1968. The first was an unassuming building at 34 Boston Place that would serve as the laboratory of Apple Electronics.

The second property purchased by Apple was a far more impressive affair. Situated in the heart of fashionable Mayfair, Apple's new building was a five-storey Georgian townhouse purchased for approximately £500,000 on 22 June 1968. Located at 3 Savile Row, the elegant townhouse would be Apple's headquarters for the next five years. Prior to Apple purchasing the property, the building had housed a theatrical management firm owned by bandleader Jack Hylton.

Although the building would require substantial refurbishment, members of Apple's staff began moving in as early as 15 July 1968. For the next two months, workmen swarmed in and around 3 Savile Row, turning the stately, albeit somewhat run-down, townhouse into a space suitable for a company that was set to revolutionize the entertainment industry. In addition to reconditioning the facade, the building's interior was painted a rich cream colour and the floors were covered in thick apple-green carpet.

Though primarily intended to be Apple's headquarters, the four Beatles also envisaged their new building as being something along the lines of their personal London clubhouse. To cater for their whims and the soon-to-be-frequent business lunches, Apple hired several young chefs to man the small kitchen on the fourth floor. In keeping with Apple's utopian spirit, The Beatles decreed that even Apple's junior staff would be allowed to order lunch from the kitchen.

To ensure that The Beatles would have constant access to a first-rate recording studio, Apple Electronics was contracted to construct a state-of-the-art studio in the basement of the new building. Even before the plans for the studio had been drafted, The Beatles had lured several Abbey Road Studios employees to come over to help establish Apple Studios. One of the first was former Abbey Road engineer Malcolm Davies, who was hired to run the cutting room in the Apple basement for The Beatles' exclusive use.

Back when vinyl records were the primary medium of recorded sound, it was the responsibility of the cutting room engineer to transfer the music captured on the recording studio tapes to a metal "master" that would be used to manufacture a record. In addition to mastering records, the cutting room engineer also "cut" acetates, which were essentially short-lived records that were pressed in small numbers in order to check the sound of a performance or a mastered recording.

To assist Davies in the cutting room, Liverpool musician George Peckham was hired to train as an Apple Studios cutting room engineer. Like The Beatles, Peckham was a veteran of the Liverpool music scene. "I started out playing bass in a band called The Fourmost, who were also managed by Eppy," he explains. "In early 1968 when I was

23, The Beatles told me that they were thinking of getting a studio together. I went to speak to Peter Brown and told him I wanted to work in the studio, start at the ground level, no favours or anything, and work my way up. So when The Beatles decided to put a studio together at Savile Row, I had these interviews with Peter Brown. Peter introduced me to Ron Kass and then said 'OK, you can start in September, but there won't be any favours. You'll start like any other employee.' So I gave my notice to the band and started at Apple. I was already living in London while the rest of the band was still in Liverpool. With The Fourmost, I was always interested in what Geoff Emerick was doing in the control room. I used to drive Geoff mad with asking about what all the different meters did and all that. A few months later when Geoff came over from EMI to become the Apple Studio Manager, I had already been at Apple for a while. When I was introduced to him, and he saw me and it was like, 'Oh my god, what are you doing here!'

"The actual mastering room was up and running in Savile Row by the summer of 1968... they were still putting walls around it when I got there. *Hey Jude* was being cut when there were still three walls there... there wasn't a fourth wall yet. When I started, Malcolm Davies did the mastering and he let me do all the acetates. But that changed around because the better I got, the easier it became for Malcolm, so he could spend more time at the pub around the corner."

Although originally intended for the exclusive use of The Beatles, many other artists were soon clamouring for an opportunity to cut their records at Apple. Peckham remembers: "I used to go out clubbing every night after work and I would bump into a lot of musicians that I knew from when I played music. When they found out I worked at Apple, they used to ask me to cut their records. Eventually I had to sit down with George Harrison and the others and tell them that people want to come and cut at Apple and I asked if we could open Apple up to outside clients. They agreed, and the next thing you know, Apple Studios was up and running. It was busy as hell after that.

"At other studios of the time, you would have these guys in white coats cutting your records... they wouldn't say anything and they wouldn't let you give any input... but with me as an ex-musician, I'd say, 'Oh you need more bass on that,' and you work with the artist. So Apple got a reputation for cutting records that had that magic, which was what The Beatles wanted... they wanted to make a better record. Soon I was cutting records for The Stones, Clapton, Led Zeppelin, those early Genesis albums... all these artists were coming in. It was like working day and night."

Although Apple Electronics would not be able to complete a fully functioning recording studio until at least January 1969, a high-quality cutting room would be operational by late July and The Beatles and Apple would soon begin cutting all of their acetates and test pressings in the Apple basement cutting room instead of at EMI.

With the music publishing, film and retail divisions fully functional, Apple then turned its attention to finding talent for Apple Records. Peter Asher explains, "The A&R Department was really just me and then I hired some people. There was no aspect of going out and looking for people because everyone was coming to us. We ran that campaign where we said, 'Send us your tapes and we will listen'. So basically, I ended up with quite a number of people there just listening to tapes and they would select the best moments and I would finally listen to the best of the best. None of it was much good unfortunately. Out of the myriad of tapes we got in the mail, we didn't sign anyone. We tried to have A&R meetings once a week or so... whenever we could get a quorum of Beatles. But again, The Beatles tended to be more interested in their own favourite projects.

"We worked pretty hard but most of our time was taken up with the process of listening to all those submissions. The actual A&R part didn't take much. Once you said, 'OK, Jackie Lomax, George is producing,' boom, that's done. Nowadays, A&R people do a lot more interfering with how records are made, but that didn't happen then. We did have some A&R meetings when all four Beatles would be there and I would play maybe six of the best submissions, so that they would know what was going on. They would discuss their pet projects and I would bring them up to date with the ongoing projects. There would be occasional arguments and stuff because they had fairly abrasive relationships, but things got done."

As Asher noted, Apple had been actively looking for artists since the company had officially opened for business in January and several promising artists had been signed to Apple. The first was James Taylor, an American singer-songwriter from North Carolina. Peter Asher remembers that Taylor had been given his number at Apple by a mutual acquaintance, Danny Kotchmar. "Danny and James were old friends and Danny and I became close friends because Danny had been in a band, The Kingbees, that had backed Peter and Gordon on a US tour," recalls Asher. "Danny and James had been in a band together called The Flying Machine... I apparently met James at a Flying Machine rehearsal here in New York, which I don't remember. So Kootch gave James my phone number and said, 'If you get to London, here's my friend, you should give him a call.' So James called me up, came over and played me a tape and I loved it. It wasn't what was happening then, but the songs were brilliant. Coincidentally, I had just started this job with Apple, so I asked if he wanted to make an album. So within a week of arriving in London, he was hanging with The Beatles and signing with Apple. So at an A&R meeting I said basically, 'Here's this guy, an American, he's here and we're going to sign him.' And Paul went, 'Oh yeah, he's great.' John, I think, didn't care one way or the other and I think George kind of liked it." In addition to being signed to Apple Records, Taylor was also given a contract with Apple Music Publishing.

In early 1968, everyone involved with Apple seemed to be looking for talent. For several months, Mal Evans and Apple Music Publishing's Mike Berry had both been keeping an eye on a young, London-based group called The Iveys. Consisting of three Welsh teenagers and Tom Evans from Liverpool, The Iveys were a talented, yet decidedly unspectacular pop group that was just one of a hundred bands that could be found performing around London in 1967 and 1968. Through a mixture of hard work and raw talent, The Iveys had managed to make a name for themselves on the London live circuit, playing inventive versions of songs by The Beatles, The Animals and other popular groups, as well as some of their own promising compositions.

Drummer Mike Gibbins believes that it was through the efforts of their manager, Bill Collins, that Mal Evans first became aware of The Iveys. Collins, a Liverpool native, claimed to have once played in a jazz band with Paul McCartney's father, James. Having also worked as a road manager for his son Lewis' group, The Mojos, Collins knew Mal Evans from Liverpool. It was at Collins' suggestion that Mal Evans first came to see The Iveys. Gibbins remembers, "Mal got really friendly with us... he really liked the band and he used to hang around our house with us. We used to do acid with him. Peter Asher came to the Marquee to see us with Mal and he didn't like us... he thought we sucked, but then so did Peter and Gordon in my book."

Gibbins maintains that Peter Asher never really supported The Iveys, noting that Asher tended to focus on James Taylor and several other groups that he was considering for Apple. "Peter Asher was producing Yes for a while too then. We were in the next studio. This was before Yes was big... he was doing a demo with them. Peter wasn't really our A&R man at Apple... everybody was A&R at Apple. Everybody at Apple was stoned constantly... I mean everybody. We used to hang out there all the time. Mal was our main guy at Apple. Peter Asher took a few photographs, he did what he had to do. Everybody was a photographer at Apple... everybody was everybody.

"We owe it to Mal for getting us to Apple more than anybody," explained Gibbins to Peter Skiera in an interview for *Good Day Sunshine*. "Mal and Bill of course, because Bill put his foot in the door big time. Bill was turning down record deals and stuff... we were starving but he was holding out for an Apple deal. He knew that Apple was going to be a happening thing. Mal used to come around to our house way before we signed. We would make him tape after tape on Revox recorders... cheap demos. The tapes that we gave Apple... if I gave that same tape to a record company today, they'd laugh at us. It was really chinzy, but they saw something in the sound."

The Iveys submitted three sets of demo tapes to Apple before Harrison, Lennon and Derek Taylor agreed that Apple should sign the group. On 31 July, Apple Records signed The Iveys to a three-year contract with two one-year options. For reasons no longer remembered by any of the participants, it would not be until 31 October that The Iveys signed a five-year contract with Apple Music Publishing.

Mary Hopkin, a young Welsh folk singer, was another one of Apple's early discoveries. Signed to Apple Records in May, Hopkin had come to Apple's attention after British fashion model Twiggy saw her perform on a TV talent show called *Opportunity Knocks*. As Hopkin recalled in an interview with *Goldmine Magazine*: "I did the show on the day after my eighteenth birthday. Twiggy saw the show, and I think the next day saw Paul McCartney. He was telling her all about the new Apple label, and she said she had seen this girl on *Opportunity Knocks* and he should check me out. So I received a telegram, two days after the show, which I ignored for a few days. It said, 'Ring Peter Brown at Apple Records' and I'd never heard of either of them. I was a great Beatles fan and I'd heard of the Apple Boutique, but nothing else. We didn't know that Apple Records was on the way. I left it on the shelf for three days, and then my mother said it would be polite to ring back. So I did, and I was put on to who I thought was Peter Brown, and this chap had a distinct Liverpool accent.

"I started wondering at that point, making the connection with Apple... but he asked me if I'd come to London and sing for him. I said 'Well, that depends'... and he realized I was being very cautious, so he asked my mother to come to the phone. So my mother came to the phone, and he said, 'Oh, this is Paul McCartney. Would you like to bring your daughter to London to sing for me?' That was it really, I was whisked off there the next day and I sang for him. We demoed at the little Dick James Studios. I sang a few songs for him, then I was called back about two or three weeks later, and he sang a little song for me, sort of hummed it, and said, 'I've had this song lying around for years. It's called *Those Were The Days*. Let's go in and do it.'"

McCartney had apparently been looking for the right singer to record *Those Were The Days* ever since he had first heard the song performed at the Blue Angel nightclub by an American duo, Gene and Francesca, sometime in 1966. McCartney was convinced that given the right vocalist and arrangement, *Those Were The Days* could be a massive hit.

After hearing Mary Hopkin sing, McCartney knew that *Those Were The Days* would be the perfect song for Hopkin's Apple debut and decided that he would personally produce the record. Envisaging *Those Were The Days* with an "old-time" arrangement, McCartney instructed Peter Asher to secure an appropriate arranger for the recording session. Having only been working as a producer and A&R man for several months, Asher had some difficulty coming up with a suitable arranger for the session. Asher eventually brought in Richard Hewson, a London musician who had played drums in a jazz trio in which Peter Asher had once played stand-up bass. Arranging *Those Were The Days* was Hewson's first job out of music college.

"Apple was a funny old place," recalled Hewson in an interview with *Good Day Sunshine*. "It was very haphazard. Nobody really knew what anybody else was doing. Peter didn't know anything about arrangers. All he knew was he knew me, and that I'd been to the Guildhall and studied classical music and he thought, 'OK, Paul wants some orchestra on this, Richard probably knows how to write classical orchestra arrangements, let's try him.' That's how I got the job, cause they didn't know anybody else. If they'd looked around, they could probably have found a real arranger."

Hewson proved to be an inspired choice and McCartney was delighted with the results of Mary Hopkin's first recording session for Apple. Out of all of The Beatles, it was Paul McCartney who had the most interest in using Apple as an outlet for his songwriting and record production skills. Soon after completing work on *Those Were The Days*, McCartney was already planning to produce a recording session for a brass band called The Black Dyke Mills Band. The song that McCartney wanted to record was an instrumental entitled *Thingumybob* that he had written a few months earlier as the theme song for the new London Weekend Television show starring Stanley Holloway. Having failed to capture the sound he wanted when he recorded *Thingumybob* with London session musicians, McCartney hired the award winning Black Dyke Mills Band to record a new version of the song. To capture an authentic brass band feel, McCartney opted to record the song in the band's hometown of Shipley in Yorkshire.

On Saturday 29 July, Paul McCartney and several Apple staff members drove up to Shipley to "produce" an outdoor recording session by The Black Dyke Mills Band. The band were part of a long-standing English tradition of factories sponsoring employee brass bands and orchestras. Given that the members of The Black Dyke Mills Band spent most of their days toiling in a distinctly unglamorous area of the textiles industry, even the older members of the band were thrilled to be making a recording with one of The Beatles.

Accompanying McCartney on his trip to Shipley were Peter Asher, Tony Bramwell, Derek Taylor and McCartney's sheepdog, Martha. On Sunday morning, Peter Asher set up the portable recording equipment they had brought from London for the recording session. Apple had booked the local Victoria Hall to use in the event of rain, but the morning turned out to be the start of a lovely English summer's day and over a hundred fans turned out to see McCartney and Martha grace the streets of their small, usually quiet town. The session went well and at the end of the day, Apple had a fine recording of *Thingumybob* as well as a rousing brass band version of The Beatles' *Yellow Submarine* to use as a B-side.

Though not as prolific as McCartney, George Harrison also spent several months during 1968 producing records for Apple. Harrison's first Apple project was to record an album for Jackie Lomax. Lomax recalls: "I think it was before they went to India with the Maharishi trip that George came to me and said, 'I heard some of your songs from upstairs. I really like them and I'd like to produce something when we get back from India. Are you into that?' I said 'yeah yeah yeah of course.'" Lomax was in for an even bigger surprise when Harrison returned from India. While in India, Harrison had written several new songs, and upon returning to London, Harrison offered one of those songs – *Sour Milk Sea* – to Lomax to record as his first Apple single. With Harrison producing, Lomax recorded *Sour Milk Sea* and his own composition, *The Eagle Laughs At You* in the late spring of 1968.

It was during the sessions for *The Eagle Laughs At You* that Lomax remembers first meeting fellow Apple artist James Taylor. "James came into Trident Studios where we were recording, and he comes into the control room and plays me the first verse and chorus of a song. I said, 'Hey James, that's great, if you finish that up we'll put it on the album, I'll do my own version,' and he thought that was great. Then he went away and disappeared shortly after... the song was *Fire And Rain*... I would have loved to have done it."

Having signed James Taylor, Mary Hopkin, The Iveys and Jackie Lomax to the label, Apple now had more than enough acts to launch Apple Records. Apple soon concluded, however, that if they were truly going to fulfill their promise to discover and promote undiscovered talent, they needed to encourage such talent to contact Apple. To get the word out about The Beatles' new company, Paul McCartney came up with an advertising concept that was sure to entice even the most humble artist to submit samples of their work to Apple.

Under McCartney's direction, an advertisement was created featuring a photo of Apple Office Manager Alistair Taylor dressed up as a one-man band. The accompanying text read:

This man had talent... one day he sang his songs to a tape recorder (borrowed from the man next door). In his neatest handwriting he wrote an explanatory note (giving his name and address) and, remembering to enclose a picture of himself, sent the tape, letter and photograph to apple music 94 Baker Street, London W1. If you were thinking of doing the same thing yourself – do it now! This man now owns a Bentley!

The advertisement was placed in several British music papers and was so successful that more than 200 tapes arrived at Apple within two weeks of the ad appearing. Even though Peter Asher noted that Apple really didn't need to run such a campaign, he still defends the project, explaining that, "We hated the way that record companies were. It's hard to remember now, but back then the artists had no power, the companies were run by serious suits – people who had never listened to a rock record. We really felt that it had to be changed so we said, 'Listen, here's a new label run by people who actually like music and therefore we will listen to your stuff. Bring us your ideas.' It was a worthy ambition and it didn't do any harm. It made us a little nuts for a while... all these mailbags of tapes and weirdoes on the doorstep. But it was fun. Even the weirdoes were great."

While a few would be given cursory listens by Peter Asher's assistants in the A&R Department, most of the tapes were never even played. When interviewed by Geoffrey Giuliano in *Dark Horse*, Alistair Taylor recalled how, "Everything collected dust in the corner, we just couldn't cope... the kids were sending all sorts of tapes and sheet music in constantly. You'd come in the morning, switch on the answering machine and get some guy auditioning on the message tape. We used to send a lot of them around to the [Lew] Grade Organization."

Amidst all of the sheet music, tapes and film outlines that were making their way to Apple, there was also an alarming number of book and poetry manuscripts turning up, presumably due to one of The Beatles casually mentioning that Apple would be getting into the book publishing business. Unbeknownst to the literary hopefuls who sent in their unpublished works, Apple had no plans to start a book publishing division and most of the poetry and book manuscripts would end up unread in a closet known as "the black room" next to the press office on the third floor of the Savile Row building.

At one point during the summer of 1968, Apple assigned a young American named Francine Schwartz to start going through the poetry to find the best work to be used for a possible book project. Schwartz herself had come to Apple in April with the hope that Apple would finance a film of a script she had written. Though her script was probably never seen by anyone at Apple, she did manage to have a brief fling with Paul McCartney, who secured her a position in the Apple press office.

Having Schwartz review some of the accumulated poetry manuscripts was probably the closest that Apple ever got to having a book publishing division. Apple Books would actually put out one book in early 1970, which was the book that accompanied the initial pressing of the "Let It Be" album. Although the book was credited to Apple Publishing, all of the work on the project was actually done by freelancers.

Still, in the few months that had elapsed since Apple had opened for business, it seemed that struggling artists from all around the world had pinned their creative hopes on Apple. Each day, bulging mailbags full of demo tapes and manuscripts would be dragged up to the Apple mailroom, where the office boys would make a vain attempt to direct the packages to the intended recipient. While a majority of the submissions arriving at Apple were from the United States and England, Apple also received inquiries from musical groups from France, Sweden and several other countries.

But before any of these undiscovered artists could be presented to the world, Apple still needed to secure a distribution outlet for the record division. After several months of negotiation, Apple finally signed a worldwide manufacturing and distribution deal with EMI in late June of 1968. Under this agreement, Capitol Records would distribute and promote Apple in the United States and EMI would handle the distribution and promotion for the rest of the world. It is important to note that The Beatles did not become Apple Records artists as part of this deal. Although all Beatles records would now be issued with an Apple label, The Beatles were under contract to EMI until 1976 and the money earned from sales of Beatles records issued with an Apple label would go to Capitol and EMI and not Apple. Apple would not earn any money from the sale of Beatles albums until the Apple contract with Capitol and EMI was renegotiated in 1969.

To represent Apple at Capitol's Hollywood office, Capitol's Director of Independent Labels, Ken Mansfield, was hired to be North American Manager of Apple Records. Mansfield remembers, "Capitol President Stanley Gortikov called me one day and told me that The Beatles, mainly Paul McCartney and Ron Kass, has asked for me to head up Apple Records in America. 'You don't have to tell us where you are or what you're doing and you don't have to clear your expenditures. You only have one responsibility – to keep it together with The Beatles.'"

Ken Mansfield had first met The Beatles in 1965. "I was head of Capitol's Artist Relations and District Promotion Manager for the West Coast out of the Hollywood office. So when The Beatles first came through they were like any other band and they were my responsibility. Any time an artist was in my area, which was Southern California, Arizona, the western quadrant of the United States, it was my responsibility on any major tours and stuff to set up all the press conferences... anything to do with artist relations, and if it was a major act, to just fall in with the band and spend the time with them. So when they came to L.A. to do the 1965 Hollywood Bowl concert, that was my job. We did the press conference downstairs in the Studio A recording studio in the basement of the Capitol Building and we were going to present them with a gold record for *Help!* We had incredible security. The Beatles were really enamoured with L.A., with California, and Hollywood. George was asking me where all these things were, Paul turned to me and asked me if I could get him any Gene Vincent records, and Ringo asked me if he could meet Buck Owens while he was at Capitol. They just really wanted to know more about California. Because we kept on getting interrupted, I said to them we have a day off tomorrow and that we could take care of all their questions then. So the next day we just spent the day by the pool at this house in Benedict Canyon and I got to know them pretty well.

"So when they decided to set up Apple, I was kind of the only young executive they knew. Everyone else was a lord at EMI or a chairman of the board. Everyone was old and grey, while I was twenty-four and starting to grow my hair long. When they set up Apple, America was unquestionably the market. So they flew me, Stanley Gortikov and Larry Delaney over to London, and we put it together over there, then I came back and ran Apple for them in America. It wasn't like I changed offices or that they put up a special logo or sign.

The only thing that happened was that my stationary changed to US Manager of Apple Records. But Capitol paid my salary. I became their personal liaison. Everything had to go through me; I was responsible for everything: promotion, release dates, American mastering, keeping track of the parts and artwork. Most of my day-to-day work and dialogue was with Jack Oliver in London.

"It was crazy," continues Mansfield, "but it was more to do with the sheer volume of the work. The unfortunate, in a way, announcement that Apple was open to the people and that they wanted to do this different thing just made everyone in the world think that Apple was their home and that would drive you crazy. And Apple was not just a record company, there were five companies there. When I got to London, they had already made me a special packet of acetates of the first four records. We spent the days in London going over how we were going to present and position Apple in America. They were really gearing up for the American release because America was *the* market. The office at Savile Row had just been painted white on the outside and white on the inside, and they had put in green carpeting, but there was no furniture. When they brought me over to London, we would have our meetings in a hotel in Hyde Park, and then we'd go to the Apple building and we'd sit on the floor. The only thing in the whole building was a big sound system that Paul had brought in so that we could decide what our first releases were going to be and a portable table where they put food on.

"It was always very clear what the first four records were going to be, except for *Hey Jude*. Paul was really concerned about *Hey Jude* because it was seven minutes long and unlike any other single at that time. We spent a lot of time going back and forth, whether we should do *Revolution* as our first record instead of *Hey Jude*. Finally, because we kept playing it over and over every day and going back and forth, I said, 'Tell you what Paul, I'll just go back to America, I'll work my way back to L.A. and I'll hit the major cities and I'll run the two songs by the big stations.' Because I had been National Promotion Director for Capitol, I had good relationships with a lot of the major music directors and program directors across the country. I flew into WFIL in Philadelphia, Jim Hilliard was the hot ears in Philadelphia at the time, and then WQAM in Miami, a fellow named Jim Dunlop was there, and I went into St. Louis and they all fell all over *Hey Jude*, so I called London and told them we had to go with *Hey Jude*.

"When I came back to L.A. I set up a special promotion team to handle independent labels, but it was really because of Apple. I took my best six men out of the fifty national promotion people I had at

Capitol and created a six-man team to promote Apple. But I was the only person in America working specifically for Apple. Neil Aspinall once told me that the London office never had a clue what was going on with me in the States. I was their only contact in America. Paul Wasserman was their American PR man, but other than that it was just me. I just got inundated all the time... it was madness, but it was fun."

With Mansfield in place to manage Apple in the United States, Ron Kass fine-tuned Apple's London office with a few last-minute personnel changes. To round off Apple's record division in the UK, Kass moved Jack Oliver out of the press office and into the record department on the ground floor of the Savile Row office.

Jack Oliver recalls: "I had moved from Apple Publishing to working with Derek Taylor. Ron Kass wanted me to work with him, and Derek wanted me to work with him, and I chose to go into records, because I thought I could go further, which I did. Ron Kass was very gentlemanly, a gentle person. He was a very smooth, Californian type American. He was a very good businessman. He was very together and made some good decisions. When I first went into the label and worked with Ron in the record division, he gave me the foreign department, so I handled all of the foreign licensees. And then they gave me the advertising department and then the production department, so I did all the workings of a label and I knew exactly how it all worked and I would go meet with the people at EMI and took care of everything basically. Then Tony Bramwell did the promotion and I did everything else."

Looking back on those hectic days, Oliver recalls: "I thought Bramwell was pretty good. He knew a lot of people. To be honest, I don't see it as being too difficult to promote anything that came out of Apple Records. We were with the fab four and everyone would listen to us, no matter what we said. At that time we could do anything we wanted because we were so big. It wasn't a difficult job, but he played it very well."

With Apple Records fully staffed, all that was left to do was to put the final touches on the four singles that Apple had selected to inaugurate the Apple label. Everything appeared to be running smoothly for Apple, until the company made headlines around the world with the sudden and dramatic closing of the Apple Boutique. Although the real reason why The Beatles decided to close the boutique will probably never be known, many of the people involved with Apple at the time – and The Beatles themselves – have claimed that The Beatles simply got tired of being involved in the retail clothing business.

Only the remarkably prescient Derek Taylor seemed to comprehend that closing the Apple Boutique signalled the beginning of the end of the Apple dream. Despite Taylor writing an impassioned letter to The Beatles, imploring them not to give up on "promising openings for the hopeless, riches and Bentleys for clerks, shops for the young where even the counter was for sale, adventurous music, progressive films", The Beatles decided that they were no longer interested in running the Apple Boutique and they came up with a rather original plan for extracting themselves from the retail business.

On the evening of 29 July 1968, The Beatles and Neil Aspinall entered the boutique after it had closed for the night and gleefully set about taking whatever clothes they wanted. All of them left with some choice merchandise, except for Ringo Starr, who lamented to *Rolling Stone* that he had been unable to find anything in his size.

The next morning, Apple Boutique employees informed shocked customers – the first being American actor Michael J. Pollard – that there was no need to pay for their selections and then set about giving away the remaining £10,000 worth of stock. Once word spread that the Apple Boutique was giving away all of its merchandise, a frenzied mob gathered on the corner of Baker Street and Paddington Street, intent on taking away anything they could lay their hands on. Bolts of unused fabrics from The Fools' workshop, ashtrays and even the carpeting that covered the floor of the shop were taken away by the ravenous horde.

Future Apple recording artist Joey Molland even managed to get a piece of the shop itself as a souvenir of the final hours of the Apple Boutique. "I got a hold of the Apple Boutique door handle," recalls Molland. "It used to be a hand sticking out that you could put your hand in. I was in London with Gary Walker and The Rain and our manager, Morris King, his office was right off of Baker Street, about two blocks north of the Apple shop. I still have a jacket from the Apple shop. It was beautiful. It was a little far out with a lot of velvet."

Then it was all over and on the evening of July 30, after only eight months in operation, the Apple Boutique closed its doors for the last time. In a statement, Paul McCartney explained: "Originally, the shops were intended to be something else, but they just became like all the other boutiques in London. They just weren't our thing... All that's happened is that we've closed our shop in which we feel we shouldn't, in the first place, have been involved." McCartney whimsically concluded his prepared statement by proclaiming that "Apple is mainly concerned with fun, not frocks," and assured the public that the staff of the Apple Boutique would be given three weeks pay and an opportunity to get a job with another division of Apple. In addition to shutting the boutique, Apple made arrangements to close down the entire retail operation. Though the King's Road shop would continue operating into the autumn of 1968, Apple signed the entire operation over to John Crittle soon after closing the Apple Boutique.

One Apple Boutique employee that The Beatles were particularly keen to keep on Apple's payroll was the enigmatic Caleb. Not wanting to lose the services of a good mystic, The Beatles brought him over to Savile Row, where, with the aid of his i ching coins, he proceeded to contribute to the decision making process at Apple. He remained at Savile Row for several months, until one of his coin tosses suggested that it was time for him to move on. Peter Brown later claimed that Caleb ended up in a mental institution.

The closure of the Apple Boutique meant that Apple was now free to concentrate on what it would presumably do best, which was to make music. After months of careful preparation, the first four Apple records were finally released in the United States on 26 August 1968. The Beatles' *Hey Jude*, Mary Hopkin's *Those Were The Days*, Jackie Lomax's *Sour Milk Sea* and The Black Dyke Mills Band's *Thingumybob* were to be Apple's introduction to the world. Due to scheduling problems with the record pressing plants that Apple used in England, The Beatles and Mary Hopkin singles came out in the UK on 30 August, while the Black Dyke Mills Band and Lomax singles came out the following week, on 6 September.

To promote Apple's inaugural singles, Apple hired the prestigious Wolfe and Ollins advertising agency to develop a campaign to introduce Apple to industry VIPs and the press. The agency came up with a plastic presentation box on which a sticker reading "Our First Four, 3 Savile Row, W3" was affixed. Each box contained the four records along with a photo and short biography of each artist.

Hoping to get maximum press coverage of Apple's launch, Jeremy Banks devised a plan to have Richard DiLello deliver "Our First Four" presentation boxes to the residences of English Prime Minister Harold Wilson, the Queen Mother and other members of the royal family. Driven to the residences by Apple's chauffeur Joe Marchini and accompanied by favoured Apple photographer John Kelly, a slightly inebriated DiLello delivered the packages with little incident. Afterwards, George Harrison was reportedly less than pleased that DiLello delivered a set of records to Prime Minister Wilson (the Mr. Wilson featured in Harrison's *Taxman*). However, the publicity stunt worked well and Apple even received a thank you note from the Queen.

In a more offbeat attempt to publicize *Hey Jude*, a few weeks earlier Paul McCartney and Francine Schwartz found themselves spending a few hours of the evening of 7 August in the vacant Apple Boutique on Baker Street. Scraping away the whitewash that covered the abandoned shop's windows, the two proceeded to write "*Hey Jude*", "*Revolution*" and an Apple logo on the windows of the empty shop. Unfortunately, when local residents and merchants saw McCartney's handiwork the next morning, many mistook "Hey Jude" to be an anti-Semitic slur and the windows had to be hastily covered over.

By almost any standard, Apple appeared to get off to a spectacular start. In Britain, The Beatles shot to number 1, only to be replaced in the number 1 spot by Mary Hopkin. Both singles also reached the top ten in America. While Apple was ecstatic with Mary Hopkin's success, the company was disappointed that the Black Dyke Mills Band and Jackie Lomax singles failed to get into the top 100 in either the United States or Britain.

Apple was particularly confounded by the failure of *Sour Milk Sea*, a catchy, high-energy rock song that had been written and produced by George Harrison and featured instrumental support from Harrison, Ringo Starr, Paul McCartney, Nicky Hopkins and Eric Clapton. John Hewlett, who had been hired by Apple mid-summer as a promotions manager, admits that his attempt to promote Lomax's single did little to help make *Sour Milk Sea* a hit. Hewlett, the former bass player of the notorious UK pop band, John's Children (which also featured a young Marc Bolan), remembers that he joined Apple after the band split in the summer of 1968. "I came back to London and Simon [Napier-Bell, the manager of John's Children and several other groups] introduced me to a woman who worked at Apple. She was leaving and Simon happened to know her and he asked if I wanted to step into her job. So I called Terry Doran and went to meet him at the Baker Street office and Terry... who was gay and coming on real strong... I guess me being from John's Children and having that whole cute young-looking boy image, he just hired me instantly, so I had a job. He was a really nice man. Initially I was hired to do promotion. The first day I was asked to go to the BBC with a Jackie Lomax record. I had never been a promotion man so I just went over with the record. And I recall clearly what I said to the BBC guy, which was, 'My job is to get it played... I think it's pretty crap, but would you play it?' When I left, the BBC producer called Apple and told them that I said that 'the record was crap, but would they play it?' So when I got back they called me up to the office and fired me. But Terry was cool and gave me another job. They gave me the job of sifting through all the tapes that had been sent in after they did that promotion where they announced that anyone could send in a tape."

In a 1968 interview with *Melody Maker*, Lomax admitted that he never expected his association with The Beatles to make his career, although he probably also never thought that his record label promotions man would be as frank and as opinionated as John Hewlett. "When people heard that I was on Apple, they said, 'You got it made,'" he told *Melody Maker*, "but I'm not really connected with The Beatles, just with George as an individual." In the same interview, Harrison added: "When we started Apple, we thought that, even if we don't have a hit, as long as the record is good, that's all that matters. We never think of anything as A or B-sides. We just try to make them all very good with what's around us, with the musicians and the studios."

Due to the exposure that came with the immense success of *Hey Jude* and *Those Were The Days* and the media interest generated by The Beatles' direct involvement with the company, Apple quickly became an almost mythical part of the youth culture of the day. For many, Apple was idealized as a place where you could go and meet The Beatles, find a receptive outlet for almost any sort of creative idea, or to just go and "hang out". Speaking on behalf of Apple in a 1968 press interview, Derek Taylor summed up the goal of Apple: "What we are trying to create is a situation where an unknown can walk through our door, be welcomed and talk ideas, work projects over with, say, a Beatle. If they are good, he'll be backed and given artistic freedom for his work." With such warm, well-publicized invitations, it was little wonder that Apple was soon besieged by legions of would-be artists, well-wishers and tourists.

To the company's credit, Apple was exceptionally tolerant of the unusual individuals it attracted. During the first year of operation, Apple would be visited by Hell's Angels from San Francisco (who charged the cost of shipping their motorcycles to London directly to Apple) and even a family of American Hippies – dubbed "Emily's family" – who came to London to convince John Lennon and Yoko Ono to join them on a proposed trip to the Fijian Islands. Emily's family were a particular nuisance given Emily's penchant for walking around naked and breast-feeding an infant while her older children ran unsupervised through the office. It would have been very easy for Apple to have barred these people from the building, but instead, they were given day time use of the fourth floor guest lounge and access to the Apple kitchen.

The Hell's Angels eventually grew tired of London and left on their own accord, but Emily's Family and the other hippies who had come to Apple with the Hell's Angels would only leave after George Harrison – who had developed a strong aversion to hippies after an unpleasant visit to San Francisco in 1967 – finally took it upon himself to rid the building of the hippies that had taken over the guest lounge. In *The Longest Cocktail Party*, Richard DiLello recalled the day that Harrison came into the guest lounge and asked, "Well, you moving all your stuff out of here tonight?" There was then a long silence in the room, which was only broken when one of the stunned hippies asked Harrison, "Do you dig us or don't you?" Harrison's simple reply was, "Yin and Yang, head and tails, yes and no." Apparently Harrison's cosmic response managed to connect with their hippie logic and the lounge was empty by the end of the day.

The popular public perception was that the Apple office was a haven for crazy hippies and wide-eyed, post-adolescent dreamers, yet once past the imposing front door at Savile Row, Apple actually looked like any other mid-sixties record company. For most of Apple's first year of operation, Peter Asher, Derek Taylor, Tony Bramwell and many of the other male staff would be attired in stylish jackets and ties, while senior executives such as Peter Brown and Ron Kass were renowned for their fine suits and keen sense of style. Although drinks – and to a lesser extent, drugs – flowed freely at 3 Savile Row, the Apple staff probably had more in common with London's young businessmen than with the bands of disaffected students who were spreading civil unrest across Europe in 1968.

Still, Apple was a much more hospitable place than your typical mid-sixties British record company and Apple did attract a good number of the more extreme members of the thriving counterculture movement. The focal point of this idealized utopia was unquestionably Derek Taylor's chaotic press office on the third floor. Fuelled by his experience in Los Angeles during the summer of love, Taylor was the perfect person to preside over The Beatles' daring attempt to bring youth, culture and commerce together under one roof. More than anyone else at Apple, Derek Taylor fully believed in what The Beatles were trying to do and say with Apple.

In addition to his Press Officer duties, Taylor rapidly evolved into Apple's unofficial master of ceremonies. Sustained by a daily diet of alcohol and psychedelic drugs, Taylor would prove to be as adept at dealing with the Hell's Angels and hippie families who stopped in at Apple as he was setting up record receptions and fielding incessant press inquiries.

For most of 1968 and 1969, there seemed to be a perpetual party in the Apple press office. Each morning Richard DiLello would stock the apple-shaped ice buckets with ice, make sure the drinks cabinet was fully stocked, secure a fresh supply of Benson and Hedges cigarettes, and then wait for the daily parade of artists, staff and visitors to pop into the press office for some entertainment, gossip and refreshment. At the peak of Apple activity, the drinks bill often reached £600 a month.

Among The Beatles, Paul McCartney was Taylor's harshest critic (though he justifiably admonished Taylor for tripping on LSD during work hours) and, as illustrated in Taylor's *Fifty Years Adrift*, he frequently sent Taylor mean-spirited post cards and letters that questioned the relevance of his press office. One of McCartney's more pointed notes featured a cartoon drawn by McCartney himself showing two people drunk at a bar, over which he wrote, "We probably don't want a press department. Do we?"

Peter Brown explains that while Taylor often seemed quite caught up in the high spirit of the times, the press office "also served as PR for Apple, not just in the sense that they handled Apple's publicity, but rather that they conveyed Apple's style at the time. Derek and the Press Office certainly helped shape the public's perception of Apple. It was swinging London as everyone imagined it to be."

George Peckham readily agrees with Brown's assessment of Taylor's press office. "Derek Taylor's office was the nucleus of Apple. Everyone used to hang out there and there was always something happening with Derek. Many a time, his missus would call and ask if we'd seen Derek, and we'd have to go up and get him. He'd be in his office on the floor of the bog, out cold, pissed or stoned. We'd have to get him in a cab and send him home."

John Kosh, a graphic artist who designed several Apple album covers and who spent many happy hours at 3 Savile Row, sums up the feelings of many of Apple's staff: "Derek enjoyed himself a lot and he liked his substances," adding that "he was older than everyone else, so it was a little more shocking."

Sheltered from the loud, chaotic environment of the press office by two sturdy floors and by their more traditional view of the record business, Ron Kass and Jack Oliver had little time to spend lazy afternoons in Taylor's press office. Though pleased with the international sales of *Hey Jude* and, in particular, *Those Were The Days* (the first true Apple hit) Kass knew that Apple Records could not afford to be lulled into complacency by their early success. Throughout the waning days of summer, he worked tirelessly to build up Apple's artist roster. Being an avid jazz fan, Kass even went so far as to make a deal with Atlantic Records to have the venerable Modern Jazz Quartet record several albums for Apple, reasoning that an established jazz act would give Apple's roster some immediate prestige.

Establishing Apple Publishing in the United States was another priority project for Kass. In late 1968, he hired an American named Mike O'Connor to oversee Apple's American publishing operations. Before being sent off to open an Apple Music office in Los Angeles, O'Connor was brought to Savile Row for a few months so that he could get a feel for Apple's way of doing business.

Though hired as Director of Apple's American publishing, Mike O'Connor had also been asked to help make Apple Music's London operation more efficient. Part of this effort included replacing the well-liked but somewhat unconventional Terry Doran. In November, Doran would leave Apple Music Publishing to focus on managing Grapefruit, who also severed their links with Apple around the same time. Although Grapefruit would no longer be on an Apple retainer, George Alexander would remain signed to Apple Publishing until early 1970.

Neither the members of Grapefruit nor Terry Doran could ever explain why The Beatles' patronage seemed to have blighted Grapefruit's career so decisively. Speaking to *Melody Maker* soon after leaving Apple, George Alexander stated that, "What we want to do now is lose the Beatles tag. Sure, it helped us in the beginning and everybody knew us as The Beatles' group, but we want to make it on our own. If any mistakes were made in the past, it was getting four blokes off the streets and saying, 'You're Grapefruit' and getting fantastic publicity."

After leaving Apple, Grapefruit signed to RCA Records and attempted to update their sound by adding a new lead vocalist and a keyboard player to the original line-up (with Pete Swettenham leaving the band, Alexander switching to rhythm guitar and lead guitarist John Perry to bass). They replaced their tuneful psychedelic pop style with earthy, riff-driven rock songs to fit the gruff voice of their new front man, Bobby Ware. Their subsequent recordings were rather pedestrian efforts that lacked the charm and catchy pop melodies of their early singles and the group failed to find an audience for their new sound (except in Germany, where the Apple-published *Deep Water* was a top 20 hit in early 1969). Realizing that Grapefruit's days with RCA Records were numbered, Terry Doran relinquished management of the floundering group and returned to Apple in mid-1969 to work as George Harrison's personal assistant.

Like Grapefruit, The Iveys were another Apple act who were often accused of sounding too much like The Beatles and both Apple and the band tried to downplay the Beatles connection. The Iveys' debut single *Maybe Tomorrow* was released in November 1968 and it showed the band to be developing a distinctive style of their own. With a bold melody, sweeping strings and an ultra-catchy chorus, *Maybe Tomorrow* perfectly captured the best elements of British pop circa 1968. The record's flip side, *And Her Daddy's A Millionaire,* – a bouncy pop-rock number powered by a driving, fuzz guitar riff – was equally impressive and both the band and Apple were certain that one of the songs had to be a hit.

Maybe Tomorrow was the first Apple Record to be issued since the release of the highly-publicized "First Four" and they desperately wanted to get a hit in order to prove that there was more to Apple Records than The Beatles and their assorted pet projects. Yet despite receiving decent airplay from the BBC, *Maybe Tomorrow* had only modest sales in the UK. The single fared somewhat better in the United States, where it became a regional hit in some parts of the country and ultimately climbed to number 56 in the national charts.

Out of the early Apple artists, The Iveys were perhaps the most difficult to market. The Iveys had come to Apple at a time when the British and, to a lesser extent, the American pop scene was moving away from the traditional show business approach that fuelled such teen-oriented bands as The Herd and Amen Corner, into the rapidly evolving progressive rock scene that spawned bands such as Cream and The Jimi Hendrix Experience. With their tight harmony singing, two-and-a-half minute melodic pop songs and matching outfits and haircuts, The Iveys were neither mired in the past, nor were they on the vanguard of the looming rock revolution. On the liner notes to their debut album, Derek Taylor himself wrote: "They are not adventurous innovators, but they are ready to be."

Given the rapidly changing tastes of the music buying public, Apple seemed unsure of how best to market The Iveys. Indeed, the promo film that Apple shot for *Maybe Tomorrow* featured the uncomfortable-looking Iveys playing the song in the unfinished Apple basement studio. Under the advice of Mal Evans, the group were dressed in matching suits, although they had turned up the collars of their jackets in a vain attempt to appear hip. Still, *Maybe Tomorrow* was a significant step for Apple in that it was the first record released by the company that had no direct involvement from any of the four Beatles.

Ken Mansfield had very high hopes for The Iveys in America. "I believed in *Maybe Tomorrow* so much that I had 450,000 copies pressed up. We came out full blast, had radio play and acceptance from the stations, but we ended up probably selling 200,000 copies. With James Taylor's *Carolina In My Mind* we had more airplay than any other artist that I have ever worked with and still nothing sold. It was a total non-sale record. Nothing was wrong – they just didn't sell. From the business standpoint, we put all our resources behind Apple. What we spent on Apple was so out of proportion I don't know how Capitol could have made money on Apple. We did everything on those Apple records. Philosophically we were supposed to treat the Apple records as a Capitol record. We were supposed to work Jackie Lomax equal to Glen Campbell or whatever. Apple was a plum for Capitol – it was the greatest thing we ever did."

Despite Capitol's supposed enthusiasm for Apple Records, it proved to be very difficult to break The Iveys and James Taylor in the American market. Even being the pet project of Apple's A&R Director seemed to be of little help to James Taylor. Asher was so personally involved with Taylor's career that he took special care to make sure that everything to do with James Taylor – the single, the album, the promotion – was just right. Largely due to Asher's attention to detail, it was not until late 1968 that Apple finally got around to releasing the first James Taylor record.

Working with Asher and arranger Richard Hewson, Taylor had spent most of the summer of 1968 recording his debut album at Trident Studios in London. Taylor's Apple album was Peter Asher's first album-length production project. Upon hearing the tapes of Taylor's songs for the album, Apple was particularly excited by a song called *Carolina In My Mind* and it was selected to be Taylor's debut single. In a show of support, Paul McCartney played bass on the track and Peter Asher remembers that George Harrison also dropped by to add backing vocals to the song. Having only recently given up performing music, Asher too found it difficult to remain in the control room during the recording sessions and he contributed backing vocals and percussion to several of Taylor's songs.

Unlike the sparse, acoustic-based hits like *Fire And Rain* that Asher would produce for Taylor in 1970, Taylor's 1968 recordings featured some exceptionally ornate production. Building on the production style he first explored on the 1968 Peter and Gordon single *I Feel Like Going Out*, Asher added punchy brass arrangements, intricate backing vocals, harpsichords and even a harp to Taylor's simple folk-influenced tunes.

In the UK, Apple worked hard to promote both Taylor and The Iveys, yet Britain proved to be no more receptive to the music of both acts than had America. Tony Bramwell recalls: "The biggest problem we had with The Iveys was with their manager Bill Collins... he just had no idea about the music business. Then later when they were

Badfinger they had this American... Stan Polley... they had no idea of what they had. Collins always expected the impossible, but not do the obvious, they would say, 'Oh, we don't want to do that.' And Tommy [Tom Evans] wanted to be Paul McCartney, but he didn't know how to behave like Paul McCartney. And that little drummer was a bit of a Welsh git. They were great performers, but they had this rock and roll lifestyle of living in the country before they'd earned it. Mal Evans was a bit overprotective of them... he thought they were the next Beatles and he pushed them as the new Beatles before they were ready for it. But as songwriters they were dreams... fantastic songwriters."

More than anything else, Bramwell remembers the first years of Apple as being a very hectic time. In between trips to the BBC and to Capitol's Hollywood office to coordinate the promotion of Apple releases, Bramwell was also charged with creating almost all of Apple's promotional film clips. "I had a brief training course in TV direction in the mid-sixties," he explains. "I directed a couple of editions of *Ready Steady Go*... a few quiz shows. Brian [Epstein] sent me out to learn how television worked. He thought it would be a good idea to have somebody at Nems who knew TV, film speeds, lighting and all that. So when it came to Apple, I did all of the Apple videos... I can't remember all of them... they were usually something along the lines of taking a camera out for a day and shooting people running around in Hyde Park... I remember filming Mary Hopkin in Paul's garden... Paul playing his guitar in the studio."

In addition to their efforts to transform The Iveys and James Taylor into successful recording artists, the final months of 1968 found Apple rushing to complete the recording of Mary Hopkin's debut album. Paul McCartney had devised an idea of including a Valentine-like card in each copy of the album and Apple wanted to finish the album in time to release it on Valentines Day 1969.

Following the success of *Those Were The Days*, McCartney had agreed to produce Hopkin's debut album and he had come up with a concept of having her record a combination of show business standards and new songs written by some of the top pop songwriters of the day. Critically-acclaimed American singer-songwriter Harry Nilsson, whose work was greatly admired by Derek Taylor and all four Beatles, contributed a song called *The Puppy Song* which was recorded for the album and almost released as a follow-up single to *Those Were The Days*. McCartney had also asked Derek Taylor to contact Randy Newman about contributing a song to Hopkin's album, and Taylor dutifully sent a telegram to Newman's home in November 1968. While Newman eventually did manage to write a song for Hopkin called *I'll*

Be There, it was completed too late for inclusion on Hopkin's debut.

The best songs on Mary Hopkin's album were certainly the folk-pop compositions written by McCartney's friend Donovan, who contributed no less than three songs to the project. Singing to the simple accompaniment of the acoustic guitars of McCartney and Donovan, Hopkin's performances of *Lord Of The Reedy River*, *Voyage Of The Moon* and *Happiness Runs* showed her to be an exceptionally gifted folk vocalist.

In the course of searching for songs for Mary Hopkin, Apple also came across another addition to the company's roster of artists. A trio of American teenagers who called themselves Mortimer were visiting London after having released an impressive acoustic-folk album for Mercury-Phillips Records earlier in the year. As Mortimer's drummer Guy Masson remembers: "We were managed by an Englishman named Danny Secunda and we went to London for just a few weeks in the late fall of 1968 and we went over and knocked on Apple's door. We had heard over the radio in England that Apple was looking for songs for Mary Hopkin and for you to bring your tape to Apple Records because they were looking to finish Mary Hopkin's album."

"So the three of us went down to Apple Records – we were still signed to Mercury-Phillips – and we walk in and we go, 'Hi, we're Mortimer and we heard on the radio that you were looking for songs.' We walked in with our acoustic guitars and the receptionist said, 'You have to leave a tape.' So Tony Van Beeshotten [another member of Mortimer] was pretty sharp and said, 'We can't make a tape, we don't have time, we're going back to the States tomorrow.' So she says 'Alright, let me call up to the publishing office,' and she tells Mike O'Connor 'Mortimer is here,' and he goes, 'Mortimer, John gave me their album... send them all up.'"

The three members of Mortimer were shocked to hear that Mike O'Connor knew who they were and that he had even already listened to their debut album. Earlier that summer, Masson and a friend had attempted to deliver a copy of Mortimer's debut album to John Lennon and Paul McCartney when the two Beatles were staying in New York City at Nat Weiss' (The Beatles' American attorney) apartment. "We had heard on the radio that The Beatles were in town," recalls Masson, "and a friend of mine kept pushing me to take a copy of our record to Weisman's (sic) office/apartment which was only around ten blocks from where we lived. So my friend and I went off down the street with our little album to give to The Beatles. I said to him 'I don't know how we're going to get in there,' and when we got there, the whole block was surrounded... there were girls and cops everywhere. So we're stuck in the middle of this crowd when suddenly one of the girls looks at us and screams, 'Oh, it's The Hollies!' So one of the cops thought we were The Hollies and they grab us and pull us through the crowd. My friend Gary told them that we had to see John Lennon and Paul McCartney so we went from being stuck in a crowd as Mortimer to being led into the apartment with a police escort as The Hollies! I could hear through the door that there was a party going on so we knocked on the door and Nat Weiss answered it. We told him we were Mortimer and I said, 'I want to give this album to John and Paul.' He took the album and went back inside and came back a little later and said, 'I gave it to John and he said he would seriously give it a listen.'" John Lennon was apparently a man of his word and Mortimer's album not only made it back to London with Lennon but had also been passed on to Mike O'Connor in Apple Publishing."

Masson continues: "We went up to the office and sat around with our guitars and sang our songs. While we're going along singing a song called *Life's Sweet Music*, there's two doors in this office, one opens up and George Harrison walks in dressed in this Indian-styled green long jacket. He comes bopping in and he's clapping and he's dancing all around, and the three of us are going, 'Holy Toledo, that's George Harrison,' and he says, 'Sign them up' and he went out the other door. So we told our manager and he followed up, and the next thing you know, they bought us off of Mercury, and we're signing contracts with Apple Publishing and Recording."

With a growing list of artists now signed to the label, the first Apple album was finally issued in November 1968 – George Harrison's "Wonderwall". Harrison's album was recorded as the soundtrack to a quirky psychedelic film of the same name, a delightful period piece that starred English actress Jane Birkin. George Harrison's score, which was essentially the first solo album issued by a Beatle, was suitably colourful, featuring an eclectic set of instrumentals that ranged from Indian ragas to more rock-oriented recordings.

Since Harrison – like the other three Beatles – was unable to read or write music notation, he had to hire an outside music arranger to assist him with the "Wonderwall" recording sessions. His arranger of choice was London native John Barham, who would go on to be Harrison's principle arranger until the mid-seventies.

"I was 25 when I started to work with Apple in 1968," recalls Barham. "I had gone to the Royal College of Music in London and then the Trinity College of Music. In my third year there, I met Ravi Shankar and started working with him on the *Alice In Wonderland* film in late 1966. I met Ravi because I had been writing some music that used Indian scales and that's why Ravi took an interest in me. George came down to some of our sessions at the BBC and Ravi introduced me to him. From my work with Ravi, George knew that I could compose and arrange music, so he asked me to do 'Wonderwall'. We started recording in early 1968 after George had returned from India where he had recorded the Indian music. I also played trumpet on the "Wonderwall" sessions. I hadn't played the trumpet for around six years... it was Paul McCartney's trumpet... it was a flugelhorn... just lying in the studio, so I asked George if I could use this. So after I warmed up, George asked me to play this melody he had. He played it for me on piano, and I made up a melody to go above it, which was based on a tune that Ravi had given him to practice on the sitar."

Barham remembers: "For 'Wonderwall', I would go up to George's house in Esher and he would play things on guitar and sing them to me and I would write down the music. Most of the 'Wonderwall' music wasn't composed when we went into the studio. It was usually improvised. We recorded it at EMI with Tony Ashton and the Remo Four. We also did overdubs on some of the Indian tracks. It was very much a collaboration with all of the musicians. Obviously George knew what he wanted and he was guiding it the whole time. He played on almost all of the sessions... guitar, bass and piano. Ringo Starr and Eric Clapton were at the sessions. After the first day of playing the flugelhorn, George went out and bought me one. I ended up playing it on Jackie Lomax's *The Eagle Laughs At You*. So I got a trumpet and a very generous fee for my work on 'Wonderwall'." Impressed with Barham's work, Harrison would later hire him to play piano and score the string arrangements of some of the songs that Harrison was producing for Jackie Lomax.

Despite being a soundtrack album with no vocal performances, "Wonderwall" sold well and was a promising start for the Apple Records album catalogue. "The Beatles" double album – better known as "The White Album" – and John Lennon's and Yoko Ono's "Two Virgins" were the next Apple albums to follow "Wonderwall" into the shops. While The Beatles' album was yet another critical and commercial triumph, it was John Lennon and Yoko Ono's "Two Virgins" that received the most attention. Housed in a sleeve that displayed a fully naked John Lennon and Yoko Ono on its cover, the album sent shock waves throughout the world.

Featuring "music" that consisted of little more than Lennon's tape recorder experiments and Ono's voice manipulations, the record itself was of little consequence. However, the risqué cover of "Two Virgins" was another story altogether and it caused the album to be banned from sale in many American cities. The very conservative EMI refused to have anything to do with "Two Virgins", so Apple had to contract two independent record companies to distribute the album.

In Europe, "Two Virgins" would be distributed by Track Records, an independent label founded by the managers of The Who. In America, it was distributed by a small label called Tetragammon. "What happened was that EMI wouldn't touch it," recalls Jack Oliver. "They wouldn't even sleeve the record, so I had a bunch of the Apple scruffs sleeve the record in the basement of the old Apple shop and then Track picked them up to distribute to the shops."

A few weeks after issuing "The White Album" and "Two Virgins", Apple ended their first year by releasing James Taylor's self-titled debut and "Under The Jasmine Tree" by the Modern Jazz Quartet.

Driven by Peter Asher's boundless enthusiasm for James Taylor, Apple expected Taylor's album to be a big seller. Packaged in a lavish gatefold sleeve that featured musician credits and lyrics, Apple had put substantial resources into the release. It was an excellent album, featuring the definitive versions of such well-loved Taylor songs as *Carolina In My Mind*, *Rainy Day Man* and *Something In The Way She Moves* (a line that George Harrison would later "borrow" for his own composition, *Something*). Taylor, backed by strong musicians including guitarist Mick Wayne, turned in twelve superb performances that still sound fresh and vital, especially when compared to his subsequent work.

"Under The Jasmine Tree" was also an exceptionally strong album. The Modern Jazz Quartet were different from any of the other acts on the Apple label. Since the mid-fifties the MJQ had been one of the most respected jazz outfits in the world and there was clearly little that Apple could offer them that they could not find at any other label. The MJQ's leader, John Lewis, explains: "When we signed with Apple, it was an interim time between our obligations to Atlantic Records where we had been for many years. The Beatles had just started their record company and the president of the company, Ron Kass, was an old friend of our manager Monte Kay. We had known Ron Kass for many years. We were visiting Ron in Switzerland and we were having dinner and the whole thing came up and Monte Kay made the deal. We never thought anything about it... we were busy making music. At the time, the deal was open, we could have done other albums, but we did two albums. We recorded 'Jasmine Tree' in New York City and sent it to Apple." Packaged in a colourful post-psychedelic cover designed by Alan Aldridge, "Under The Jasmine Tree" was a superb, if perhaps incongruous, addition to the Apple catalogue.

Given the exceptional quality of both albums, Apple's staff were dismayed when neither managed to sell many copies in either the United States or Britain. Since the James Taylor album had sold so poorly in the UK, Apple decided against releasing *Carolina In My Mind* as a single there.

Frustrated by the commercial failure of his Apple debut, James Taylor began to feel that The Beatles and Apple had lost interest in him. His growing frustration and drug-related health problems led him to return to the United States in December 1968.

Looking back on James Taylor's initial difficulty in finding an audience, Peter Asher stresses that Taylor's album "got a lot of attention because the songs were so good. In retrospect, both James and I feel that I kind of overproduced it in an effort to get people to pay attention because at that time the feeling was that if he was just some sort of folkie guy with a guitar, no one was going to pay any attention. That's why I added all that different instrumentation and links. In the end, I think the album still stands up due to the songs."

By the end of the year, it was clear that Apple would need to work very hard in 1969 if they were going to make stars out of Jackie Lomax, James Taylor and The Iveys. As the year wound down and the UK record industry entered the pre-Christmas lull, Apple had a brief opportunity to re-evaluate some of the departments and personnel that were not living up to Apple's ambitions. Only months after having opened for business, Apple had already come under attack in the British music press for not having discovered any new stars other than Mary Hopkin and for the unkept promises and general chaotic atmosphere at Apple.

In a November 1968 article entitled "Has Apple Gone Rotten?" *Melody Maker* painted a bleak picture of an Apple that had failed to live up to the grand ideas that had been announced earlier in the year. Speaking on behalf of Apple, Derek Taylor was forced to admit, "We are now more or less a record company," though he added in typically Tayloresque fashion, "We started off with grandiose ideas but it's difficult to be grandiose in a glum society like the one which we have here."

In the course of the article, journalist Alan Walsh clearly put Taylor in defensive mode. When Walsh brought up the subject of Apple appearing not to respond to most of the letters and tapes that were sent to Savile Row, the usually enthusiastic Taylor bitterly answered, "Why should we reply? We didn't ask for the letter in the first place and we don't owe them a letter back at all." Trying to sum up Apple's first year, an exasperated Taylor concluded: "We certainly haven't brought about a revolution in the music business... we've failed in that. But all the other revolutions this year have failed, too!"

Paul McCartney was especially stung by this criticism of Apple and on several occasions he became obsessed with making Apple a more efficient company. Upon reading that Apple was full of freeloaders and unnecessary staff, he asked Neil Aspinall, Peter Brown and Derek Taylor to come up with lists of non-essential personnel, but none of the three Apple managers ever had the heart to draw up an Apple hit list. McCartney even tried to take matters into his own hands by asking Derek Taylor to cut the head count of the press office and fire one of the department's several secretaries. In *Many Years From Now*, McCartney remembers how his attempt to cut costs in the press office was ultimately foiled by George Harrison, who bluntly informed McCartney that if he were to fire the secretary in question, he and the other two Beatles would "reinstate her immediately".

In the end, Jeremy Banks was the only employee to be declared redundant and he was fired in November 1968. During his six months at Apple, Banks did coordinate some successful publicity photo opportunities and he set up several deals which gave Apple a royalty for all Beatles photos that were provided to the press. However, he was also notorious for spending most of his time at Apple pursuing freelance work and consuming a potent mixture of champagne and diet pills. To help out in the press office after Banks' departure, Derek Taylor hired Mavis Smith to be his assistant. She started at Apple on 16 December.

For the most part, Apple's staff were unfazed by the press criticism and Apple celebrated their generally successful inaugural year with a Christmas party held at the Apple office on 23 December 1968. Surprisingly, Ringo Starr and John Lennon were the only two Beatles to attend as Paul McCartney had already gone up to Liverpool for the holidays and George Harrison claimed to have overslept (Harrison would not admit that he skipped the party because he feared possible violence – on the part of the Hell's Angels who were attending the party – until he was interviewed for *Anthology* in 1997).

Having entertained a steady flow of holiday visitors since midday with an ample supply of alcohol and drugs, by the time the party officially started at six o' clock in Neil Aspinall's office, Apple was swimming in good cheer. The idyllic mood was unexpectedly shattered when Frisco Pete – one of the more menacing members of the California Hell's Angels biker gang that took up George Harrison's innocent offer to "drop by and see us when you're in London" – decided that he was unwilling to wait any longer for Apple's cooks to serve the holiday turkey.

Within moments, Frisco Pete had felled Mavis Smith's husband, journalist Alan Smith, with a single punch after Smith had tried to reason with the belligerent biker. In his book, *The Longest Cocktail Party*, Richard DiLello recounted how Frisco Pete was moving towards John Lennon and Yoko Ono when Peter Brown intervened to head off any physical harm coming to Lennon. With his calm, collected manner and gift for being able to find the right words for any situation, Brown was able to get Frisco Pete to quieten down and the party was soon able to get back under way.

Despite the unfortunate incident with Frisco Pete and the presence of only two of The Beatles, the party was, by all accounts, a wonderful affair. In addition to the magician who was hired to entertain the children in attendance, Apple's guests were treated to a costumed John and Yoko playing mother and father Christmas. As the evening wound down, John Lennon, Yoko Ono and Mary Hopkin would lead Apple's guests on a rousing round of Christmas carols, before bidding everyone good night, ending 1968 in fine style.

3
1969 - The Pre-Klein Era

Compared to the blur of activity that marked the final months of 1968, the first weeks of 1969 were relatively quiet at Apple. This brief respite gave Apple's management the opportunity to tend to some housekeeping and attempt to bring some much needed order to Savile Row. One of the first tasks to be tackled in 1969 was to move Apple's accounting department into a fourth floor office in the Savile Row building. With Apple's one-year lease at Wigmore Street due to expire at the end of January, all of the Apple departments that had remained at Wigmore Street – which included the accounting department, the travel office and Apple Films – were brought over to the Savile Row building.

Even the relatively simple task of consolidating all of Apple's departments into one building was a daunting project for Apple's young, inexperienced staff. While most of the furniture and files from the Wigmore Street office would arrive intact at Savile Row, important paperwork was mislaid and some even lost. Terry Doran recalls that he and the other Apple Publishing employees simply dumped all of their paperwork into the back of a black cab and had it driven over to Savile Row.

With all the Apple departments finally housed in a single building, the Savile Row office was soon filled to capacity. To help support the additional personnel and workload that came over from Wigmore Street, Apple added another office boy to their staff – 18 year-old Nigel Oliver.

Like so many English teenagers who grew up during the peak years of Beatlemania, Oliver was captivated by the music and allure of The Beatles. But he never thought that he would meet a Beatle, let alone work for the band. "I used to stand outside of the Baker Street shop just looking in, but I was scared to go in," he remembers. "I had left school and was working in a clothes shop at the time. One day, this Irishman I knew from my job asked me what I wanted to do and I told him I wanted to work for The Beatles, so he wrote a couple of letters to Apple for me. They didn't have any jobs, but I kept writing to Apple each month until Alistair Taylor hired me in January 1969. The office boy who trained me was the one who nicked the lead off the roof, but never got caught." The incident to which Oliver refers – when Apple realized that someone was actually stripping the lead off of the office roof, dragging mailbags full of lead through the office, and then sell-ing it to a scrap dealer – did little to dispel the popular, though somewhat exaggerated, image of the Apple office being so chaotic that visitors could walk away with almost anything they wanted.

But theft was certainly a problem at Apple. In *The Longest Cocktail Party*, Richard DiLello details a partial list of items that walked out of Apple's front door, which ranged from employee paychecks and electric typewriters, to record player needles and cases of alcohol. One of the more enterprising thieves went as far as to remove the expensive speaker cones from some of the speakers in the basement studio. The thief simply unscrewed the back panel of the speaker cabinet, removed the speaker cones, and then re-sealed the cabinet, leaving the studio staff none the wiser until they attempted to use the now-worthless speaker cabinet.

While tales of missing typewriters, cameras, and roof lead are now a fundamental part of Apple lore, thefts such as these were generally isolated occurrences. Typically, the items most likely to be removed from the premises were copies of Apple singles and LPs that were stored in the building. In addition to the records being stolen, the Apple staff were apparently also quite generous when it came to giving them away. When Ron Kass finally realized just how many records were being given to employees, friends of employees and even people who came in off the street, he was forced to initiate a policy under which each employee would be given a single copy of each Apple release and the option to purchase up to three additional copies at wholesale price.

Nigel Oliver confesses that he too was not always able to resist the temptation of helping himself to some of the record riches that could be found around the office. "We used to take sacks of albums out of Apple. All of the albums that were supposed to be posted to America we never sent. I was the best office boy though; people thought I was the one who could be trusted, I wore a suit and I was making seven pound fifty. The fiddles were amazing, but if you had to go somewhere late at night, Paul's house or over to the studio, Derek would give you a couple of albums or a bottle of scotch. I took the job very seriously."

After integrating all of the Apple departments into one building, the next task undertaken by Apple's management was to evaluate the overall business performance of the company. There had already been several half-hearted attempts to identify inefficient or impractical divisions of the company, but in general, efforts to downsize the under-performing departments of Apple would prove to be quite troublesome for the young company. Apple had managed to abandon the Apple Foundation for the Arts and Apple's retail operations, but little progress had been made when it came to evaluating the performance of the many other divisions of Apple.

Given that Apple Films was run by an experienced executive, Dennis O'Dell, it was surprising that Apple Films had done relatively little during its first year in operation. By early 1969, all of the projects planned for Apple Films had been put on hold and the film division was relegated to doing little more than overseeing the distribution and rentals of The Beatles' *Magical Mystery Tour* and John Lennon and Yoko Ono's *Smile* films. While Apple Films was involved with coordinating the filming of The Beatles' upcoming "Get Back" project, O'Dell is remembered by many of his Apple co-workers as having spent most of his time watching TV in the office and taking long lunches.

By early 1969, the only fully functional Apple divisions were Apple Records and Apple Music Publishing, which was fine as far as Ron Kass was concerned. Former Apple staff members remember that Kass was quite pleased to not have to devote Apple resources to non-music projects and that he was anxious to give Apple a proper launch in the United States. In mid-January, Kass had announced an ambitious plan to establish an Apple office in Los Angeles, noting that Apple had already been searching for a building to house a proposed six-person staff. Since Apple's American distributor, Capitol Records, was responsible for most of the record production issues, Kass envisaged Apple's California office as focusing primarily on Apple Publishing, which he promised would soon grow larger than the British publishing operation.

Kass took an active interest in Apple's music publishing business and he put his full support behind establishing an American presence for Apple Publishing. To represent the company's music publishing interests in America, Apple Music Publishing was split into two companies – one to correspond to each of the two major American performing rights organizations, BMI and ASCAP. Apple Music Publishing Co. Inc. was aligned with ASCAP while Apple established a new company, Python Music, to focus expressly on American writers and to be affiliated with BMI.

As part of Kass's plan to expand Apple operations in America, on Saturday 4 January 1969, Peter Asher was dispatched from London for a two-month stay in Hollywood, California. Kass knew that the United States would ultimately be Apple's key market and he sent Asher to California so that Apple's relatively inexperienced A&R Manager could get a sense of the American market, look for American talent and assist Ken Mansfield in setting up Apple's American operation.

Once settled in California, Asher was given an office in the Capitol Records tower and he quickly immersed himself in learning the intricacies of the American record business. Asher also used his California sojourn as an opportunity to reunite with James Taylor and to start preliminary work on Taylor's second album for Apple. During his stay, Asher recorded several songs with Taylor, including a fully-produced early version of *Fire And Rain* featuring strings and gospel-style backing vocals.

Back in London, Apple's staff were equally busy gearing up for a new Beatles project, which was to be a film of The Beatles recording their new album, "Get Back". In addition to coordinating the details of the "Get Back" album and film, Apple was also pushing Magic Alex and Apple Electronics to put the finishing touches to the state-of-the-art recording studio that was under construction in Apple's basement so that the studio could be utilized for "Get Back" if needed.

All of The Beatles were anxiously awaiting the completion of Apple Studios. Tired of the corporate bureaucracy and outdated 4-track recording equipment at EMI, The Beatles had spent a good deal of time in 1968 recording at several of London's new independent 8-track studios. Between not having 8-track facilities at EMI and sometimes not being able to record at EMI or Trident due to the studios being booked by other artists, The Beatles were looking forward to having an 8-track recording studio available for their exclusive use.

Having confidently assigned the task of creating the studio to Magic Alex and Apple Electronics, The Beatles expected to have the studio completed by January 1969. Instead, they were dismayed when they went down to the basement and found out that not only had Magic Alex been unable to create such promised technical innovations as a 72-track recording console and invisible sound barriers, but that the recording studio – which Magic Alex had cobbled together from assorted components of commercial recording equipment that he claimed were his own creations – was barely even functional.

In Derek Taylor's *Fifty Years Adrift*, George Harrison remembers that, "Alex's recording studio at Apple was the biggest disaster of all time. He was walking around with a white coat like some sort of chemist, but he didn't have a clue of what he was doing. It was a 16-track system and he had 16 tiny little speakers all around the walls. The whole thing was a disaster."

From his vantage point in the Apple cutting room, George Peckham spent many hours watching Magic Alex working on the studio and he remembers his creation quite vividly. "Magic Alex had some good ideas in principle, but it didn't work. All down one side he had these big stainless steel panels that inside were like sponge, so you had this reflection and absorption... which is how modern studios are today. But what let it down was that he didn't float the floor so it was solid and you got reverberation everywhere. He also kept the old fireplace that was down in the basement, so the sound would reverberate up the chimney and then back down again.

"There was also this big set of lovely oak doors," continues Peckham, "and he kept them in and neglected to soundproof the other side of them, so the sound would hit the doors and the passageway behind the doors would become this kind of sound box and you'd get all these rumbling sounds that you would pick up on the mics. He also made what we called the white elephant desk... it was a big old white leather thing with bloody big knobs on it. We called it the white elephant because if somebody switched it on it wouldn't function. It would just make some nasty sounds and switch itself off. I think the only thing we ever recorded on it were some demos for John... his Saturday morning demos we used to call them. Alex had some great ideas... they had a window that shined light into the studio and Alex was putting in these lights that would change with the different sound frequencies but we eventually realized that it wasn't going to float. So we ended up buying a desk from a guy called Dick Swettenham which cost about 15 grand. They had to gut out all of Magic Alex's work when they rebuilt the studio." According to studio manager Geoff Emerick, the entire recording console that had been built by Magic Alex was eventually sold to a scrap metal dealer for five pounds.

Out of all of the Apple department heads and close associates of The Beatles, Magic Alex was perhaps the only person whose activities were never really questioned. "They should have called him Crazy Alex," offers Jackie Lomax. "That guy Alex kept promising that he could make a fantastic studio out of cheap bits, but he never could... I never heard it play more than two tracks at a time. That's Magic Alex for you... every time something went wrong he had a heart attack and went into hospital... it was a nice studio, well done except for the machines."

Jack Oliver agrees: "The studio was a waste of money; it never came together. When I was there it was nothing – it was a hole in the ground. We had a room down there, but there was never any electronics in it, all that would happen was that bands would rehearse down there. Most of the bands would have rehearsal studios elsewhere, but people would come and play now and again. Billy Preston would jam down there a lot and Doris Troy would come in and sing and people would sit in. It was great fun. They were always in there at night, we would all descend down there at night after work and they would play until two in the morning."

Even though Magic Alex's efforts had left the Apple Studio as little more than an astronomically expensive rehearsal room, The Beatles decided that they wanted to move the recording sessions for the "Get Back" project to Apple. Having spent two weeks recording on a cold, desolate soundstage at Twickenham Film Studios, they were adamant they would finish "Get Back" in the more hospitable environment at Apple. Since The Beatles were midway through filming and recording, Apple had to borrow mobile recording equipment from EMI so that the project could continue.

It was not only the location that changed when The Beatles abandoned Twickenham for Apple. When filming and recording finally resumed at Savile Row, The Beatles were now accompanied by a guest musician, American organist Billy Preston. Preston was in England performing with Ray Charles when George Harrison had spotted him on stage with the Ray Charles Band at the Festival Hall. The Beatles had first crossed paths with Preston while in Hamburg in 1962 and they had been very impressed by his dynamic playing. In the ensuing years, Preston had become an even more accomplished musician and after seeing him at the Festival Hall, Harrison extended an invitation to drop by Apple and sit in on a Beatles recording session. Within an hour of arriving at Apple, the good-natured Preston had clearly hit it off with the entire band and he would stay with The Beatles until the end of the "Get Back" sessions.

To thank Billy Preston for his contribution to the "Get Back" sessions, The Beatles would bill the forthcoming *Get Back* single as being by "The Beatles with Billy Preston," an honour that was never bestowed on any other session musician who graced a Beatles' recording. George Harrison was so impressed with Preston – who at the time was signed as a solo artist to Capitol Records – that he requested Capitol re-assign Preston's contract to Apple Records. Capitol seemed to be more than happy to pass Preston to Apple and he was soon signed to the Apple Records label and given a contract with Apple Music Publishing in February 1969.

All four Beatles would later admit that Billy Preston's presence greatly improved the tense atmosphere that had characterized the initial "Get Back" sessions at Twickenham. Prior to Preston joining the "Get Back" sessions on 22 January, George Harrison had even quit the group on Friday, 10 January after having a row with Paul McCartney. The argument – which was captured on film – was touched off when McCartney attempted to give Harrison a suggestion on how to play a guitar part. The argument quickly escalated and ended when Harrison left the soundstage and drove home. Harrison would return on 15 January to meet with the other three Beatles to outline the conditions for his return to the group. Harrison was adamant that The Beatles abandon all plans to resume live performances and that the "Get Back" sessions – which were initially intended to be the basis of a television documentary – become the foundation for a new album. After heated debate, The Beatles agreed to Harrison's demands and the sessions resumed at Apple Studios the following week.

Even though the "Get Back" sessions are now generally regarded as the nadir of The Beatles recording career, a good deal of exceptional music was recorded during the project. Perhaps the finest moment of the Apple era took place at 3 Savile Row on 30 January 1969, when The Beatles made their last public performance on the roof of the Apple building.

Throughout the "Get Back" sessions, The Beatles had been arguing amongst themselves about whether they should give a live performance as the finale of the "Get Back" film. After dismissing such ambitious ideas as filming a performance in a Roman amphitheatre in Tunisia or on an ocean liner at sea, the group elected to simply give a live concert on the roof of the Apple building.

This final chapter of The Beatles' career – which was captured for posterity by the film crew – began on an overcast Thursday morning when road managers Mal Evans and Kevin Harrington loaded the band's equipment into the elevator at the back of the Apple building. Once on the roof, Evans and Harrington set up the drums, amplifiers and Billy Preston's electric organ in stage formation and then watched and waited as the film crew made their preparations. A few hours later, around lunchtime on that cold winter's afternoon, The Beatles – augmented by Billy Preston – made their final public performance as a group on the bleak rooftop of the Apple office.

With the film cameras rolling, The Beatles played for forty-two minutes, running through several versions of songs that they had been rehearsing in the Apple basement and at Twickenham. Performing five stories above Savile Row, few people could actually see the band, but the raw, amplified sound that they made reverberated throughout the surrounding neighbourhood. As The Beatles played, the film crew captured people scampering onto the rooftops and fire escapes of neighbouring buildings to get a better look at the group that had not performed in public since 1966. The unannounced performance brought traffic in the street below to a stand-still. The Beatles managed to perform only seven songs before the police arrived at Apple's door and requested that they cease performing.

While it has since been suggested that someone at Apple or with the film crew called the police to add some drama to the proceedings, those who were at 3 Savile Row that afternoon are adamant that the police raid was genuine. "The police raided the building during the rooftop concert and there was a whole chorus of toilets being flushed when the fuzz arrived," recalls resident Apple designer Kosh. "Ten minutes before the raid, someone called from Savile Row police station to say, 'You've got ten minutes.' We knew they were coming and everyone was ready for it... the toilets had been securely flushed by then... there was all sorts of stuff around."

By the end of the day, however, neither The Beatles nor any of the Apple staff had been arrested for disturbing the peace or for possessing any illicit substances. Though The Beatles would return to Apple's basement studio the next day to finish filming what certainly ranked among the most dispirited recording sessions of their career, there was no denying that for one brief moment on that windswept Apple rooftop, The Beatles had managed to come together as a band one last time, each member seemingly charged to be playing in front of a live audience and remembering what it felt like to play in a real working rock band.

Apple Publishing's John Hewlett, who was on the roof along with Ken Mansfield, Peter Brown and other Apple staff members and guests, remembers: "The Beatles were fantastic. It was amazing, I had never seen them close-up like that. I had seen them in the studio... every now and then, but I never heard them playing a whole song. It was great, it really was. I was blown away. It was so much fun seeing them playing and they were really, really good. They were all enjoying it, Lennon in particular. I was most impressed with Lennon and with Ringo Starr... his drumming was knocked a lot, but he was great and really unique. I came in from lunch and heard all this noise and we went up on the roof and just sat and watched them play."

The rooftop performance may have been one of the most exciting moments on Savile Row, but by the next day both the group and the Apple staff had put the excitement behind them and had returned to their usual work schedule. While The Beatles struggled to finish the "Get Back" project in the makeshift studio in Apple's basement, in the record office directly above the studio, the small staff of Apple Records was working round the clock to establish Apple as a hit-making record label in its own right. Apple's first new record in the UK for 1969 was the debut single of White Trash, a five-man band from Glasgow that had come to Apple in late 1968 while they were still performing as The Pathfinders.

In contrast to their beat group-inspired name, The Pathfinders – whose guitarist Fraser Watson had been a member of the seminal

Scottish band, The Poets – had a progressive, hard rock sound that was very much in vogue in late sixties London. Their debut single was a song called *Road To Nowhere* that had been independently recorded by their manager, the former Shadows drummer Tony Meehan, and it was Meehan who had brought the finished tape to Apple. In the book *Blue Suede Brogans*, Fraser Watson remembers: "One night we were sitting in the Cromwellian Club, totally depressed after a rotten gig, when Tony came in and said, 'Apple – The Beatles' company – want to release *Road To Nowhere*!' It was like a dream."

The Pathfinders had come to Apple's attention when Meehan visited Savile Row in late 1968 and played The Pathfinders' tape to George Harrison and Paul McCartney. Both Beatles were impressed by the tape and The Pathfinders were given a contract with Apple Records and Publishing. When the newly signed group voiced concerns that their name might not be suitable for the progressive music scene of 1969, they asked Apple to come up with a new name. It was Richard DiLello who came up with White Trash.

Their single was a moody, magnificent version of a seemingly obscure Carole King song called *Road To Nowhere*, backed with *Illusions*, a driving slice of poppy psychedelia written by ex-Poet Hugh Nicholson and assigned to Apple Publishing. *Illusions* was arguably even better than the A-side and either one of the songs had the potential to become a hit for White Trash.

Only weeks after the band was signed, it was discovered that English singer Lesley Duncan had recorded her own rendition of the song and Apple suddenly found itself with only a few weeks to get the record into the shops. Copies of White Trash's powerful performance of *Road To Nowhere* were quickly pressed up and released in late January. As soon as finished demo copies of the record arrived at Apple, Tony Bramwell rushed the White Trash single over to the BBC to try to get *Road To Nowhere* added to the Radio One play list. Confident that Apple had found themselves a new hit act, Ron Kass and Jack Oliver were extremely disappointed when a sheepish Tony Bramwell returned from the BBC and informed them that the BBC considered the name "White Trash" to be offensive and that they would not be airing the song unless the group came up with a more suitable name.

Apple's first instinct was to refuse to give in to the BBC, until Ron Kass pointed out that the name would certainly face even more resistance in the more conservative American market. As a compromise, Apple simply had the group shorten their name to Trash and then re-pressed the record under the group's revised name. Unfortunately, by the time the re-pressed *Road To Nowhere* was issued, the single's initial commercial momentum had been lost. Despite the quality of the recording and the group's well-received live shows, the single failed to chart. Iveys drummer Mike Gibbins was quite fond of White Trash and is still surprised that they were unable to get a hit. "White Trash went over real well in London," he recalls. "We used to hang out with White Trash... we used to hang out and get stoned. They used to come to our house, we used to go to theirs. I loved them, they were a powerful band. They were heavy but they weren't very successful with Apple. Their drummer is a taxi driver in London now."

Trash's failure to get a hit with *Road To Nowhere* is one of the many unsolved mysteries of the Apple story. Unlike The Iveys, whose upbeat Kinks/Hollies/Beatles-influenced style was several years out of date with what London's taste-makers considered to be cutting edge, Trash's hard rock guitar and neo-gothic organ sound placed them at – or at least near – the forefront of the heavy rock style which was quickly becoming all the rage in England. Trash's only real liability was that none of the group members were accomplished songwriters. Tony Bramwell notes that the main problem faced by *Road To Nowhere* was that, "White Trash were too heavy... there was no heavy radio station at the time to play it. Also there was a bit of a rejection of the name, although they were never actually banned."

Despite the cool reception that *Road To Nowhere* received in the UK, the single was issued in the United States in March 1969. Similar to The Ivey's single, the record sold well in some regional markets but never managed to break on a national level. James Taylor's debut single *Carolina In My Mind* was also released in March 1969 and it too met with only limited success.

Ironically, less than a month after the Trash debacle, Apple would have yet another of its records run into censorship problems, although this time it was Apple's distributor, EMI, that would be the censor. The controversy was over *The King Of Fuh*, a single by an American artist called Brute Force that Apple had planned to issue in February 1969. A pretty, melodic song that combined subtle flower-power sentiments with an exceptionally funny and risqué lyrical hook, *The King Of Fuh* was a perfect record for Apple circa 1969, and it could have been a hit had it received a proper release at the time.

Brute Force was (and still is) the stage name of Stephen Friedland, a singer/songwriter from New York City specializing in satirical music and surreal performance art. Prior to coming to Apple, Friedland had been a staff songwriter for Bright Tunes Music Publishing (where he wrote songs covered by UK pop-art sensations The Creation and several other groups) and a member of the vocal group, The Tokens. Friedland had also previously recorded a solo album for Columbia Records in 1966, featuring quirky songs such as *Sitting On A Sandwich* and *Tape Worm Of Love* – earning him a good deal of notoriety but little in the way of record sales.

Like fellow New Yorkers Mortimer, Friedland came to Apple's attention through The Beatles' American attorney, Nat Weiss. "I had a girlfriend who eventually became the girlfriend of Tom Dawes from The Cyrkle and they were managed by Nat Weiss," explains Friedland, "so, I got Tom Dawes to speak to Nat Weiss about a song I had recorded with The Tokens. This was early 1968... it took me a long time to convince The Tokens to do *King Of Fuh*. I had produced the song with The Tokens at Ohmstead Sound Studios which was on 40th and 6th Avenue in New York... they had a mellotron and we used that for violins, so we made the track. We did the B-side *Nobody Knows* at a different session around the same time.

"So we brought the song to Nat Weiss with the idea that it would go on Apple," recalls Friedland. " I wanted them to hear it, and it came back to me one day that they wanted to do it – that's what I heard from Nat Weiss. So Weiss sent the master tape to Apple in London and George Harrison took the track that I did with The Tokens and put on strings with the London Philharmonic. I believe he also re-did the bass and he might have done something with the drums too. He changed the melodic line of the strings and made it prettier. I wasn't there when he did that. So they pressed it, put it on a 45 as Apple 08, and then they didn't do it. EMI banned *The King Of Fuh*... they found it offensive."

John Barham, who was summoned by George Harrison to write a string arrangement for *The King Of Fuh*, remembers the session well. "There was a lot of laughing when they played the tape in the studio... I did the strings for *The King Of Fuh* when George produced the overdub session at Trident." While the assembled session musicians were quite taken by the subtle wit and good-natured fun of *The King Of Fuh*, EMI's senior management were not so easily amused.

In fact, when the EMI management heard *The King Of Fuh*, they flatly refused to press or distribute the record. Unwilling to once again be undermined by corporate censorship, Apple ultimately elected to press up the single themselves and they gave a small run of records a very limited distribution in mid-May. Friedland recalls that, "They distributed it as much as they could – they must have pressed around 3000 copies. They just sent it to friends and disc jockeys. I had two boxes of them, around a hundred copies."

Friedland claims to have never signed a contract with either Apple

Records or Publishing (although he has a letter from Mal Evans that mentions that Peter Asher had received his contract), nor did he receive any money from Apple. "I had no management at the time... I was a young artist, 28 or 29, on Apple Records! I should have sat down with a manager, but it didn't happen. So in the spring of 1969, me and my wife Cynthia went to Savile Row. I essentially went to pick up the tapes because it wasn't happening... I couldn't understand it. I never did meet George. I remember when I was at Apple that I was hoping to meet George Harrison and Derek Taylor said to me, 'Well, he's rather provincial,' meaning that George wouldn't come into the city to meet with me. I did get to meet with the other guy, Neil Aspinall and Richard DiLello... it was a pretty sedate office."

Even as Apple waged war with Britain's conservative record industry while simultaneously launching an all-out assault on the pop charts of the world, they somehow found the time to launch a subsidiary "art" label called Zapple. Since Apple's inception, Paul McCartney and John Lennon had been very interested in launching a budget-line label to issue what would essentially be known three decades later as "audio books". In October 1968, Apple hired Barry Miles, who co-owned the Indica bookshop with John Dunbar and Peter Asher, to manage the proposed spoken word label. The initial idea of Zapple was that it would release avant-garde and spoken word records at a reduced price that would be comparable to that of a paperback novel. While the idea looked great on paper, the reality was that when the few records actually put out by Zapple finally made it into the shops, they were priced like any other full-priced music album.

Zapple's first (and last) two releases were George Harrison's "Electronic Sound" and John Lennon and Yoko Ono's "Life With The Lions". Although the records were supposed to be issued in February, both records were not released in the UK until 9 May 1969.

Apple had initially considered putting out every Zapple release in a custom designed generic Zapple sleeve, but of the two Zapple Records to be released, both had traditional album cover art and the regular Apple label with a silver "Zapple" superimposed over the top of the Apple. Curiously, neither Harrison's nor Lennon's record really seemed to fit the original Zapple concept. "Electronic Sound" was an undistinguished recording of Harrison experimenting with his recently purchased Moog synthesizer and "Life With The Lions" was essentially "Two Virgins" part 2, being little more than recent field recordings made by Lennon and Ono.

The next Zapple project was to be more in keeping with the original idea for Zapple – an album of American author Richard Brautigan reading some of his poetry. Although the album "Listening to Richard Brautigan" was recorded and actually scheduled to be issued on 23 June, it was never released on Zapple.

In spite of the difficulties that Apple was having getting recordings issued on the Zapple imprint, plans for Zapple continued to flourish throughout 1969. In the spring of 1969, Zapple announced plans to release spoken word recordings by such acclaimed underground writers as Allen Ginsberg, Charles Bukowski, Kenneth Patchen, Ken Weaver and Lawrence Ferlinghetti. Zapple even proposed issuing a 24-album set of Lenny Bruce recordings. John Kosh remembers that, "There was a lot of Lenny Bruce being played at Apple. Derek Taylor decided to convert everyone to Lenny Bruce, which he did successfully."

American author Ken Kessey – of *One Flew Over The Cuckoo's Nest* fame – went as far as to venture to Apple's London office to begin work on an Apple-sponsored project. When Kessey got to London, Apple supplied him with a tape recorder, typewriter and the use of a small back office in the Apple building and asked him to record his impressions of late-sixties London. Though Kessey allegedly submitted a finished tape to Peter Asher, Asher never got around to doing any further work on the project and it remains unreleased to this day.

One of the few Apple projects to successfully reach fruition in early 1969 was Mary Hopkin's "Postcard" album, which was issued by Apple in late February. Despite Apple failing to get the album into the shops by the Paul McCartney-imposed target of Valentines Day, the album was still a massive success in Britain where it reached number 3 in the charts. In America, where Apple had added *Those Were The Days* to the album to help boost sales, the album sold reasonably well and it became Apple's first non-Beatles album to break into the American top thirty, reaching number 28 in March 1969.

Having been involved with almost every aspect of "Postcard's" creation, Paul McCartney was exceptionally pleased with Hopkin's success. In addition to having produced the sessions and having played on the album, McCartney had even come up with the concept for the album cover and had his American girlfriend, Linda Eastman, take the pictures that graced the record sleeve. To drive home the postcard theme, McCartney hand wrote the album credits on the back of a postcard, which he then sent to Apple. The post card – now complete with authentic Royal Mail postage stamps – was then used for the credits that were shown on the album's back cover.

Seemingly not content with the positive response that Mary Hopkin had enjoyed in Britain and America, Apple put a good deal of effort into establishing Hopkin as a true international star by having her record non-English language songs for specific foreign markets. Her *Those Were The Days* single had been released in English, Spanish, German and French language versions and Apple was keen to have Hopkin record additional foreign language material.

In an effort to capitalize on the success of the foreign language versions of *Those Were The Days*, Hopkin recorded a new single, *Lontano Dalgi Ochie* for release in Brazil, Italy, and a few other European markets in early 1969. Around the same time, Apple also tried to crack the French market with *Prince En Avignon*, a French language song from "Postcard" that was released as a single in France. Both singles were backed with *The Game*, a pleasant pop song written by Beatles producer George Martin and published by Apple Music Publishing.

Jackie Lomax may never have been brought down to Trident Studios to record foreign language versions of any of his songs, but Apple did put a big promotional push behind his "Is This What You Want" album on its worldwide release in March. Featuring Lomax's sensational overlooked single, *Sour Milk Sea*, plus exquisite ballads like *I Fall Inside Your Eyes* and sturdy pop-rock like *Speak To Me*, the George Harrison produced "Is This What You Want" was expected to be a big seller for Apple. Instead, it garnered only modest sales in the United States, sold relatively few copies in the UK and fared no better in other European territories. In an effort to stimulate sales, Apple even added an apple-shaped sticker on the cover proclaiming that such famous guests as Paul McCartney, George Harrison, Ringo Starr and Eric Clapton appeared on the album, but it was to little avail.

Ken Mansfield maintains that Apple expended a great deal of effort and care launching Jackie Lomax's career in America. "I took Jackie Lomax and Mal Evans on a radio promotion tour around the country hitting up all the DJs and music directors in all the major markets. We really worked it. With Apple though, we didn't have to do too much. It was The Beatles... it was Apple... so we were sort of above having to do too much. Anything on Apple had immediate acceptance and it was considered to be very hip, very cool. Jackie got a really good listen because of it. Unfortunately, Jackie seemed to believe his publicity a little too much. I thought he was making great records and George was into it, but it didn't sell." Though Mansfield and the Apple Records staff were stumped as to why the Lomax album didn't make a big commercial splash, both Lomax and Apple were consoled by the fact that the album sold steadily for several years as record buyers slowly discovered the exceptional quality of the music on "Is This What You Want".

At the start of 1969, Apple was still riding high on the momentum generated by their spectacular and highly-publicized summer of '68 launch, but Ron Kass and the other Apple managers were growing concerned with the lacklustre commercial performance of James Taylor, The Iveys, Trash and Jackie Lomax. Though few would admit it in public, many of Apple's staff had assumed that the quality of the music and the fact that it was associated with Apple and The Beatles would boost the commercial fortunes of Apple artists. It came as quite a surprise then when Mary Hopkin seemed to be the only Apple artist to benefit from that theory.

As it was, Apple was taking no chances with Mary Hopkin. To ensure that Hopkin would retain her initial level of commercial success, Apple took great care in developing Hopkin's recording career. Certain that there was no way that Hopkin could ever repeat the success of *Those Were The Days*, Paul McCartney instinctively knew that there was no need to rush out a second single by his young protégée. When McCartney felt that the time was right for a new Mary Hopkin single, he presented her with a specially written Lennon and McCartney song called *Goodbye*. Boasting a breezy McCartney melody, a winsome arrangement by Richard Hewson and McCartney's highly commercial production, *Goodbye* reached number 2 on the British charts following its release in March. Issued a month later in America, the song returned Hopkin and Apple to the American top ten, where *Goodbye* went all the way to number 8.

The B-side to *Goodbye* was a dark, folk-jazz song called *Sparrow*, composed by Apple Publishing's Gallagher and Lyle. Apple Publishing's John Hewlett recalls that "McCartney really loved their stuff and he was responsible for the Mary Hopkin cover. McCartney was the only one taking any interest in publishing. He was actually genuinely interested and he was thrilled when Gallagher and Lyle came through because the man's got a good ear. McCartney would actually come into the office on a regular basis and sit on the floor and listen to the songs with me... listen to these people singing in the bath in Wales sending a tape in. We'd laugh about a lot of it, but he'd also listen to the stuff that was half-way any good, and Gallagher and Lyle were really one of the better writers, or writing partnerships, that we signed during that period. The majority of the tapes were awful. I don't recall coming across anything else that was particularly good. The only guy I signed was a guy called Peter Cooper who we got a record deal with Giorgio Gomelsky's label. But Peter was a little shaky. He had ability but his marriage broke up and he had problems. It was an interesting sort of psychedelic guitar based band. Giorgio produced some songs for him but it never got released."

In *Blue Suede Brogans, The History Of Scottish Rock*, Graham Lyle recalled how Paul McCartney had asked all of the Apple Publishing writers to submit a song for consideration as a B-side for Hopkin's second single: "He came in and said, 'We need a B-side.' There were six or seven teams of songwriters... The Badfinger and Grapefruit guys... and McCartney said whoever writes the song for Mary will win a cake! And we won a cake. It was a song called *Sparrow*... extremely exciting times. Paul McCartney was genuinely concerned that the publishing side of Apple would develop. We got two or three B-sides and it was good for us."

Mortimer's Tom Smith also remembers the competition, recalling that, "We got a memo from McCartney saying that he wanted material for Mary Hopkin's new single and he had everybody in the company trying to write her something. We wrote a song and put it down but nothing happened. I remember I was down in the main studio... I was at Apple by myself... and I went down to the studio and heard a guitar strumming... it was just George Martin and Paul McCartney in the studio and the lights were out. I sat in the corner and listened to Paul put down a version of *Goodbye* and George was putting it down on tape. The studio was in shambles, but they recorded that demo there."

Despite the relative lack of success of any (other than Mary Hopkin) of the initial wave of artists signed to the label, Apple continued to sign new acts in the early months of 1969. During the sessions for Billy Preston's debut Apple single, George Harrison became reacquainted with an American R&B vocalist from New York City named Doris Troy. Troy, who had been living in London for several years, remembers that she had been asked by her friend Madeline Bell to help out on Preston's session and that she had no idea that the session was being produced by George Harrison.

Harrison, a great admirer of Troy's early 1960s hits like *Just One Look*, was knocked out by Troy and her dynamic voice and several weeks after meeting Harrison in the studio, she had been signed to a record, publishing and production deal with Apple. Doris Troy was given an office next to Peter Asher's on the fifth floor of the Apple building and she immediately started writing new songs for herself and other artists. Her first Apple project was on behalf of Apple Publishing, co-writing several songs with Billy Preston.

From his small office next door to Doris Troy's, Peter Asher still oversaw Apple's entire artist roster, although he dedicated most of his time to developing the career of James Taylor. Having gained a taste for the American market while he was in Hollywood, Asher was more confident than ever that Taylor would be Apple's next star. As he waited for Taylor to complete a new set of songs for a second album, Asher agreed to produce an album by the new Apple group Mortimer. As he had done with Taylor, Asher assumed control of the whole project, which included taking promo pictures and even penning a biography for the group.

Mortimer's Tom Smith recalls that Asher had high hopes for Mortimer and that Apple spared little expense when it came to recording the album. "We recorded mostly at Trident Studios. We did lots of sessions over a span of six months. Peter brought in some outside musicians to help us. We had an upright bass player named Spike Heatley playing on our song *People Who Are Different.* On our song *Dolly*, Richard Hewson brought in a choir of twelve people to sing the parts he had written. Richard Hewson also played piano on a song we hoped to make a single, *Pick Up Your Heart.* Peter Asher sang on *You Don't Say You Love Me* and he also played bass on a track."

Mid-way through the recording sessions, Mortimer were paid a visit by Paul McCartney. Smith remembers: "McCartney popped in on us – he used to drop in and see how things were going with all the artists that were signed to Apple – and we had just recorded a song, *You Don't Say You Love Me*, and Peter thought that it might be the single, so he played it to Paul. Paul said that he liked it but said, 'I don't know if it's a single.' Paul noticed that we played a lot of acoustics and he said 'I've got a song I think you guys would be perfect for,' and he played us *Two Of Us*, which was then still called *On Our Way Home.* He played us an acetate of him and John playing it on acoustic guitars... they were joking together like The Everly Brothers saying, 'Take it Phil' and things like that. It was nice, but honestly I don't think any of us thought that it was a single. But the fact that Paul gave it to us and that Peter said 'Let's go and try it,' we went and recorded it. When we finished the album Peter invited us out to his place in the country to take pictures for the album cover. It was a frantic time. Apple showed interest in our finished album but no one was raving about it. I wouldn't say we took the place by storm."

Listening to the eleven songs that Mortimer recorded, it is difficult to understand why Apple chose not to release the Mortimer album. Recorded in London's top studios and having even been given expensive orchestral overdubs, Apple certainly spent a good deal of money on the recordings. While by no means a ground-breaking work, it is an excellent collection of folk-influenced harmony rock, and several tracks, including the poppy *You Don't Say You Love Me* and *Pick Up Your Heart* – a soulful rock ballad on which Mortimer's acoustic guitars and conga drums are blended with forceful piano and a swirling Richard Hewson string arrangement – are commercial, late sixties rock songs that sound similar to the style with which the band America would have great success in the early seventies.

Like Smith, percussionist Guy Masson recalls most of Mortimer's tenure at Apple fondly. "We rehearsed at Apple in The Beatles' storage room which was upstairs on the top floor of the Apple building where they had all their equipment and the Apple kitchen. There was still plenty of room and it was quiet, they had all of their original Beatle drums, George's painted guitar that he played in *Magical Mystery Tour*... it was something, a great place to rehearse."

Masson remembers how, "the group visited arranger Richard Hewson's apartment several times, where we worked out beautiful orchestrations. We also had a full tilt, ten person chorus sing on some of the songs... I remember that for *On Our Way Home* he worked out this little trumpet sound, a popular sound back then. As far as I know, Apple never did any test pressings, only acetates and they never did a cover." Finishing the album in the late spring of 1969, Mortimer played a few shows around London and then waited for Apple to release their record.

By mid-1969, Apple seemed to be operating at full capacity. Indeed, Neil Aspinall and Peter Brown found themselves overwhelmed by all of the Apple activity and the increasingly busy personal lives of the individual Beatles. To help out with the administrative duties at Beatles and Co, Brown had been given permission to secure an assistant and in April 1969, he hired a 20 year-old Londoner named Bill Oakes.

Oakes – who had previously worked as an entertainment reporter for the news wire service UNS – first met Brown while covering a press reception for Mary Hopkin. "I had already met Paul McCartney and Peter Brown at St. Paul's Cathedral of all places," remembers Oakes. "It was in the summer of 1968 at a press reception for Mary Hopkin, who was performing in the cathedral. I caught the tail end of it and then coming out of it were Peter Brown and Paul McCartney. I ended up writing an article on Apple. The next time I ran into Peter and Paul was in April 1969, I had just come back from hitchhiking around Europe.

"I happened to be cutting down Savile Row as a shortcut to Oxford Street, when I saw Peter Brown and Paul McCartney coming out of Nutter's, the tailor. Tommy Nutter was Peter Brown's friend and tailor to The Beatles. I said hello and was amazed that Peter Brown recognized me. Peter Brown said, 'Hello, come into Apple,' so I went past the scruffs and went in with them, and the next thing I know, they were offering me a job. Although I had a couple of O-levels no one was interested in my qualifications. It was more of, 'Oh, he seems like a good geezer, when can you start?' Paul had just got married and I think he was already moving away from Apple mentally. Klein hadn't been hired yet, but he was in the wings. So I was to work for Peter Brown, but there was no question that my first and foremost priority was meant to be McCartney. That was quite clear, although the others of course regarded me as being their slave too, so you had to juggle it."

Unbeknownst to Oakes, he was joining Apple just as The Beatles and Apple were both starting to fall apart. After roughly a full year of having all of their money funnelled into Apple, by early 1969 all four Beatles were increasingly alarmed as they realized just how much money was actually flowing out of the company. Of course, it never occurred to any of The Beatles that much of the money that Apple had paid out during 1968 was directly attributable to their personal spending.

Slowly coming out of his acid induced lethargy, John Lennon was especially concerned by the developments at Apple. Speaking to Ray Coleman in an interview for *Disc and Music Echo*, the brutally frank Lennon exclaimed that Apple "needs a new broom and a lot of people will have to go. It needs streamlining. It doesn't need to make vast profits, but if it carries on like this, all of us will be broke in six months." Clearly on a roll, Lennon continued to bare his soul to Coleman, adding: "We have enough to live on, but we can't let Apple go on like this. We started off with loads of ideas of what we wanted to do... but like one or two Beatles things, it didn't work out because we aren't practical and we weren't quick enough to realize we needed a businessman's brain to run the whole thing."

Lennon was correct in his assessment that a substantial amount of The Beatles' money was flowing out of the offices at 3 Savile Row. Due to the lavish spending habits of The Beatles and in some part to the rapid expansion and carefree business practices at Apple, the company was simply spending more money than it was bringing in. In an interview with *Record Collector*, Derek Taylor noted that the problem at Apple was that, "the weirdness was not controlled at the start. You can't control weirdness anyway... weirdness is weirdness."

"The Beatles weren't together: they didn't know what they wanted out of Apple," explained Taylor in 1988. "George and Paul wanted different things, while John and Ringo didn't know what they wanted at first. What Paul wanted was a publishing company, a record company, the Apple shops. I'm not sure that he wanted Apple Electronics and Magic Alex: John was the big sponsor there, but George liked Alex and Paul didn't dislike him. I don't know what Ringo's idea of Apple was."

Eventually, it became apparent that Apple had to find a suitable person to take control of the company. Peter Brown clearly recalls: "There was a point when Paul, with the support of the others, went looking for a major figure to run Apple, on the basis of they were so big and powerful that Neil and I were not qualified to do it. Paul felt that The Beatles needed the biggest and the best to run their corporation. They interviewed English tycoons like Cecil King and Dr. Beeching, but these people were not interested. Not only that, they knew nothing about the music business."

Having rapidly exhausted the list of potential saviours for Apple, it suddenly dawned on Paul McCartney that Lee Eastman, the father of his girlfriend, Linda, would be the perfect person to run Apple. Eastman, a successful New York City music industry attorney who had extensive experience with music copyrights, was certainly a viable candidate for the job. Although the other Beatles were not particularly comfortable with the idea of Paul McCartney's prospective father-in-law running Apple, the other three agreed to discuss the issue with Eastman and for a short while, even let Eastman and his son John act as business advisers to Apple.

It was Derek Taylor who convinced Peter Brown to put Allen Klein in touch with The Beatles. By 1969, Klein, a New York City-based manager who had been involved in the music industry since the early sixties, had already developed a formidable – and somewhat unsavoury – reputation on both sides of the Atlantic. Klein, an accountant by trade, had started in the music business by auditing the books of agents, managers and music publishers that he believed were short-changing artists on their royalties. Since undertaking his first audit on behalf of singer Bobby Darin, Klein roared through the New York City music industry, becoming the manager of Sam Cooke and later acting as the American manager of such top British acts as The Rolling Stones, Donovan and Herman's Hermits amongst others. Only 37 when he began courting The Beatles, Klein had already managed to "acquire" the American music publishing interests of The Rolling Stones, Ray Davies and Pete Townshend, leaving some of the most important British songwriters of the era bitter and resentful of their association with the self-styled "Robin Hood of pop".

Klein's dubious business dealings were common knowledge to most people in the music industry, yet he was also celebrated for being a ruthless negotiator who had a remarkable ability to secure fantastic deals for the artists he represented. The Beatles, and Paul McCartney in particular, were far from happy about the fact that The Rolling Stones had a much better record deal than The Beatles.

Klein's interest in securing a meeting with The Beatles had first been conveyed to Derek Taylor by Tony Calder of Immediate Records. Taylor, who commuted daily to London from his home in Surrey, was driving to the train station with Calder when Calder mentioned that Klein had been trying to get in touch with The Beatles. Klein had apparently read the Lennon interview with Ray Coleman where Lennon had proclaimed that if Apple continued on its present course, the company would be broke in six months. Klein was anxious to tell John Lennon how he could solve all of Apple's problems and Calder intimated to Taylor that Klein was under the (false) impression that the reason he was not getting through to John Lennon was due to interference from Taylor. Taylor, never wanting to appear to be the bad guy, explained that he had no idea that Klein was trying to secure a call with John Lennon but he agreed to bring Klein's request to the attention of Peter Brown.

Unbeknownst to Taylor, Allen Klein had been actively pursuing The Beatles and Apple ever since he had heard the news report of Brian Epstein's death in August 1967. Peter Brown and Clive Epstein had even met Klein, but as Brown noted in *The Love You Make*, "He was so foul-mouthed and abusive that I ended the meeting in a few moments and had him shown the door." Yet despite Brown's less than favourable first impression of Klein, Brown did arrange a phone call between Klein and John Lennon as a personal favour to Taylor.

A call was placed and by the end of the conversation, an intrigued John Lennon had agreed to meet Klein in a London hotel, out of sight from the prying eyes of Apple's staff and his fellow Beatles. The beleaguered Beatle was particularly interested in getting Klein to sort out his and Yoko Ono's personal business matters. Speaking to *Playboy Magazine* in 1971, Klein explained that, "He [Lennon] made it clear that he was there for himself and Yoko, period. He told me that the Eastmans were handling The Beatles' financial affairs."

After his initial conversation with Lennon, Klein moved quickly to court The Beatles and he was soon in London for a face-to-face meeting with Lennon and Ono. The meeting was by all accounts very fruitful and both John Lennon and Yoko Ono were highly impressed by Klein's down-to-earth manner, knowledge of The Beatles music, and obvious business savvy. Lennon would later characterize Klein as a real person, as opposed to the Eastmans, whom he thought were pretentious. Lennon also liked the fact that Klein didn't look like a businessman. Unlike the reserved Eastmans, who were always attired in immaculate suits with fine silk ties, many former Apple staff members vividly recall that Klein's favourite attire appeared to be dirty polonecked sweaters.

Lennon found Klein's attitude refreshing and at the end of the meeting, Ono typed out a letter authorizing Klein to look into Lennon's business matters and Klein agreed to see what he could do on behalf of John and Yoko. It was during a lunch meeting at Apple the next day that the other Beatles first found out that Klein was looking after Lennon's financial affairs. Klein later admitted to *Playboy Magazine* that during the meeting, "Paul was pretty cool. I don't think he made up his mind about me."

Reflecting on how Allen Klein came to power at Apple, Peter Brown feels that the other three Beatles were ultimately motivated to choose Klein over Eastman due in part to a feeling that Apple was becoming too dominated by McCartney. John Lennon was especially disturbed by what he perceived as McCartney's dominance at Apple. Brown concedes, "The day-to-day driving force at Apple was Paul and therefore it was Paul that Neil and I dealt with. I would be there all day, Neil would come in the late morning and Paul would come in most days. So naturally, Paul was the person we spoke to. Paul was the most reliable about making decisions. He was the most conventional about structuring a business. He liked the idea, so Apple was built in Paul's image. What happened was that when John woke up, partly as a result of Yoko's prodding, he found the structure in place. Then when he said he'd like to do this or like to do that, we had to say, 'Well, you can't do that because we've already got a structure, it's already done.' And that was the start of many of the problems, because John came along and said, 'I want something different', and we would say, 'it's already done, this is how it's done'. So he would say, 'Well, I don't like it,' and we would say, 'Well, it's too late, you should have been here before.'"

Peter Brown still considers Lennon's enthusiasm for Klein to have been particularly perplexing due to the simple fact that Klein's shady business dealings were no secret to the London music community. "Part of John's perverseness was shown by that awful situation when Mick Jagger wanted to come around and tell The Beatles what Klein was really like. He went to John and told him: 'Before you make a commitment to Klein, let me tell you my experience.' And I told John that Mick was gonna come around and do this which was a very sensible thing to do. Mick was a very bright man and he was far more business orientated than either John or Paul. So Mick was going to say, as a friend, 'Listen, before you make any decision I should tell you what happened to me.' So John tells Klein that Mick was coming and when Mick arrived he was presented with not only the four Beatles, but also with Klein. So there wasn't much that Mick could say. It was a very, very bizarre thing for John to have done."

1969 - The Pre-Klein Era

Lee and John Eastman, who a few weeks earlier had assumed that they would soon be representing The Beatles, were extremely upset by Klein's arrival at Apple. They knew Klein from New York City and they did not relish the thought of having to battle Klein for control of Apple. For the next few weeks, both parties worked hard to curry the favour of all four Beatles, yet the balance of power soon tipped towards Klein as John Lennon grew disenchanted with the upper class Eastmans and threw his full support behind the scrappy, middle class accountant from New York City.

The fierce competition between Klein and Lee and John Eastman to become The Beatles' business manager could not have come at a worse time, given that the group would need to address two major business deals in the spring of 1969. As a result of the protracted power struggle between Klein and the Eastmans, The Beatles would be forced to rely on the often contradictory advice of Lee and John Eastman and Allen Klein.

The first order of business would be to find a way to extract The Beatles from their commitments to Nems. Ever since Brian Epstein's death in 1967, Nems – now known as Nemperor Holdings and run by Brian's brother Clive – had continued to receive 25% of The Beatles' income, despite the fact that the company now provided little in the way of management services to the group. The company had languished under Clive Epstein's leadership and it was thought that Nemperor would not have the cash required to pay the death taxes on Epstein's estate, due to be paid on 31 March 1969. John Eastman realized that this presented an excellent opportunity for The Beatles to purchase Nemperor outright, which would bring the 25% of The Beatles' income that was being paid to Nemperor back to the group. Eastman even arranged for EMI to loan The Beatles – as an advance against future royalties – £1.4 million to purchase Nemperor.

It seemed like a done deal, until Allen Klein arrived on the scene and told The Beatles that they would have to earn twice as much in pre-tax royalties to pay back the EMI loan. Klein even made claims that he could get Nemperor for free. A stalemate ensued and little action was taken until McCartney and John Eastman abruptly left a critical meeting after coming to a major disagreement with Klein. With McCartney and Eastman out of the room, Klein was able to convince Harrison and Starr to side with Lennon and support Klein's plan for securing Nemperor.

Klein's acquisition tactic was to threaten to initiate a rigorous audit of Nemperor's books, reasoning that the company owed The Beatles money from the pre-1967 tours and merchandising. Klein then sent an ominous letter of intent to Nemperor via John Eastman, warning Epstein of an imminent audit. Klein suffered a serious setback in his campaign to become The Beatles' business manager, however, when Clive Epstein reacted to Klein's threat by promptly selling Nemperor to a London-based consortium of investors, called the Triumph Trust.

Shaken but unbowed, Klein quickly changed targets and turned his sights on Triumph, again assuring The Beatles that he would secure Nemperor for nothing. Klein then met Triumph head, Leonard Richenberg, making the same claims he had used on Clive Epstein. Richenberg turned out to be a far more formidable adversary than Klein had anticipated, and he was not overly concerned by Klein's threats. Unable to get Richenberg to capitulate to his demands, Klein decided to up the ante. His next move was to instruct EMI to pay approximately £1.3 million in royalties that they were due to pay to Nemperor (who would traditionally deduct their 25% share and then pay the remainder of the royalties to The Beatles) directly to Apple.

The matter quickly ended up in court, with Klein insisting that Nemperor no longer represented The Beatles in any way, with Nemperor insisting that The Beatles contract with Nemperor was still valid, and with EMI wisely not willing to pay out the royalties to any party until the conflict was resolved.

A settlement was eventually reached only after Triumph engaged a detective agency to investigate some of Klein's more dubious business dealings back in the United States. The resulting report was exactly what Triumph expected and they proceeded to leak the document to London's *Sunday Times* newspaper, who used the findings as the basis of a less than favourable article on Klein. Klein realized, now that his past dealings were exposed, that it would be difficult for him to prevail in court and that it was in his and Apple's best interests to settle with Triumph as soon as possible. Klein eventually negotiated a settlement that stipulated that Apple would pay Triumph £750,000 in cash, plus 5% of The Beatles gross royalties earned between 1972 to 1976. Triumph would also get 25% of the royalties that were being held by EMI and £50,000 for the shares of Subafilm that were owned by Nems.

As John Eastman would later point out in a memo to The Beatles, the figure that Klein paid to free The Beatles from Nemperor far exceeded the original one million pound deal that Eastman had negotiated with Clive Epstein several months earlier. While it had cost Klein a good deal more to free The Beatles from Nemperor, there was a financial upside to Klein's deal, in that The Beatles became Triumph shareholders when they traded the Nemperor shares held by the group

– which represented 10% of the company – for close to one million dollars worth of Triumph stock. At the end of the day, freeing The Beatles from Nemperor had been a costly and questionable victory for Klein, but Lennon, Harrison and Starr did not hold Klein accountable for the inflated price that they were forced to pay for Nemperor.

Even as Klein waged battle with Triumph, it was still not certain if it would be Klein or the Eastmans who would ultimately assume management responsibility for Apple and The Beatles. John Lennon finally broke the managerial stalemate when he decreed that he wanted to be represented by Allen Klein. Peter Brown remembers: "John wanted to bring in Allen Klein and John managed to persuade George and Ringo to support him, so it was a case of they were the majority shareholders and they wanted Klein to come in and take charge. And the way that Klein wanted to take charge was to eliminate costs, because that could be seen to be doing something, and to remove anyone who could stand up to him that he could get rid of. So he got rid of everyone effectively – except for Neil and myself, and he would have liked to get rid of us. But there was a line drawn where they wouldn't let him go. I stayed long enough to prove he couldn't get rid of me, and once I made my point, I didn't want to stay any longer. He would have liked to have had a clean sweep of everyone so he could run Apple as he wanted, but as it was we were left with so little authority anyway that it was very difficult for us to be a problem for him."

With the backing of John Lennon, George Harrison and Ringo Starr, The Beatles and Apple signed a three-year management contract with Allen Klein in March 1969. Celebrating the agreement by taking press pictures of a staged signing ceremony, all four Beatles were shown gathered around a desk with Klein. Contrary to the collective image presented by these photos, Paul McCartney's signature was still missing from the contract. In fact, McCartney would never sign the document.

Several of the photos taken as The Beatles "signed" the document show McCartney playing around with a magnifying glass, as if he were scrutinizing every detail of the contract. Given the deal that Klein had negotiated for himself, one wonders if The Beatles – or the Eastmans – ever even looked at the contract before it was signed. Once the smoke had cleared, it was obvious that Klein had negotiated an exceptionally lucrative deal for himself. Peter Brown admits he had no idea of why The Beatles would offer Klein such generous compensation. "They had no idea of what the going rate was," he concludes. "They had no idea how to negotiate. I don't know where their heads were."

In exchange for Allen Klein and his company, Abkco, assuming management of The Beatles and Apple, Apple would pay for a London apartment for Klein and for "reasonable expenses" incurred by Klein and other Abkco employees in the line of Beatles and Apple business. Klein would also receive 20% of the gross income earned by The Beatles and Apple during the period in which Klein was acting as manager. In addition to his base commission, if Klein were to renegotiate any existing deals on behalf of The Beatles, he would earn 20% of the gross income generated from the difference between the original royalty rate and the new royalty rate that Klein had negotiated.

McCartney appeared to be the only Beatle to have raised an objection to the handsome commission that Klein had negotiated for himself. Given that The Beatles operated under the concept of majority rule, he knew that it was inevitable that Klein would assume control of Apple, but he didn't think The Beatles had to pay him 20% of their gross income. In *Many Years From Now*, McCartney relates how on 9 May, Klein came down to a Friday night recording session at Olympic studios with the express purpose of having McCartney sign the management contract. Klein claimed he needed to have McCartney sign the document so he could return to New York. But McCartney reasoned that The Beatles were "the biggest act in the world" and that Klein would take 15% instead of 20% so he attempted to convince the other three Beatles to get Klein to accept 15%. To McCartney's dismay, the other Beatles were insistent that Klein should get 20%, and they angrily accused McCartney of "stalling". McCartney simply wanted to have his lawyer review the contract the following Monday and he refused to sign the document. On realizing that McCartney was not going to sign the agreement, Klein and the other three Beatles abruptly left, leaving McCartney alone in Olympic Studios.

4
1969 - Life After Klein

Acknowledging that he would not be getting McCartney to sign the management contract any time soon, Klein returned to New York where he informed the Abkco staff that the company would now be representing The Beatles and Apple. Klein had been especially secretive about his courtship of The Beatles and even his closest business associates were surprised when it was announced that Klein had been appointed to manage Apple. Al Steckler, a New Yorker who had been looking after the record production side of Abkco's business since 1966 recalls that, "In early 1969, Klein suddenly became less available to us in New York. He spent a lot of time in England and nobody really knew why. We heard rumours that he was doing something with Apple but we didn't know. He was there for almost a year straight at one point. Then all of a sudden he just told us that we were involved with Apple. So I flew over, met all the people and started getting involved. Peter Asher was already gone, but Tony Bramwell and Jack Oliver were still there."

With the ink still wet on his partially signed management contract, Klein immediately turned his full attention to Apple. His first project would be to take a close look at Apple and find a way to reduce the company's mounting expenses. But before Klein could even begin this task, he found himself having to contend with a totally new and unforeseen crisis that surfaced when The Beatles' long-time music publisher, Dick James, sold his shares of Northern Songs to ATV Music publishing in mid-May.

Upon hearing the news that James was planning to sell his Northern Songs shares, The Beatles were rightfully infuriated. Their songs had built Northern Songs into a successful, publicly traded company, and then suddenly, without evening offering The Beatles a chance to buy his shares, Dick James sold the fruit of their labours to another company. With Lennon, McCartney and Klein out of the country when James announced his intention to sell, Apple sent George Harrison, Derek Taylor and Neil Aspinall to attempt to get James to postpone the sale. As Peter Brown later noted, the meeting quickly got out of hand and the anger that the Apple contingent directed towards James – however justified it may have been – only fortified his resolve to sell.

Harrison, Taylor and Aspinall may have been unable to stop James from selling his shares to ATV Music, but there was still a good chance that The Beatles would ultimately be able to get control of Northern Songs. While James did own a significant portion of the company, he did not own a majority share. After purchasing the shares of James and his partner Charles Silver, ATV held roughly 35% of Northern Songs.

Given that the four Beatles and Apple collectively controlled approximately 29% of Northern Songs, either The Beatles or ATV could have conceivably ended up with the majority share of the company. An all-out fight to secure the outstanding shares of Northern Songs stock still held by private investors was soon underway. It would be a long, difficult and, for The Beatles and Apple, an expensive undertaking. Complicating the battle for control of Northern Songs was a consortium of London stockbrokers who had noticed that Northern Songs was "in play" and quickly amassed their own block of Northern Songs stock that represented approximately 14% of the company.

For the next few months, ATV and The Beatles would be locked in an intense contest to come up with the winning bid for the outstanding shares of Northern Songs. The key to winning control was to win over the consortium, and by mid-May, it appeared that the consortium was prepared to sell its shares to The Beatles. It looked like a done deal and ATV had even conceded defeat.

It only took a few choice words from John Lennon to bring the entire deal crashing down. As Peter Brown noted in *The Love You Make*, it was during a meeting to finalize the details of the deal that John Lennon lost his temper and exclaimed to a key member of the consortium: "I don't see why I should work for a company in which I have no say. I'm not going to be fucked around by men in suits sitting on their fat arses in the City." While it is highly unlikely that Lennon's statement alone cost The Beatles the deal, it was certainly a factor in the consortium's prompt decision to sell its shares to ATV.

Negotiations would drag on for several months – with Klein coming close to securing a very good deal for The Beatles with ATV – but McCartney refused to agree to the deal that Klein had negotiated. Once it was clear that ATV would gain control, The Beatles wanted nothing to do with Northern Songs and they converted their shares into ATV stock, which ATV was legally compelled to purchase at the premium price that they had offered during their takeover bid. From a short-term financial perspective, The Beatles had profited from ATV's takeover of Northern Songs, but they also lost any chance they would have of ever getting ownership of their songs. To add insult to injury, Lennon and McCartney would both be required to have their songs published by ATV until 1973.

If there was any bright side to the Northern Songs debacle, it was that both George Harrison and Ringo Starr had not renewed their songwriting contracts with Northern Songs when their original contracts had expired in March 1968. Instead, they had both signed to Apple Publishing, which meant that The Beatles at least owned the songs that Harrison and Starr would write after 1968.

Looking back, Klein's first few months working for The Beatles had been largely unsuccessful. After leading the costly acquisition of Nemperor and then losing the battle for Northern Songs, Klein needed a successful deal to prove his worth to The Beatles. Klein's first coup would be his re-negotiation of The Beatles' contract with EMI. By early 1969 The Beatles had already produced the minimum number of records required under their 1967 contract with EMI and Klein realized that this presented a perfect opportunity for the group to renegotiate their contract.

Klein immediately went on the offensive against EMI, threatening that The Beatles would not make another album until their demands were met. While Klein's aggressive tactics during meetings with EMI head Sir Joseph Lockwood nearly cost him another deal, an agreement was finally reached where, in exchange for The Beatles supplying two albums a year until 1976 (either collectively or as solo artists), the group would receive an unprecedented royalty rate of 58 cents per album in the United States until 1972, at which time the royalty rate would escalate to 72 cents per album. It was an excellent deal – even Paul McCartney was impressed.

In addition to negotiating a greatly increased royalty rate for The Beatles, (since early 1967 they had received, excluding publishing income, 39 cents per album – prior to 1967, they had only earned 6 cents per album) Klein also secured a piece of the action for Apple Records as part of the deal. The deal was quite inventive and it stipulated that EMI – who retained ownership of The Beatles' master recordings – would grant Apple the right to manufacture and sell Beatles albums in the United States. Apple would then pay Capitol to manufacture the actual records.

The finished records would then be purchased from Apple by Capitol, who would then sell them to record stores. The difference between what Apple paid Capitol to manufacture the records and the amount that Capitol would purchase the finished albums from Apple, was Apple's profit. Prior to this deal, Apple made no money from the sales of Beatles albums, so it represented a significant flow of income for the company.

Klein's masterful negotiation with EMI was a turning point in his relationship with The Beatles and John and Lee Eastman were soon eased out of any Apple business, other than to the extent that they would still represent McCartney. Bill Oakes recalls that the new record deal sealed Harrison and Starr's support of Klein, noting that, "Klein's mandate from George and Ringo anyway was go and get us a better deal. They were tired of hearing of all these rock groups coming along with these huge percentages... they wanted a better deal and they were right, they really had a stupid deal... Paul couldn't argue with that. His point was that Eastman could have got them the same deal or more and they didn't have to go with a suspect felon or someone with as unsavoury a reputation as Klein. Paul was always conscious and protective of the group's image, even when he didn't want to be known as a Beatle. He felt that Allen Klein was a poor representative for The Beatles. Linda was providing him with the dirt on Klein as she came from New York and knew of his reputation: he was really seedy, he was a horrible creature, but John didn't give a shit about that. No one was going to argue with John except Paul, and Paul did it his way, which was he didn't talk to him. I think he knew he was going to be outvoted three to one. So Klein's mandate was get the money and he fulfilled it. It was when he started doing things like the 'Hey Jude' repackage (an album of miscellaneous Beatles tracks that Klein released in the United States in 1969) that Paul's teeth really got on edge. The interesting thing was that almost within weeks of them signing with Klein, there was Mick Jagger appearing. My first encounter with Mick was when he came breathlessly into The Beatles' room to talk to John, to tell him, 'Don't sign man, cause we're suing him,' but it was too late, they had already signed."

Having secured a suitable record deal for The Beatles, Klein was finally able to devote some time to sorting out Apple. Predictably, he soon determined that excessive staff levels and lax business practices were to blame for Apple's financial problems. Though it has long been assumed that it was the excessive Apple-related spending that led John Lennon and the other Beatles to start worrying about their financial well-being, Bill Oakes, the employee who had to sign off and log all of The Beatles' personal expenditures, takes a very different view of The Beatles' financial predicament at that time. In fact, Oakes is adamant that Apple was responsible for only a small part of the band's financial woes.

"White Trash was really Apple's only flop up until that point," says Oakes. "People think that there was a lot of money spent, but the money at Apple wasn't being spent on things like records. I remember that EMI were horrified at the cost of 'All Things Must Pass', which they said was the most expensive album ever made in EMI history, but the total was just around £70,000. But the money haemorrhaging out of Apple was never really a creative thing. It was not the fact that The Beatles were investing large sums in creative endeavours, it was the rampant kind of waste of things, the houses and things they were treating themselves to. I don't think that Apple could ever be accused of pumping money into creative projects. Klein was able to save The Beatles a little money by having stricter things put on, but The Beatles continued to live exactly as they had before – he couldn't control that. Effectively, I was working for a company called Beatles and Co. which was their own partnership. Apple was a separate entity and I assume that Apple Records was subject to the usual Capitol and EMI structure when it came to spending. Beatles and Co. was The Beatles' own holding company from which they paid themselves and all their own expenses, their helicopters, planes, all of that. So Beatles and Co. was where there was a large expenditure."

Conceding that it would be impossible and politically unwise to attempt to curtail The Beatles' lavish spending habits, Klein immediately attempted to lower the group's overheads by cutting back the expenditure associated with Apple. Having been assessing Apple's situation for several months, Klein's first action was to introduce more traditional business practices to the loosely structured Apple organization.

Where it had once been possible for an Apple employee to go to a shop and charge an item to Apple or to simply get reimbursed from petty cash, Klein instituted a strict purchase order system so that every Apple expenditure had to be cleared through his office. Klein was so determined to cut costs anywhere he could that he even instituted a policy where staff members were able to order a sandwich from Apple's kitchen only if they were actually working through their lunch hour. But this was just the beginning. Apple's staff knew that it was only a matter of time before Klein would start cutting jobs.

They didn't have to wait long before Klein's axe started to fall. The first wave of dismissals came on a sunny spring day in the first week of May. After several months of close scrutiny by Klein, Apple Records President Ron Kass was one of the first people to be fired, as was Apple office manager and long-time Beatles aide Alistair Taylor.

Taylor, a hard-working, modestly paid Beatles employee since 1962, was devastated to find out he had been let go by The Beatles. Taylor repeatedly tried to get a phone call through to John Lennon or Paul McCartney to find out why he was being fired, but neither Beatle would take his calls. The British music press – which had been looking for cracks in the Apple facade since late 1968 – gleefully ran stories of Taylor's dismissal and the other Klein-imposed firings. When finally asked about the way that Apple was handling the termination of employees, Paul McCartney curtly replied, "It isn't easy to be nice when you're sacking someone."

While it was certainly Klein's intention to make Apple more efficient by getting rid of non-essential personnel, many Apple insiders felt that Klein was also trying to consolidate his power at Apple by firing anyone who was too close to, or too influential with, The Beatles. The problem was that Klein was not exactly sure which employees were truly close to the group, so he fired almost all of Apple's senior management just to be on the safe side.

Dennis O'Dell, Brian Lewis and Apple Films were other early casualties of Klein's firing spree. Given that Apple Films had almost nothing to show for Apple's investment, it came as little surprise that Klein chose to eliminate the film division. Yet Peter Brown, who had considerable post-Apple success in film production, is adamant that Apple Films was simply shut down too soon. "With Apple Films, there wasn't enough time... film projects take a while to develop. Several things could have happened... it wouldn't have taken a lot of Apple money. It wasn't meant to be a full-blown film studio, it was more of a film development or production company. One project I do remember was that we started a documentary on the Royal Ballet... there was footage of Margot Fontaine... I don't know what happened with all that. It was a project that I brought in. There was some historic footage there. I guess Neil still has it somewhere."

Given his reputation for being a ruthless businessman, Klein uncharacteristically put Peter Brown in charge of carrying out the actual firing. Wanting to avoid any direct confrontation, or perhaps in an effort to not look like the bad guy to The Beatles as he fired loyal long-time employees, Klein had Brown serve notice to the targeted Apple employees while he was either back in America or out to extended lunches.

Jack Oliver and Tony Bramwell had both stated to their fellow Apple employees that they would resign if Ron Kass was ever fired, but they both stayed on after Klein dismissed Kass. Jack Oliver's decision to stay at Apple was rewarded when, shortly after Kass was fired, Oliver was appointed the new President of Apple Records.

Jack Oliver feels that, "Klein pushed Kass out because Ron Kass knew what Klein was up to. Ron tried to bring it up to The Beatles, but they didn't want to listen. What happened was that John brought in Klein and Paul hated him. Paul wouldn't even want to talk to the guy. In fact, one of the only meetings Paul had with Klein was with me, and that's when he told Klein that he wanted me to be head of the label... I was 23. Looking back on it, I thought I was equipped to run the label, but I wasn't."

In the wake of the mass firings and Klein-mandated changes at Apple, the British staff quickly came to resent Klein and his heavy-handed way of doing business. Peter Asher was one of many Apple employees who grew disenchanted with Apple once Klein took control of the company. At first, Asher tried to work with Klein, but within months of Klein taking over, Asher resigned as head of Apple's A&R on 14 June. Soon after announcing his departure, Asher explained to *Billboard*: "Apple has been changing a great deal recently and it made it more and more difficult for me to do my work with the same enthusiasm and effectiveness as before," although he diplomatically added, "I shall also be happy to produce for Apple on a freelance basis." In Asher's absence, the responsibility for booking and coordinating recording sessions for all of the Apple artists was assigned to his American secretary Chris O'Dell.

In a subsequent interview with *Disc*, Asher explained: "When I joined Apple, the idea was that it would be different than other companies in the record business. Its policy was to help people and be generous. It didn't mean actually that I had a tremendous amount of freedom; I was always in danger of one Beatle saying, 'Yes, that's a great idea, go ahead,' and another coming in and saying he didn't know anything about it. But it did mean that it was a nice company to work for. Now that's all changed... it's lost a great deal of its original feeling."

At the time Asher made those statements, both he and James Taylor assumed that they would be recording a second album for Apple Records. "There were some discussions about an album," remembers Asher. "We did some recording in L.A., which we had no trouble doing. If we had wanted to do an album, I don't think anyone would have stopped us. Capitol would have paid the bill." James Taylor did eventually return to England early in the summer of 1969 to begin work on a new album, but as he related to *Rolling Stone* later that year, when he finally returned to the Apple offices, "nothing was happening... I wanted to record, we were ready to record. They knew I was coming to record, but we couldn't get moving. So I did two television shows, a radio show, two guest club appearances, and came home again." Undaunted by their unsuccessful attempt to record a second album in England, Taylor and Asher made tentative plans to record a new Apple album in New York City sometime in August.

After leaving Apple, Asher moved to the United States, where he set up a management company and hoped to find work as a freelance record producer. Asher was very anxious to record a new album with

James Taylor, yet Apple seemed unable to come to a decision on what to do with Taylor. After another failure to get Taylor into the studio, Asher made several attempts to determine Taylor's status at Apple. Unable to get any commitment or definite answer, Asher went ahead and signed James Taylor to Warner Brothers Records. For the time being, no one at Apple seemed to notice or even care that Asher and Taylor had simply walked away.

Looking back on Taylor's exit from Apple, Peter Asher is still amazed by how simple it was for James Taylor to leave the label. "He just kinda left. I knew about Allen Klein before… well, I knew people who had dealt with him. There were certain admirable things about him, but I knew I didn't like his style. It was clear that it was going to be a very divisive issue between The Beatles with John being for him and Paul so against him. All that stuff was going on and James met with him in London. Allen was convinced he impressed the hell out of James. But James came out of the meeting going, 'I never want to come near that guy again,' so I told him I thought we should get off of Apple. So we just sort of left. Eventually I met with Joe Smith of Warner Brothers and made a deal for James Taylor, which included them indemnifying us completely from any lawsuits. I told him that James and I couldn't afford to get sued and they gave us complete indemnification, which nowadays a company wouldn't do. Allen Klein served me some sort of legal paper – a notice to appear – but I didn't have to do anything. He did this interview with *Playboy* where he said he sued us for some massive amount. I got one bit of paper, which was like some notification of a suit being filed. I consequently heard that Allen really was going to sue us and that The Beatles talked him out of it… I don't know that for a fact, but I think George told me, 'Oh no, Allen was going to do something,' but then he and Paul had said, 'No, this is not how we wish to be perceived. If an artist is unhappy and wants to go, let them go.' So in that sense, I may indeed owe George and Paul a debt."

To help pay the bills while he waited for James Taylor to strike it big, Asher took an A&R job with MGM Records, where he would report to his former Apple boss, Ron Kass. Soon after leaving Apple, Kass had been hired to be the new president of MGM, and he quickly recruited several ex-Apple employees to help him reorganize the faltering MGM label. In addition to Asher, Kass hired Ken Mansfield to be the Director of Exploitation and Artist Relations. Ken Mansfield remembers: "I ended up leaving Apple at the end of 1969. Peter Asher, myself, Mike O'Connor and Ron Kass all went together to MGM Records. MGM had been through five presidents at that time and they thought that their salvation, by taking advantage of what was going down at Apple, was to slice off the top of Apple and plug it in on top of MGM. Then three months after we started at MGM the company was sold and the new owner got rid of Kass and brought in Mike Curb as President of MGM."

Once Klein had brought the record division firmly under his control by eliminating Kass and Asher, Apple Music Publishing became Klein's next target. The same week that he fired Ron Kass, Klein fired Apple Publishing's Director Mike O'Connor, song plugger Wayne Bardell and most of the department's support staff. The only people that Klein retained were Copyright Manager Bernard Brown and John Hewlett, although Hewlett left on his own accord soon after Klein let go of O'Connor and Bardell. "I quit Apple when I got the opportunity to go to the States to work for Tetragammon Records, which was Bill Cosby's label. Allen Klein was around. I didn't get fired. I know Mike Berry had gone, Wayne wasn't there... I think I was the only one left in publishing when I left Apple."

Out of all the Apple departments that were cut by Klein, his decision to effectively close down Apple Publishing made the least sense from a business perspective. Located on the fifth floor of the Apple building and operating in a quiet, efficient manner, Apple Music Publishing had signed some excellent songwriters, including James Taylor, George Alexander of Grapefruit, Tony Hill of High Tide, The Iveys, future Strawb Dave Lambert, and Gallagher and Lyle. Apple also held the European publishing rights for several promising American acts, including The Steve Miller Band, Van Dyke Parks and singer-songwriter Kenny Rankin, who had his song *Peaceful* turned into a top 20 hit by Georgie Fame in early 1969. Although Apple Publishing was a large department with a staff that ranged from five to seven people, it was one of the few Apple divisions that saw any return on Apple's investment. According to Mike O'Connor, Apple was ready to sign UK publishing agreements with both Randy Newman and Harry Nilsson when Klein shut the department down.

Once most of the Apple Publishing staff had been let go, Essex Music – a large publishing company headed by David Platz – was assigned to oversee the catalogue of Apple Music Publishing. From this point on, no new songwriters would be signed by Apple, although several artists who signed to Apple Records would also be given contracts with Apple Music Publishing. Any Apple Publishing songwriters who were not under contract to Apple Records would remain so until their existing contracts expired.

After being fired from Apple Publishing, Mike O'Connor joined

Ron Kass at MGM Records in America before leaving the music industry to become a professional photographer. Wayne Bardell, who was also dismissed from Apple Publishing, became the manager of High Tide, an English progressive rock group who were led by Apple Publishing songwriter Tony Hill.

Apple Music Publishing songwriters Graham Lyle and Benny Gallagher went on to enjoy considerable success after leaving Apple. In 1969 they joined former Manfred Mann guitarist Tom McGuinness' new band, McGuinness Flint, and in 1970, scored a British hit single with *When I'm Dead And Gone*. Former Apple Publishing staff member John Hewlett managed the group. Hewlett had grown close to Gallagher & Lyle during his year at Apple and when he decided to start managing bands after leaving Apple, Gallagher & Lyle were his first clients.

Having seen firsthand the troubles that Lennon and McCartney were experiencing as a result of having an outside party control their publishing, both George Harrison and Ringo Starr left Apple Music Publishing and established their own individual publishing companies. Harrison was the first to launch his own company. In June, he set up Sing Song Music, which would be administered by Apple Music.

The first and only song to be copyrighted by Sing Song Music was *Old Brown Shoe*. Harrison soon changed the name of Sing Song Music to Harrisongs. Both Harrisongs and Ringo Starr's Startling Music would operate out of Apple's Savile Row office and the copyrights to all Starr and Harrison compositions that had been originally published by Apple were transferred to their respective new companies. Although Apple Publishing would still earn money from administering Harrisongs and Startling Music, Apple Publishing lost a substantial source of their revenue when the two Beatles struck out on their own. In addition to losing out on the income derived from the copyrights of George Harrison's 15 compositions on "The White Album", Apple Publishing lost its lucrative share of the Cream hit *Badge*, which Harrison had composed with Eric Clapton in late 1968.

After Klein had cleaned out the Savile Row office, Magic Alex and his cosy electronics den in Boston Place was the next Apple department to be identified as a drain on Beatles' money. Klein moved in and suspended all of Apple Electronics' research and as of Friday 29 August, Apple Electronics ceased operations. To get some return on Apple's investment in Apple Electronics' Boston Place location, Klein discarded most of Magic Alex's equipment and prototypes and moved Apple Studios' disc cutting operations into the building.

George Peckham explains: "When they got into rebuilding the studio, they turned the Apple Electronics space into Apple Studios... they moved the desk there and any other equipment that we could move. You'd walk into the reception area of Boston Place and that was where we put John Smith and the tape copying area... you'd walk into the main area that was the Apple Electronics area and that was where we had the lathe and did the cutting. We were there for a couple of years. All we had there was copying and cutting... Magic Alex was long gone... he must have gone in the Klein purge... but he still got away with an armful of goodies."

There was no denying that the arrival of Allen Klein totally transformed the working environment at Apple and by the summer of 1969 there were noticeably fewer employees at 3 Savile Row. From a once inflated staff of fifty, approximately thirty employees were left after Klein's purge. Unfortunately, a few promising projects also seemed to fall through the cracks due to the personnel changes. With Peter Asher gone, Mortimer had lost their representative at Apple and their single and album were put on temporary hold as Klein determined how best to proceed with non-Beatles Apple artists.

With a reduced number of staff handling the former workload of fifty people, the remaining Apple staff soon found themselves struggling to keep up with their additional responsibilities. Apple Records' newly appointed President, Jack Oliver, clearly remembers the frantic pace in the aftermath of Klein's reorganization of the company. "I had two secretaries, and then there was Bramwell. I did everything. I worked all the time – it was my entire life. I worked from maybe nine, nine-thirty in the morning, to maybe four in the morning, because we would go out to dinner and maybe clubs and socialize. Bramwell and I would hang out all the time, we would go out every night together to the Revolution or one of those clubs. They had a table there for us. Klein cut us down a bit, but not a lot. But we never spent outrageous amounts of money. I was always one of the first ones in. The record department was pretty sane and the press office sometimes would look down on us with disdain because we did so much work. We'd go up and hang out with them because it was so much fun up there.

"Anyone that ever came to London from the States would come to our building and would end up in Derek's office. Jerry Moss from A&M would be in our office all of the time. I never had any problem with Klein. I kept out of his way and I did my job. He knew that. We worked most weekends, not in the office, but outside. We would take off on Sundays and go to the pub."

Of all the remaining Apple staff, Apple Director Neil Aspinall was perhaps the most affected by the arrival of Allen Klein. Once totally consumed with the responsibility of setting up the company and then with keeping Apple running as smoothly as possible, Aspinall found his duties at Apple greatly diminished once Klein took over operations. Jack Oliver points out that, "When Klein came in, Neil became, I suppose, a lame duck President. He came in every day and worked on his Beatles film and basically acted as a referee between The Beatles and Klein and everybody else."

While Klein seemed unable – or unwilling – to fire employees who had come with The Beatles from Liverpool such as Aspinall and Peter Brown, he was able to limit their power and The Beatles did nothing to intervene on their behalf. Peter Brown believes: "With all of us who came up from Liverpool with them, it was a case of, 'How could they be good since they came from Liverpool with us?' With Neil for instance, Neil is a very good businessman who is savvy with artists and patient, but he's never been rated like he should have been by The Beatles, because they still think, 'He's our roadie.' The only reason he's survived is the fact that he's the only one that everyone can tolerate. Basically, he's been underestimated in terms of all he's achieved over the years. He's made The Beatles millions of dollars. Not even the generous-minded Ringo valued Neil as much as he should be."

As Jack Oliver noted, after Klein assumed control of Apple, Aspinall spent most of his time working on a new Beatles film. With most of the fifth floor at Savile Row now vacant due to Klein's liquidation of Apple Music Publishing, Aspinall was able to set up film editing equipment in Apple Music Publishing's old space and bring in several assistants to help him compile a film history of The Beatles. In 1996, Aspinall would explain to *Mojo* magazine: "In '69, in all that chaos, the traumas – things were falling apart but they were still making 'Abbey Road' – Paul called me saying, 'You should collect as much of the material that's out there, get it together before it disappears.' So I started to do that, got in touch with all the TV stations around the world, checked what we had in our own library, like *Let It Be*, *Magical Mystery Tour*, the promo clips, what have you. Got newsreel footage in, lots and lots of stuff. We edited something together that was about an hour and three quarters long."

While Aspinall toiled on his Beatles film, Allen Klein was cooking up a Beatles movie project of his own. Realizing that Apple had hundreds of hours of film footage from the "Get Back" sessions at their disposal, Klein decreed that "Get Back" should be a feature film rather than a TV documentary as originally intended.

From that point on, the "Get Back" project seemed to take on a life of its own. Somewhere along the line it was decided that the project should also include a book. Much of the responsibility of putting together the "Get Back" album cover and book was assigned to 23 year-old London artist John Kosh. Kosh – who was to become one of the best-known album cover designers of the seventies – remembers that it was John Lennon who brought him to Apple. "I was working in the design department of the Royal Opera. The Royal Opera House housed the Royal Ballet and the Royal Opera and it was real fashionable for pop stars like Mick Jagger and John and Yoko to sort of show up in the royal enclosure as it were. I was also working as a creative director for a magazine called *Art and Artist* who did a piece on Yoko. All of these things sort of converged at the same time and the next thing I knew I had to go and see John. I got this phone call from John, 'This is John Lennon, will you come and see me?' I was like 'Yeah, right.' I was convinced it was someone playing a joke on me, but I showed up at Apple anyway, and it wasn't. We hit it off immediately and we had a lot of fun and I suddenly found myself working at Apple.

"I wasn't exactly staff, but I had an office. I started out on the ground floor in Ron Kass's old office until Lennon kicked us out because he wanted the office, then I ended up on the third floor with Derek Taylor. They didn't have an art studio; we just had an office. I used to do the design work at night, come in at lunch and get stoned and then go home again. I was just hanging out, I actually did the work at home."

Kosh considers the "Get Back" project to be one of his greatest professional memories. "Looking back on it, Apple's fees were ridiculously low, but you didn't need much money in those days. We would sometimes get paid in substances, though I don't know how it was channelled. None of the suits and ties ever got an idea of what was going on. But wherever we went, we went first class. Apple sent me to New York for six months and I lived off the fat of the land – all paid by Apple. We were trying to get the "Let It Be" book published. I had an office on the 45th floor [of the Abkco building in New York]. I got on very well with Allen Klein, he was very good to me. He was very appreciative of what I was doing and very flattering. United Artists had no intention of ever letting that book come out."

As Kosh noted, Ron Kass had barely left Apple's Savile Row office when John and Yoko commandeered Kass's spacious ground floor office in the front of the Apple building. Having become increasingly involved with activist capers such as their infamous 28 March bed-in for peace at the Amsterdam Hilton, the couple needed a base from where they could coordinate their activities, grant interviews to the world's press and work on their avant-garde films. To handle their personal projects, the Lennons hired several assistants and established a company called Bag Productions.

Despite the disruption caused by the personnel changes and the new business procedures that had been instituted by Klein, Apple was still able to maintain a healthy release schedule in the summer of 1969. In June, Apple scored their biggest hit since Mary Hopkin's *Goodbye* when Billy Preston's *That's The Way God Planned It* reached number 11 on the British singles chart. Unlike the records of The Iveys, James Taylor, Jackie Lomax and White Trash, Preston's dazzling fusion of gospel-influenced R&B and rock proved very popular with the record buying public. "Billy Preston was a dream to work with," remembers Tony Bramwell. "George gave me a finished acetate of *That's The Way God Planned It* on a Friday, I went to Kenny Everett's on a Friday night and on the following morning he played one minute sections of the song twenty-seven times and we had a hit."

That's The Way God Planned It made getting a hit look deceptively easy, but the fact remained that the majority of the artists on the label had not yet experienced any significant success. In July, Apple made an odd attempt to reach a more general audience by releasing a promotional four-song EP in conjunction with Wall's Ice Cream. Featuring Mary Hopkin's version of Donovan's *Happiness Runs*, the EP also included album tracks by James Taylor and Jackie Lomax, plus a new song by The Iveys called *Storm In A Tea Cup*. Apple hoped that the EP would stimulate some interest in Taylor, Lomax and The Iveys, but the project did not work out as planned and it is doubtful that the "Wall's Ice Cream EP" helped stimulate any interest in the featured artists.

The same month that the "Walls Ice Cream EP" was issued, Apple released a new Jackie Lomax single in America called *New Day*. Produced by Lomax and Mal Evans, *New Day* was a highly commercial pop/soul song that inexplicably failed to garner much in the way of commercial interest. The B-side to *New Day* was an old Coasters song called *Thumbing A Ride* that featured Paul McCartney acting as both producer and drummer. During the session for *Thumbing A Ride*, Lomax also recorded an original composition called *Going Back To Liverpool*. The McCartney produced track featured the talents of McCartney, Harrison and Billy Preston, but Apple didn't think that the song was particularly commercial so it was not released at the time.

Encouraged by the success of Billy Preston's *That's The Way God Planned It*, Apple issued Preston's "That's The Way God Planned It" album in August. The album was a combination of new tracks produced by George Harrison in London and songs that Preston had already recorded for Capitol Records while he was in America in 1968.

Given all of the press interest that Preston had generated through his recording activities with The Beatles, Apple was disappointed when Preston's album did not enjoy the same level of success as his single. Featuring the hit single and catchy pop-soul numbers such as *This Is It*, "That's The Way God Planned It" was a fine album that deserved to do much better than it did in both Britain or the United States.

Later in August, Apple released yet another George Harrison production, which was a single by the Radha Krishna Temple called *Hare Krishna Mantra*. It was a surprise hit for Apple, who were amazed to see the single reach number 12 on the UK charts. Even by 1969 standards, *Hare Krishna Mantra* was a record that could have only come from Apple. In the months since several temple members had arrived in England in the autumn of 1968, they had quickly become – with their shaved heads, loud street celebrations and colourful clothes – a common sight in London. It was inevitable that the Radha Krishna Temple would end up at 3 Savile Row.

One of the temple members, Mukunda Goswami, recalled that they first came to Apple after Allen Ginsberg arranged for them to meet Peter Asher in late 1968. Asher then introduced them to George Harrison, who was aware of the Krishnas and who even owned one of the records that the temple members had recorded in New York City the previous year.

Harrison was particularly interested in the hypnotic chants performed by the temple and he thought that one or two of them might make a good single for Apple. A session at Trident Studios was duly booked, and with Harrison playing guitar, bass and harmonium, the temple members added their vocals and percussion to *Hare Krishna Mantra* and created one of the most distinctive hit singles of 1969. The single did so well that the group was even invited to perform the song on *Top of the Pops*, which Mukunda Goswami claims to have delighted Harrison no end.

The Iveys debut album, "Maybe Tomorrow", was another record on Apple's summer release schedule. But the album would never be issued in Britain. Presumably due to the poor commercial performance of the *Maybe Tomorrow* single in the UK, Apple elected to only issue the album in Europe, Japan and America. While The Iveys were gutted by Apple's decision not to release their album in Britain, they were consoled by the fact that the album would at least be released in America. Or so they thought. A week before the album's 14 July American release date, Apple decided to withdraw the release of the album. The last minute decision to scrap the album was most unexpected, especially since they had already gone through the trouble of assigning the album a catalogue number and had even designed a unique cover for the American market.

The Iveys' album did come out, however, in Europe and Japan, where it was released with its original cover featuring a photograph of the group, credited to Peter Asher. Asher – who has no recollection of ever taking photographs of The Iveys – freely admits, "I didn't have much to do with The Iveys... they were Mal's project." Asher was even unaware that he had ever been credited with taking photos of the band. "I am very much into holiday snaps, but I don't think that was me. It's odd because there were so many cool photographers hanging around."

To help promote the "Maybe Tomorrow" album in the foreign territories where it was issued, Apple released the album track *Dear Angie* as a single. Apple apparently neglected to inform The Iveys of the record's existence, however, as *Dear Angie* songwriter Ron Griffiths claims that the band were unaware that the song had been issued as a single until many years later.

Featuring the A-sides to the *Maybe Tomorrow* and *Dear Angie* singles, The Iveys' debut was a solid collection of late sixties English pop. The album was assembled from tracks produced by Tony Visconti as well as tracks produced by Mal Evans that were credited as being arranged by Mal Evans and John Barham. "That was a bit naughty of Mal," chuckles John Barham, who was involved with many of The Iveys sessions. "He was a lovely guy, but he had nothing to do with the arrangements. The Iveys were Mal's first production. Mal was always around when I was working with George... he was spending a lot of time with George at that time, so I knew Mal very well. So when he came to do The Iveys, he brought me in. It was a bit strange, because he didn't have a background in music.

"I had a free hand to do whatever I wanted," recalls Barham, "so The Iveys didn't have much input on the arrangements. I remember them being very busy at the time. They were always on the road, so they didn't have a lot of spare time anyway. We did most of the recording at Trident and that studio in Barnes, Olympic. I also did some recording with The Iveys in this small studio that I haven't been to since. I remember Nicky Hopkins being at a session as well. Mal had strong ideas and opinions. It was not a question of him sitting around and being passive, he was actively involved with the recording. He would sort of suggest what he wanted by singing something or comparing it to another song. But he certainly wasn't an engineer."

Mal Evans was a tireless champion of The Iveys at Apple, yet despite Evans' obvious passion for the group, Apple seemed hesitant to get fully behind them. In retrospect, however, members of The Iveys claimed to understand why they had such problems establishing themselves at Apple. Iveys' guitarist Tom Evans recalled to *Disc* in 1970, "It was very difficult, because you had to be accepted by their [The Beatles'] standards and we weren't that good. We weren't in the bag of four different people, as everyone now knows they are. Like McCartney would like one thing and Lennon wouldn't. It was like that. It must have been a weird time for them. They'd got all these groups to promote and one would be interested and one wouldn't. But all that really doesn't matter. The main thing was that we had to please them to get a record released. That was a good thing because they wanted a record company that would be fairly well respected."

But in the summer of 1969, and with only one single to their credit, The Iveys' confidence had been severely shaken by the way that Apple was handling their career. In the 5 July issue of *Disc*, Iveys' bassist Ron Griffiths lamented, "We do feel a bit neglected... we keep writing songs for a new single and submitting them to Apple, but The Beatles keep sending them back saying that they're not good enough. We've now come up with a song that Mal Evans says he likes, so perhaps we stand a chance at last." As luck would have it, Paul McCartney read the article and was very concerned to learn that the band felt abandoned by Apple. After reading the article, McCartney decided to become personally involved with re-launching The Iveys and he soon hit upon the ideal project for the group.

Earlier in the year, McCartney had been commissioned to write the theme song for *The Magic Christian*, a film featuring Ringo Starr. Not having the time or inclination to record the song himself, McCartney convinced the producers of the film to hire The Iveys to perform the song. The Iveys found out about McCartney's gesture on 23 July when they returned home from a gig to find a letter from Paul McCartney requesting a meeting with the group. The next afternoon, they met McCartney at EMI's Abbey Road studios, where the Beatle informed the star-struck Iveys that he had read the *Disc* article and that he wanted to help. McCartney told the group about the *Magic Christian* project and The Iveys were given an acetate of McCartney's solo recording of *Come And Get It* so that they could learn how to play the song. The group was given a week to work up a suitable version and on 2 August, McCartney took The Iveys into Abbey Road Studios to record *Come And Get It*.

It would be a very memorable day for The Iveys. In addition to being given the opportunity to work with Paul McCartney, John Lennon made an unexpected appearance. In *Without You, The Tragic*

Story Of Badfinger, Ivey Tom Evans recalled seeing John Lennon and Yoko Ono walking into the studio, noting that "Lennon stopped and looked over at Paul, bowed his head, and said 'Oh wise one, oh sage, show us the light.'"

In a 1970 interview with *Disc*, Tom Evans elaborated on the uncertain environment that The Iveys found themselves in at the time McCartney offered to let them record *Come And Get It*. "We were just making album tracks and weren't doing anything as far as a single was concerned, so we began to feel depressed. We kept submitting tapes to Paul and George but they were always returned as 'unsuitable for release'. The Beatles were worried when we weren't doing well, but Paul has always taken the most interest. When he wrote *Come And Get It* he offered it to us because he knew we had nothing to do... he told us, 'I'm going to do this, but don't expect any more.' When we did the single, we thought it was too simple because only piano, bass and drums are used... but now we realize what a genius Paul is... he knew what he was doing. Our music is simple – it has teeny-bopper appeal – and is aimed at middle-of-the-road people who like neither reggae or progressive music. But, like The Beatles, we're gradually going to progress... we don't intend to be a real way-out group; just a simple hard rock group."

Despite their initial lack of success, The Iveys remained confident that Apple was the best possible label for the group. Iveys drummer Mike Gibbins recalls: "Apple regarded us like we were kids. We were young lads. Little did they know we'd sell a lot of records. We'd always go to Apple for a reason, and then we'd end up staying all day because Apple was like one big happy family. George worked with us, Paul worked with us, Ringo used to hang out at our sessions. John was a bit aloof – he never bothered with us much. I saw James Taylor around, but I never got a chance to talk to him. We used to rehearse down in Apple Studios before they gutted it out. It looked great but nothing worked... Mad Alex (sic) was there all the time trying to fix things. The guy was a maniac. We used to hang out with the Apple staff a lot, go out to pubs. Especially Debbie at the front desk. She used to eat daffodils all day. They used to bring in a bunch of flowers, put them on her desk and she'd eat them. We used to be a bunch of stoners. It was later on that we got introduced to all the good stuff. Mal used to come over with The Beatles' stash and get us stoned. Mal used to come over to our house and stay all night and we'd just be tripping all night. They were good times."

Being twenty year-old musicians who were suddenly given the opportunity to work with The Beatles, it's not surprising that The Iveys look back at their time at Apple with fondness. For Paul McCartney, however, Apple was rapidly becoming a source of great displeasure. While McCartney would continue to release his records with an Apple label until 1974, The Iveys sessions would be the last production work that McCartney would undertake on behalf of Apple. Despite having been the Beatle who was the driving force behind its creation, McCartney seemed to lose all interest in Apple once Klein assumed control of the company. By Christmas 1969, McCartney had stopped visiting the Apple offices and the few times that he did come in, it was only to attend critical business meetings.

By mid-1969, it was painfully clear that no real working relationship would ever develop between Allen Klein and Paul McCartney. To his credit, Klein tried hard to gain McCartney's confidence. But while McCartney was very pleased with the increased royalty rates that Klein had negotiated with Capitol and EMI on behalf of The Beatles, he was unwilling to simply go along with the other three Beatles and let Klein assume full management of the group.

Peter Brown believes that the problems at Apple were not only due to Klein, but also to differences in opinion between McCartney and Lennon. "I think one of the problems that surfaced was because, in the early days, Paul had always been the most conventional and most business minded of The Beatles, and when Apple was set up, he took the most interest in it. He was the driving force behind the record company and virtually everything else we did. John at that time was pretty out of it, and the other two liked the idea, so they just went along with it. After Klein came in, Paul saw Apple as a place that had been taken over by someone he saw as an enemy and he wasn't going to contribute to it. He saw Apple as an obnoxious place to come to and he wouldn't come to Apple. Paul tried to avoid coming to Savile Row, so he would send John Eastman to the Apple meetings."

Looking back on the strained relationship between McCartney and Klein, Bill Oakes feels that, "Klein became absolutely obsessed with McCartney in my opinion by virtue of not being able to see him. He never had an artist who wouldn't see him, and it drove him nuts. Everyone thinks that Paul went off his rocker and was quite mad and rude about Klein, but the fact is that Paul had a nice wicked sense of humour about him. There was a time when McCartney made an appointment to meet Allen Klein at Marble Arch one afternoon. Klein kept on badgering me, asking 'Where's Paul, where's Paul?' and he wanted to know if he was in town. I told him that Paul was in town and I called Paul and told him that Klein wanted to meet him. Paul said, 'Oh yeah, I'll meet him.' At first he told me to send him around to his house on Cavendish Avenue, which obviously Paul then though better of, because how then would he get rid of Klein? So Paul said, 'Tell you what, tell him to meet me at 2 o'clock at Speakers Corner... at Marble Arch.' So I called Peter Howard and this secretary Jane who actually worked for Klein and told them what Paul had said and Klein was flabbergasted that Paul actually agreed to meet him. Then I told them, 'Well, there's a catch. He doesn't want to meet here at Apple or at Cavendish Avenue, so how about Speaker's Corner at 2 o'clock?' Then a bit later Paul called back and had me ask, 'Paul wants to know how will he recognize you?' He wanted to rub it in and he knew that this would be an insult.

"It turned out that the clouds flew over and it got dark around lunchtime and it really got raining by 2 o'clock... it was a downpour. Even if it hadn't rained, Paul had no intention of going of course. He loved the idea of Klein standing in the rain until nightfall. For him, it wasn't enough that it happened. He had to tell people, which was his downfall, and that's when he sounded a bit cruel. Klein was a charming villain... he knew all the words to The Beatles' records, which made him even more villainous to Paul. They weren't happy campers from day one with Klein... John and Paul wouldn't want to be caught hanging out together after that."

Given the tensions that existed between McCartney and the other three Beatles, it was most surprising that the group were able to put aside their differences long enough to venture into Abbey Road Studios in the summer of 1969 to record what would be their final album.

During the sessions, McCartney also found time to produce two final songs for Mary Hopkin. Unlike *Those Were The Days* or *Goodbye*, *Que Sera Sera* and *The Fields Of St. Etienne* – written by Apple Publishing's Gallagher and Lyle – were fairly standard pop numbers. In an interview with *Goldmine*, Hopkin recalled the session for *Que Sera Sera* as "just one of Paul's fun ideas. It was one sunny afternoon, we were sitting in Paul's garden, and he said 'Do you like this song?' I said, 'Well, I used to sing it when I was three,' and he said, 'My dad likes it, let's go and do it.' And so Ringo came along, it was all done in one afternoon. I was sort of swept along with Paul's enthusiasm really. By the time I was halfway through the backing vocals I said, 'This is awful.' I really though it was dreadful and I didn't want it released."

Given the catalogue number Apple 16, the two songs were released as a single in France. For some reason, Apple chose not to release either song in Britain, although they would eventually be released in America in June 1970.

Throughout the summer of 1969, there was an air of excitement around the Apple office as The Beatles put the finishing touches to their new album. Yet despite the upbeat quality of the music on "Abbey Road", the recording sessions did little to reduce the tensions within the group. With each passing month John Lennon was growing increasingly tired of being a Beatle and by September 1969, Lennon also seemed to have finally had enough of Apple.

In an interview with Zapple Records head and journalist Barry Miles (first published in *Mojo* in 1995), Lennon seemed to be particularly upset about the company. "Apple was a manifestation of Beatle naivety, collective naivety, and we said we're going to do this and help everybody and all that. And we got conned just on the subtlest and grossest level. We didn't get approached by the best artists, we got all the bums from everywhere... they'd been thrown out from everywhere else. And the people who were really groovy wouldn't approach us because they were too proud... that's why it didn't work. And then we quickly have to build up another wall around us to protect us from all the beggars and lepers in Britain and America that came to us. And the vibes are getting insane. And I tried, when we were at Wigmore Street, to see everybody, like we said, 'You don't have to get on your knees.' I saw everybody, day in, day out, and there wasn't anybody with anything to offer society or me or anything. There was just, 'I want, I want,' and 'Why not?' – terrible scenes going on in the office with hippies and all different people getting very wild with me."

While it was certainly true that Apple – with the notable exceptions of Magic Alex and The Fool – had found no non-musical artists to back, Apple Records had done far more than Lennon seemed willing to admit. In fact, earlier in the same interview, he had been enthusiastically praising Hot Chocolate's version of his song *Give Peace A Chance*.

Contrary to what Lennon thought, many top artists had tried to align themselves with Apple. Mick Fleetwood, the drummer of Fleetwood Mac who was then also George Harrison's brother-in-law, tried to get Fleetwood Mac signed to Apple. Although the group entered into negotiations, Apple seemed to be unable to act on closing the deal and Fleetwood Mac eventually signed to another label. Tony Bramwell remembers that several of the biggest rock acts of the seventies came to Apple early in their career. "We almost signed Queen... Gilbert O'Sullivan, but no one was really interested," he recalls. "I remember going to see Yes at the Marquee club with John Lennon and he really liked them. We put them into the studio to do some demos, but nothing came of it. By the time we got to the signing stages John would say 'Aah, I don't really like it, let's just forget it.' So we did."

Peter Asher also remembers pursuing Yes for Apple. "I don't remember why we didn't sign them. I heard them in a club... maybe the Scotch... and I loved them. They did a Beatles song too – *Every Little Thing* – it was a very cool version, very original. So I did some demos with them with Andy Johns engineering at Morgan Studios. It sounded great. I don't know what happened with Yes."

Crosby, Stills and Nash had also approached Apple to see if Apple was interested in issuing their debut album. Although the group was guaranteed to be a highly commercial act, Apple allegedly passed on Crosby, Stills and Nash due to the band wanting too much money and their stipulation that Paul McCartney produce the album. In *Crosby, Stills And Nash: The Authorized Biography*, Stephen Stills recalled: "We invited George Harrison over to listen, to see if Apple might be interested in us. After we finished he went, 'Wow.' Then he turned us down. The English attitude towards American musicians was a lot more competitive than I expected."

Stills' band mate Graham Nash recalled speaking to George Harrison about Apple in the early eighties: "George told me he heard us on tape, but I don't remember making any tapes in England then. We could have. But, anyway, George tells me, 'It's damn lucky CSN didn't end up on Apple, because things were so totally chaotic you would have been swallowed up in the bullshit.' So I guess the luckiest thing that ever happened to CSN is that we didn't end up on Apple."

Future member of The Eagles and popular 1970s American solo artist Joe Walsh submitted a tape to Apple in the summer of 1968. Walsh still has a rejection letter signed by Derek Taylor thanking Walsh for submitting a tape of his soon-to-be-successful group The James Gang, informing Walsh that Apple was not interested in The James Gang at the present time. So, while Lennon may have thought that all of the truly creative artists were not coming to Apple, the reality was that Apple was routinely failing to sign these artists.

Despite at least two of the company's owners having misgivings about Apple's long-term prospects, the Apple staff who remained after Klein's reorganization did their best to carry on business as usual and to make the artists that had been signed to Apple successful. It was not an easy task, especially after Klein had decimated Apple's original management team earlier in the year. Another problem was that once Apple had released all of the records that had been planned before Klein's arrival, Apple seemed uncertain of how it should proceed. Indeed, there was a fair amount of uncertainty as to who was really running the record division in the summer of 1969. Jack Oliver had done an admirable job of assuming many of Ron Kass' duties, but in August 1969, he was still basically learning how to run an international-al record company. Without Kass or Asher, Apple had no music indus-try professionals – other than the less-than-orthodox Derek Taylor – left in its management team.

The uncertainty that had resulted from Klein restructuring the man-agement had caused Apple to cancel several projects in addition to The Iveys' album. Apple had planned to release an album by the American rock-soul act Delaney and Bonnie entitled "Accept No Substitute" on 30 May. Given the catalogue number Sapcor 7, copies of the album had been pressed and were waiting for covers when Apple cancelled the whole project due to contractual disagreements with the duo. Apple then assigned the catalogue number Sapcor 7 to a proposed album by Trash, which they hoped to release on 20 June 1969. The Trash album was never completed and any plans for an album by Trash were put on indefinite hold.

Apple's release schedule for singles fared little better than that for the albums. Apple had hoped to release Mary Hopkin's *Que Sera Sera* as their September release in Britain and the single was given the cat-alogue number Apple 16. At the last moment, however, Apple can-celled Hopkin's single and announced that Apple 16 would be Mortimer's recording of *On Our Way Home*. But by the end of the month it was apparent that Apple had not been able to decide on which single to release, and neither single came out as Apple 16.

Mortimer's Tom Smith recalls that once Mortimer had finished recording their album, they could do little else but hang around the Apple offices and wait for Apple to release it, or even a single. "We used to hang around with Pete Ham and Tom from The Iveys. We used to hang around downstairs and rehearse and go out to pubs. We didn't go to each others homes – we didn't have a home actually – but we used to hang around Apple together and have a few drinks after that."

In retrospect, it was probably just as well that neither Mortimer nor Mary Hopkin put out records in September, given that most of Apple's resources would be consumed by the release of The Beatles' "Abbey Road" album. Apple wouldn't release any new records until October, when they released three new singles in both Britain and in America. The first was Trash's version of The Beatles' *Golden Slumbers*.

Trash apparently had great difficulty coming up with a suitable fol-low-up single to *Road To Nowhere* and they had solicited suggestions from several members of the Apple staff. Richard DiLello gave them a few ideas, before Derek Taylor came up with an ideal solution. Knowing that Trash would need a really strong second single in order to get their career off the ground, Taylor suggested that DiLello ask Paul McCartney to let Trash record a song off the still-unreleased "Abbey Road" album.

In his book *The Longest Cocktail Party*, DiLello recalls how he then secured a meeting with McCartney and Jack Oliver to plead his case for Trash, only to have Neil Aspinall walk in on the meeting to proclaim that he heard Trash rehearsing in the Apple basement and that 'they were no fucking good.' DiLello argued that Aspinall had heard the band under less than ideal conditions and the house hippie was ultimately able to get McCartney to agree to let Trash listen to the still-unreleased "Abbey Road" to find a song to record as a single. Trash selected McCartney's *Golden Slumbers* and they recorded a superb version of the song. Fresh from playing an endless series of one-night-stands in clubs across England and Scotland, Trash gave McCartney's gentle ballad a much-needed rough edge and turned the unassuming album track into a highly commercial rock single.

In *Blue Suede Brogans*, Trash guitarist Fraser Watson remembered: "The Apple thing was beginning to fall apart. We had a fair bit of contact with George Harrison and I later played on his first solo album, but Lennon and McCartney had fallen out and sometimes things were pretty terrible. We spent a lot of time in the Press Office with Derek Taylor, and he got us an early copy of the "Abbey Road" album to try to get a single. We chose *Golden Slumbers* and got some of George Harrison's solo studio time. Derek was happy, but The Beatles had to be consulted and at least two of them had to agree on any project. George Harrison was away somewhere, Ringo agreed, but McCartney didn't. So we were sitting in the office waiting for a reply from Lennon. Yoko took the thing to him, then came back and said 'OK. It's going to be released.' That kept us going for a wee while, but there was a kind of an Apple backlash going on in the media and we didn't get to do *Top of the Pops*."

As Watson noted, there had been a problem with Paul McCartney when it came to getting his final approval to release *Golden Slumbers* as a single. It appeared that McCartney had been under the impression that Trash were simply going to record a demo version of *Golden Slumbers* for further consideration as a potential single. Instead, the band went off and recorded a full-blown single, complete with string overdubs and a B-side. McCartney was so incensed by what he considered to be an unauthorized recording session that he refused to authorize the release of the single. In *The Longest Cocktail Party*, DiLello remembered that it was an exasperated Taylor – who along with DiLello had become quite fond of Trash – who took the acetate to play to John Lennon in the hope that Lennon would overrule McCartney. As Taylor had expected, Lennon listened to the acetate and proclaimed, "That's a good imitation of us... it's going out."

Whether or not Lennon actually liked the single or if he was just trying to upset McCartney will probably never be known, but the song was issued as a single in October. Though extremely well done and having received the full support of the Apple Press Office, Trash's version of *Golden Slumbers* only reached number 35 in the British charts.

Unlike the Trash single, Billy Preston's *Everything's Alright*, a "That's The Way God Planned It" album track which Preston had written with fellow Apple artist Doris Troy, failed to chart at all when issued as Apple's next single. Considering that his previous single *That's The Way God Planned It* had nearly made the British top ten, Apple was surprised by the profound lack of interest in Preston's second record. Jack Oliver believes that the problem was that "things like Doris Troy and Billy Preston were difficult to break in the UK. It was a very American style of music and, at that time, that type of music wasn't selling that well."

Oliver maintains: "We had to put a lot of effort into non-Beatle acts, because The Beatles themselves would sit on us. In the case of White Trash, I think that The Beatles weren't that fond of the group. I don't think that they thought White Trash were that good. The trouble was that if they didn't like it and they didn't bring pressure to bear on everybody, then people would push their efforts in other directions. White Trash never even got the chance to record an album."

The final single that Apple issued in October was a fascinating cover version of John Lennon's *Give Peace A Chance* done in a reggae arrangement by a group that had literally walked into Apple from off the street. The group who had recorded the song came to Apple's offices with a finished master tape and asked if Apple would release the record. In an interview with *Record Collector*, Derek Taylor remembered that unlike most of the visitors to Apple at that time, "they were not awfully friendly. They didn't want a drink, they didn't want a cup of tea, they wanted to play this fucking song to John Lennon. So we went down to the record department's office with Jack Oliver, heard this fabulous little record, and John liked it. And again, they went somewhere else to succeed."

Lennon, like most of the Apple staff, loved what this mysterious group had done with *Give Peace A Chance* and the group was signed to do a single for Apple. Since the group didn't have a name, they asked Apple to provide them with one. It was Mavis Smith from the press office who came up with the name, The Hot Chocolate Band.

Although their Apple single failed to chart, Hot Chocolate would later sign with producer Mickie Most's RAK Records and go on to become one of the best-selling English bands of the seventies.

October also saw the release of the Modern Jazz Quartet's second and final Apple album. Entitled "Space", the album had been recorded in England in March. But now that their principal contact at Apple, Ron Kass, was not at the label, Apple took little interest in the MJQ and no one was surprised when they returned to Atlantic Records soon after the release of "Space". The MJQ's John Lewis remembers: "We were on tour in Europe and at the end of our tour we took a few days in London to record "Space". We recorded it at Trident and Peter Asher supervised the session. I was the music director. I like the Apple albums very, very much. They're some of the best things I think we ever did. The Beatles were having difficulties getting the company started and when Ron left, that was the end of that deal. We met George Harrison once because Connie Kay played on an album with him, so George came by the studio one day... we didn't meet the other Beatles, so after Ron left, we went back to Atlantic."

October also saw the official closing of Zapple Records, which was dissolved as part of Allen Klein's ongoing efforts to nurse Apple back to financial health. There was certainly no denying that in a few short months Klein had greatly changed the atmosphere at Apple, replacing the chaotic exuberance that had once characterized the company with a sleek, business-like efficiency. While it is likely that Klein had fired far more people than was necessary and that he had ended Apple's original goal of being an altruistic, arts-based organization, there had been a definite need for someone to step into Apple and put the company's finances in order. Preparing the financial accounts of Apple up until only the end of 1967, Klein was amazed to find that during this period, Apple's accountants had written off three cars that could simply not be accounted for and had authorized Apple Electronics to issue non-business related cash advances to art gallery owner John Dunbar for £2,000 and to Magic Alex for £1,000.

Klein had transformed Apple into a new type of company, but it was not only the foreign business practices that Klein brought to Apple that the staff had to learn to live with. Many of Apple's British staff also had to adapt to the curious cultural differences that existed between them and the sundry Abkco employees who would often turn up with Klein at Savile Row. To this day, many of Apple's former artists and staff still vividly remember Apple's American Promotion Manager, Pete Bennett.

Bill Oakes stresses that, "With Klein... when he came to England,

Grapefruit in London - 1968. (L-R) Geoff Swettenham, George Alexander, John Perry, Pete Swettenham.

Grapefruit launch party, 1968. (L-R) top row: Brian Jones, Donovan, Ringo Starr, John Lennon, Cilla Black and Paul McCartney
Bottom row: George Alexander, Pete Swettenham, Geoff Swettenham and John Perry.

(L-R) Mal Evans, Ken Mansfield and George Harrison - 1968.

The Iveys in Apple's basement studio - 1968.

(L-R) George Harrison (back of head), Ron Kass, Paul McCartney, Ken Mansfield, Ringo Starr and Stanley Gortikov - June 1968.

Allen Klein - on the move.

Mary Hopkin.

Mary Hopkin, in London 1969.

Mary Hopkin, Apple's first star.

The elusive Mortimer, snapped in Peter Asher's garden - 1969.

Richard Hewson and Peter Asher working on arrangements for the Mortimer album, 1969.

Peter Asher and Barry Sheffield recording the Mortimer album at Trident Studios, 1969.

Thursday

3. Saville Row.
LONDON. W. 1.

Dear Brute,

You have got a great
name and a lovely voice and a
beautiful Record on Apple called
King of Fuh. I felt I should
make some contact with you, (until
we meet someplace when we will
really make contact), as I have been
involved with it all so, HELLO!
I dig the "Nobody Knows" side too.
Thanks for being patient with us
and for Being: George Harrison.

A 1969 letter to "Brute Force" from George Harrison.

Former John's Children bassist John Hewlett in the Apple Music Publishing office, 1969.

(L-R) Jack Oliver, Paul McCartney, Unknown, Mal Evans and Tony Bramwell, Circa 1969.

Pete Bennett

*George Harrison and Jack Oliver introduce members of The Radha Krishna Temple
(holding a copy of their Govinda single) to French EMI executives in 1970.*

George, John and Yoko at Apple - 1971.

Apple Records president Jack Oliver in Hawaii in 1970,
on the way to Japan with Mary Hopkin.
(Dig the Apple watch!)

Mary Hopkin and Jack Oliver meet EMI executives in Japan, 1970.

(L-R) Klaus Voormann, Derrek Van Eaton, Tony King and Patti Harrison at Apple - 1971.

(L-R) Terry Doran and friend.

Badfinger - 1973.

Al Steckler presents Badfinger with a Gold Record for Day After Day onstage at Carnegie Hall.

Al Steckler, Yoko Ono, John Lennon and Phil Spector in New York City.

Apple Studios Staff, 1973. (L-R) Steve O'Donnel, George Peckham and Phil McDonald.

at that time he was about as curious a figure as the Maharishi. Suddenly there was this scruffy little guy from Brooklyn at Savile Row with a five o'clock shadow with these guys in spats. They acted like American gangsters from the movies. Pete Bennett was a boy playing at it, but Phil Spector was the real deal, going around with loaded guns. Pete Bennett was the first physical evidence that Klein had arrived. Suddenly there was this ridiculous person in a loud double breasted suit at the top of the stairs checking people's credentials in an office where they had lived and worked for two years."

Bennett himself concedes that he and many of the Abkco employees were quite unlike most of the people working at Apple at the time. "I didn't look like them, I didn't have the long hair, I was a different character... everyone was asking what the hell is Peter Bennett doing with these guys... the continuity wasn't there. They were saying what is he, a Mafia guy, a tough guy? The thing with The Beatles and Apple was that I produced... I got them hits. But when I told them I was gonna break a record, I did it. The Beatles required a lot of attention. When they came to America, I would pick them up at the airport, set up media interviews at the airport. I was acting as almost a personal manager... I was an advisor, I took them to dinner, I did everything besides the records. We had a lot of fun. We had a close relationship."

Tony Bramwell confirms that however unlikely an Apple employee Pete Bennett appeared to be, "John adored Pete Bennett. He might have been an effective promotions man, but he wasn't in The Beatles' or Apple's image."

Fortunately for Apple's British staff, Klein was still very busy running Abkco and he and Bennett were generally unable to spend too much time in England. Klein had an office on the first floor of the Savile Row building, but the office was seldom used. To ensure that Apple continued operating in an orderly fashion in his absence, Klein appointed a trusted Abkco employee, Peter Howard, to oversee the daily operations of Apple's Savile Row office. Howard was given the empty room in front of the press office on the third floor. "Klein wasn't too involved with the day-to-day running of Apple," remembers Pete Bennett. "Peter Howard worked for Klein in London and Terry Mellis helped him out, but they were mostly into the accounting end of it."

Klein also established an American office for Apple in late 1969. Although Apple had originally intended to base their American operations in Los Angeles, Klein decided to open an office in New York City so that he could be more actively involved with Apple. The Apple office was set up in space leased from Klein's Abkco Industries on the 40th floor of a new skyscraper at 1700 Broadway.

Those Were The Days

Many of Apple's staff were disappointed to learn that Apple would not have an office in California, but the shared office space arrangement with Abkco was the best possible way for Apple to establish itself in the American market. Unlike Apple's UK office, all of the employees working on behalf of Apple in the New York office were actually Abkco employees. In addition to keeping costs down by using Abkco support staff, Apple now had the services of Pete Bennett, a highly regarded independent radio promotions man. If Apple was going to break artists like Trash, The Iveys and Jackie Lomax in America, they would need a strong radio promotions man and Pete Bennett was one of the best people they could have hired.

Bennett recalls: "I ended up with Apple because The Beatles wanted the same promotion guy as the Stones. In 1969, I was an independent promoter and was working with Klein on the Stones... they actually came to me first... they wanted me, not Klein. The only reason Klein got them was because of me. He told them that he was working with Pete Bennett and that was how he got three of the Beatles to agree to let him manage them. They wanted me for promotion. Then they found out Allen Klein knew nothing about the recording business, he was just an accountant, and not even a certified accountant. I first got involved with Klein when Allen got Sam Cooke and Sam told Klein that the only way I'll go with you is if you get Pete Bennett to promote me. Cooke was a big fan of Nat Cole, whom I was promoting, and he wanted the same promotion man as Cole. So Allen says, 'I know Pete very well,' although we had never actually worked together. Allen was doing work for Scepter Records, a company which I was promoting. So Klein made a deal with me and with Sam. Then in 1964 Mickie Most came in and was involved with Klein, so I ended up working with Most too – Herman's Hermits, The Animals. But Klein didn't know anything about promotion. I was not an Abkco employee, I was independent. I was collecting a check from Abkco and Apple Records. It was a real busy time working for Apple and the Stones. I was still doing the Stones up until 1976 even after the Stones left Klein in 1970."

Having secured an American office and the services of one of the most effective promotions men in the American music industry, all that Apple needed now was some product to release. That new Apple product turned out to be a solo single from John Lennon entitled *Cold Turkey*. Inspired by the withdrawal symptoms that he and Yoko Ono had experienced during their recent flirtation with heroin, the song was a raw expression of personal pain. Though Lennon had originally hoped to record *Cold Turkey* with The Beatles, McCartney and

Harrison balked at the idea so Lennon decided that *Cold Turkey* would be the second Plastic Ono Band single. With The Beatles unwilling to put the group name on his latest creation, Lennon recruited Ringo Starr, Eric Clapton and an old friend of the Beatles from their Hamburg days, bassist Klaus Voormann, to back him on the recording.

To drive the extremely personal nature of the song home, the record came packaged in a sleeve that displayed x-rays of John and Yoko's heads. The designer of the record sleeve, Kosh, remembers: "The *Cold Turkey* sleeve was kind of scary... putting John Lennon's head under an x-ray machine... I didn't know if he was going to go blind or something. John and I thought it up on a drunken afternoon. That's really his head and his glasses, it wasn't retouched or anything and Yoko was on the other side." As could be expected from the song's unpleasant subject matter, *Cold Turkey* was only a minor hit on both sides of the Atlantic.

In Britain, Apple's final release for 1969 was scheduled to be The Iveys' recording of *Come And Get It*. Press ads were printed announcing the imminent release of *Come And Get It* by The Iveys, but when copies of the record finally materialized in the shops in early December, the band's name had been changed to Badfinger.

Apparently, The Iveys had been unhappy with their name for some time. As the sixties progressed the group felt that their name was becoming increasingly dated and they also found themselves being confused with the mid-sixties hit makers, The Ivy League. When Iveys' bassist Ron Griffiths left (or was pushed out of) the band shortly after the recording sessions for *Come And Get It* (to be replaced by guitarist Joey Molland), the remaining Iveys decided that the time had come to finally change the name of the group. After rejecting Paul McCartney's suggestions of "Home" or "Mama's Boys" and John Lennon's "Prix", the group finally agreed on "Badfinger" which had been suggested by Neil Aspinall.

The Iveys' name was not the only thing that was changing at Apple as the company prepared to move into the next decade. By the final days of 1969, most of Apple's staff had resigned themselves to being part of "an Abkco managed company" and they were learning to work within the parameters established by Klein.

Klein's influence on Apple was not restricted to new business policies. His arrival at Savile Row had also signalled an end to the free-wheeling guest admission policy that had characterized the Apple of 1968 and early 1969. With Klein in command, colourful characters like the Hell's Angels, Emily's Family, and Stocky – the drug frazzled American teen who spent two months perched on top of a filing cabinet in Derek Taylor's office drawing pictures of genitalia – were no longer welcome. The Apple staff also seemed more subdued and sights like Jeremy Banks leading a donkey that he wished to present as a gift to Derek Taylor through Apple's offices would not be seen again at Savile Row.

Still, Apple would remain open to guests who managed to get an audience with one of The Beatles or a senior Apple executive. Even after Klein had assumed control of the company, Derek Taylor remained exceptionally dedicated to keeping at least some spark of Apple's original idealistic fire alive. It was this sense of duty to Apple's original goals that would briefly pit Taylor against the future Virgin Records founder, Richard Branson.

Taylor had met Branson in December 1968 when, at the age of 18, Branson came to Apple to see if he could get one of The Beatles to contribute music for a flexi disc that was to be distributed with a magazine he was running called *Student*. Taken by the young Branson's impassioned pleas, Taylor innocently promised a tape of words and/or music by John and Yoko. In *Fifty Years Adrift*, Taylor recalled how, "Branson kept coming in to see if there was any progress and one afternoon he helped me address Christmas cards as one of a team of visitors I had seconded to essential office tasks. He looked so pessimistic and young, seated on the floor, that I wrote on a card I was signing, 'Trust me, Richard... signed Derek.'"

It was in early 1969 that Taylor finally got John and Yoko to submit a tape, which turned out to be a recording of the fading heartbeat of the couple's miscarried baby. After what Taylor described in *Fifty Years Adrift* as a "retrospectively hilarious listening session at Apple Studios", Branson and his recently acquired lawyers found the recording to be quite unacceptable.

Soon after that meeting, and using the Christmas card that Taylor had signed as evidence, Branson served Taylor with court papers and attempted to sue the hapless publicist for breach of contract claiming £10,000 in damages. Taylor was very upset by the incident and even circulated a memo to Apple management stating that they could take the damages out of his wages should Branson prevail. Fortunately for Taylor, Branson decided against taking him to court.

As for Derek Taylor, perhaps he learned – as The Beatles had done before him – that the best intentions are often abused by the very people that they are intended to benefit.

5
1970 - And Then There Were Three

To many of the younger members of London's workforce returning to their offices after the 1969 Christmas holiday, the grey winter skies of January 1970 felt a world away from the carefree days of the summer of 1969. The sixties were over and there was a palpable feeling in the air that the days of swinging London as the fashion and music capital of the world were numbered. Before the end of the year, both Janis Joplin and one-time Apple guest Jimi Hendrix would be dead and the Woodstock and Isle of Wight music festivals would prove to be high water marks of a once thriving youth culture that was rapidly starting to recede. The curtain had closed on the sixties and music, politics and society itself would face great changes in the coming years. Come December 1970, John Lennon himself would sum up the feelings of the generation who grew up listening to The Beatles when he sang in a harsh, world-weary voice, "the dream is over." While the dream may not yet have been completely over, the sixties dream that The Beatles had come to represent for so many people was certainly entering its final hour.

At Savile Row, the arrival of Allen Klein certainly contributed to a general feeling that the passing of the sixties was indeed the end of an era. Yet in many ways, Apple had not changed all that much from what it had been a mere eighteen months earlier. Despite the numerous staff dismissals that had taken place throughout 1969 and the looming presence of Allen Klein, many of the original faces could still be found at 3 Savile Row. In the third floor Press Office in the rear of the building, Derek Taylor, Richard DiLello and Mavis Smith still held court, constituting perhaps the last remaining bastion of Apple's original idealism. In the record department on the main floor, Tony Bramwell, Jack Oliver and Oliver's two secretaries remained busy running Apple Records, and from his well-appointed second floor office, Peter Brown still attended to the increasingly divergent needs of the four Beatles.

By 1970, most of the remaining staff at 3 Savile Row had come to terms with Apple's traumatic transformation into a fairly orthodox independent record label. For the most part, the Apple staff simply went about their business, largely unaware of the growing tensions within The Beatles and having no idea that the entire Apple organization was slowly being drawn into the drama of the impending split of the band.

The new decade started well for Apple when Badfinger's *Come And Get It* crashed into the British top ten in January, validating Mal Evan's intense belief in the unassuming rock band from South Wales. To guitarist Joey Molland – who had been an unemployed Liverpool musician only a few months earlier – Badfinger's sudden fame was a particularly surreal experience. One of Molland's most vivid memories from that era was the first time he met one of The Beatles. "The first Beatle I met was George Harrison," he recalled in an interview with *Vintage Guitar* magazine. "We bumped into him on the stairs at Apple. The record was a hit and he was very excited for us. It was very natural. He congratulated us and told us, 'Well, you know you'll have to play that song every day for the rest of your lives.'" Full of youth and optimism, it would be years before Molland and the rest of Badfinger would appreciate the prophetic nature of Harrison's remark.

Badfinger's *Come And Get It* was quickly followed into the UK top ten by Mary Hopkin's new single, the calypso influenced *Temma Harbour*. The bright and breezy *Temma Harbour* was a particular milestone for Hopkin in that it was her first Apple recording not produced by Paul McCartney. McCartney has since said that the primary reason he stopped producing Hopkin was that he was not particularly interested in the folk-oriented direction that Hopkin was pursuing at the time. However, many of Apple's staff remember that McCartney had simply stopped coming into the Apple office soon after the September release of "Abbey Road". Having realized that Klein had come to stay and that the rest of The Beatles had given Klein their full support, McCartney appeared to lose all interest in Apple and even The Beatles. Going into virtual seclusion, McCartney left London and moved up to his remote Scottish farm, where he spent his time recording songs on a four-track recorder that he had set up in his farmhouse.

With McCartney seemingly out of the picture, Apple needed to find a new producer for Mary Hopkin. Producer Mickie Most was eventually assigned the job. Most was a proven hit maker. Since 1965, he had produced an impressive string of hits for Donovan, The Yardbirds, Herman's Hermits, Jeff Beck, Terry Reid and many other leading English acts. Most was one of the top English record producers of the sixties and a logical and sensible choice to produce Apple's most successful pop artist. Most also had strong ties to Allen Klein (who had represented both Donovan and Herman's Hermits in the United States in the mid-sixties) so it was not surprising that he was selected to be Hopkin's new producer.

Mary Hopkin, however, was the one person who was not enthused with Apple's choice of producer. Speaking to *Goldmine* magazine in

1995, Hopkin explained: "The reason I worked with Mickie was that obviously Paul and I agreed that it wasn't going to work out, because he hadn't the time, and I had to get more material out. We came up with Mickie Most, and I thought, 'Oh, that might be good,' because he'd produced Donovan, who was very sensitive and does beautiful music. Unfortunately, Mickie took a different approach with me, and that's when the rot set in. The crunch came when Mickie visited me at my final summer session. We'd been going over some songs to record and he said, 'Choose the keys and I'll go away and record them. When you got a chance, you can come down and do the vocal.' I said, 'No way, I have to be there, I want to discuss the arrangements. I don't want to be a session singer.'"

Despite Hopkin's deep misgivings about both the material she was being asked to record and Most's polished, highly efficient production style, she eventually acquiesced to the wishes of both Apple and her management and recorded several singles with Most.

Mary Hopkin still claims to dislike almost all of her Most-produced recordings, but it should be noted that all of the singles did make the British top 40. Other Apple artists were far less fortunate than Hopkin when it came to getting their music into the pop charts. Billy Preston was finding that even if you could get one of The Beatles to produce and perform on your records, there was no guarantee that the record would be a hit. In January 1970, Apple released *All That I've Got*, a soulful new song by Preston, produced by George Harrison, which was Preston's first new recording since the release of his "That's The Way God Planned It" album. Co-written by Preston and Doris Troy, *All That I've Got* was an earthy R&B number. However, perhaps because it lacked the immediacy and pop appeal of Preston's earlier singles, it failed to make the charts in either Britain or America. Doris Troy also recorded a spirited version of the song, but it would not be available until 1992 when the original Apple albums were reissued on compact disc.

Like Preston, Jackie Lomax was also finding it difficult to establish himself as a pop star. In February 1970, Apple gave Lomax one last crack at stardom when they released the gospel-influenced *How The Web Was Woven*, a song that George Harrison had produced for Lomax in November 1969. Lomax remembers: "Apple seemed to have a hard time picking singles. *How The Web Was Woven* was supposed to be my commercial song that they found for me. We recorded it at Trident and Leon Russell played everything – the drums, the bass, the slide guitar, the organ – he was like a mad genius." As with Lomax's previous singles, *How The Web Was Woven* certainly sounded like a commercial pop song, yet it failed to make the charts and Apple declined to pick up their option on Lomax. *How The Web Was Woven* also failed to chart when it was released in America in March.

Lomax still believes that the failure of *How The Web Was Woven* was due in no small part to the way that Allen Klein was running Apple. "Allen Klein was not going to spend any more money, period. No one could figure out what was happening. I tried to get to see him at Apple and he wouldn't see me. I was just going to say, 'Look, am I ever going to record again, or what?' and I never did get an answer, I never did get an interview with him."

After recording *How The Web Was Woven* in November 1969, Lomax spent the next several months kicking around London while he waited for Apple to release his new single. Considering that "Is This What You Want" had sold around 50,000 copies and had – to his knowledge – not lost money for the label, Lomax assumed that Apple would be willing to continue backing his career. In a 1970 interview with *Rolling Stone*, Lomax lamented, "He [Klein] came in and put a stop to everything going out of the company, to get a chance to re-evaluate things. There I was, with a band, set to go out on the road. He didn't know me at all. It was, 'Hey kid, where do you think you're going?' I think I wound up going out with 50-watt amps... Apple was always saying, 'We're your record company, not your booking agent,' so... Klein never spoke to me to find out what I was into. They stopped answering my phone calls. I owed them a certain number of sides a year, but all I cut was a single that George produced... finally I had a solicitor's letter sent to them asking what was going on. They said the man in charge of the matter would get back to me in three weeks. Well I got some pride, so I had another letter sent saying, 'I consider our association terminated.' They haven't yet answered that one."

With his recording career at Apple seemingly on hold, Lomax returned to playing live music, touring around England in early 1970 and recording an album with a blues-rock band called Heavy Jelly in late 1969. Lomax was not the only Apple artist who was moonlighting on other projects. Badfinger's Pete Ham and Tom Evans dropped in on Heavy Jelly's 1969 recording sessions to add backing vocals to a song called *Take Me Down To The Water*. Unfortunately for Lomax, the Heavy Jelly album was never released due to business problems experienced by Head Records, the label that paid for the recordings. Finally giving up on both Apple and Britain, Lomax left for America just before Christmas 1970, settling in Woodstock NY, were he recorded several unsuccessful albums for Warner Brothers Records.

Contrary to Lomax's belief that it was Allen Klein's conservative business policies that were at the root of his failure to crack the charts, Derek Taylor explained to *Record Collector* in the mid-eighties that Klein had little to do with Lomax's failure to get a hit. "Jackie was given all the shots that a young rock and roll hopeful could have had in the sixties, both at Apple and later at Warners, but he never came through as a star. Perhaps the problem was that stars at that time had a lightness of spirit, while Jackie was a little melancholic. Anyway, his time was not to be. I agonized a lot about him, because I knew it wasn't happening for him the way that it should. I had a big joint one day on Virginia Water Station; when I got to Waterloo I went to the bar, had a couple of large gin and tonics and I thought I had it cracked. I went into the office and said, 'Jackie Lomax should go MOR.' He should become The Gaucho, dressed in incredible boots, baggy pants a moustache and a huge shirt with large sleeves and knock 'em dead in the clubs. My assistant Richard DiLello said, 'I think you need to calm down boss. This is an appalling idea, and Jackie Lomax will never forgive you for it.' So I never put it to Jackie myself..."

Jackie Lomax was not the only Apple act to be cut from the label's roster in the early months of 1970. During the same period when Lomax was breaking ties with Apple, the company also declined to extend the contracts of Trash and Mortimer. Like Lomax, Guy Masson of Mortimer clearly remembers trying to get a meeting with Allen Klein so that he could find out where Mortimer stood in relation to Apple. "In early 1970, I ran into George Harrison and said, 'Hi George, do you know when our record's coming out?' and he said it would be out in two weeks. I told him, 'I think that the group is breaking up', and he didn't know what to say, so he told me, 'Oh well, you'll make more money that way.' Our album had already been done for months and was sitting there. I had seen everything there was to see in London and the group was dissipating in front of me."

Masson finally lost patience with Apple and decided that his only option was to confront Klein directly. "At the time I might have had a warm beer from one of the pubs across the street or something," he remembers, "so I went in and said, 'Where is Allen Klein?' They said he's on such and such floor in such and such office and I just charged in there and saw this man behind a desk with a light, with these two huge business guys, all in suits. I don't remember what I was doing, but I was ranting and raving about our album and what was going on, can we get this finished and Allen Klein just kinda looked at me and said to these guys, 'Could you escort this man out please,' so they took me out, they escorted me right out of his office, down the stairs and to the lobby and said, 'Please leave Mr. Klein alone.'"

Masson claims that Peter Asher later expressed an interest in taking Mortimer with him to Warner Brothers. "Peter knew about Mortimer breaking up before it was happening, and Peter I know approached our manager and said, 'Let's go back to the United States, let's take the group with us and we'll go with James Taylor and Mortimer to Warner Brothers.'" In the end, Mortimer's management chose not to go with Asher. Masson believes that Iveys manager Bill Collins was also interested in managing Mortimer, but with the group collapsing, nothing ever developed from that offer. As Masson feared, Apple never did release any of Mortimer's recordings and the group broke up in mid-1970.

Mortimer's Tom Smith also remembers that Peter Asher was interested in Mortimer and that Asher actually invited him to join James Taylor's band. Smith explains: "After our Apple album was shelved... Peter played me a tape of James Taylor's *Fire And Rain*. By that time I had had enough of Mortimer and that acoustic business... I wanted to go back playing electric, so I had decided to leave Mortimer. So Peter was putting a band together to go to America with James Taylor and he asked me if I was interested in playing lead guitar for James Taylor. Arrangements were being made for all of this when I got a letter from my draft board in the United States. I remember both Apple and Peter sent the draft board letters saying that I was under contract for another year, but they took my passport and put out a warrant for my arrest... so I couldn't join Taylor's band. It was a big disappointment."

With Lomax, Trash and Mortimer out of the picture, a good deal of Apple's attention shifted to Doris Troy. Since the spring of 1969, Troy had been diligently working on material in Apple's basement rehearsal room and Apple decided, finally, to issue a single in February 1970. *Ain't That Cute* – a powerful R&B-infused rocker that was co-written and produced by George Harrison – should have been a big hit for Troy and Apple. It did receive plenty of favourable press, yet the single met with little commercial success. Troy is still not certain why it took Apple a year to release her debut single, although she remembers, "While we were doing the sessions at Trident Studios, George's mother died and that kind of stopped the sessions for a little while, and I had to finish it up on my own."

Unlike many of the other Apple artists who scraped by on proceeds from their live performances, Troy did not seem to have much difficulty supporting herself in London and she remembers that she didn't feel any pressure to release records. Perhaps because of her previous success in the mid-sixties, Troy appeared to have received a better deal from Apple than the other Apple artists. In sharp contrast to Jackie Lomax or the pre-Badfinger Iveys who subsisted on meagre publishing advances and the receipts from live performances, Troy recalls: "I was on a nice salary. I never had any problems with money; the money was always there. I never wanted for anything. Apple rented me a gorgeous flat. It was fun being there and we got a lot of things done. They even gave me my own office next to Peter Asher. The next thing I know Peter Asher had left with James Taylor. We had fun... it was a wonderful time."

Needless to say, the commercial failure of Doris Troy's single was a big disappointment to Apple. Fortunately, the label would have better luck in March with a new Mary Hopkin single. The single – a frothy, Mickie Most produced pop number called *Knock Knock, Who's There* – was even selected to represent the United Kingdom in the Eurovision Song Contest. Though *Knock Knock, Who's There* failed to win top Eurovision honours, the resulting publicity made the song Hopkin's biggest hit since *Those Were The Days*. Packaged in a special "Song for Europe" picture sleeve, the single eventually reached number 2 on the British charts. For reasons unknown, Apple chose not to release the single in America.

One of the more unusual items to be issued by Apple that March was *Govinda* – a second George Harrison produced single by the Radha Krishna Temple. Featuring a haunting string arrangement written by John Barham, the single had much more of a contemporary rock feel than *Hare Krishna Mantra* and it managed to climb to number 26 in the British charts. Lacking the novelty value of *Hare Krishna Mantra*, *Govinda* succeeded on its own musical merits and had the song featured lyrics sung in English, the single may have gone even higher.

Apple held an outdoor press reception on 5 March to promote the single in the UK "I remember hiring a marquee in a big garden in Sydenham... a lunchtime reception," recalled Derek Taylor in an Apple press release, "and watching with apprehension as the devotees casually wet-shaved each other's heads in the conservatory of the big house in order to look their best for the press who turned up in great numbers hunting in vain for the bar. The journalists were thoroughly puzzled, thirsty and quite annoyed by the direction in which things had taken their mop tops and their press officer."

The Radha Krishna Temple would not emulate their UK success in America, but Apple's US operation got off to a good start in March when Mary Hopkin's *Temma Harbour* climbed to number 39 in the charts. More impressively, Badfinger's *Come And Get It* made the

American top ten in March 1970. Badfinger's "Magic Christian Music" album was released later that month and by April it had reached a very respectable number 55 in the American album charts.

In the UK Apple had released "Magic Christian Music" in January, where it sold a decent number of copies but not enough to reach the UK charts. Perhaps due to the simple nature of *Come And Get It* and the fact that the song was written by Paul McCartney, Badfinger were increasingly perceived to be a teeny-bopper pop act in Britain. In fact, as far as the British market was concerned, this unfounded perception of Badfinger being a singles oriented pop band would stick with the group for the remainder of their career.

Apple promotions manager Pete Bennett remembers that breaking Badfinger in America was also far from easy. Despite *Come And Get It* being written by Paul McCartney, he claims that American radio was initially reluctant to get behind the single. "We spent 30 to 40 thousand dollars breaking that first Badfinger record. George Harrison was pleading with me to do something for Badfinger, so I broke *Come And Get It* on WLS in Chicago by buying air time, one minute commercial spots, and playing *Come And Get It*. It was like a paid advertisement, but the radio station didn't make us say it was. After we started playing the spots, people started calling in and the program director started playing it, so that's how we broke Badfinger in America."

Despite the substantial effort and resources that were being spent on Badfinger's behalf, Apple seemed to be caught off guard by Badfinger's sudden success. Once *Come And Get It* took off in England, the "Magic Christian Music" album had to be hastily thrown together by Apple in order to capitalize on the success of the single. Although "Magic Christian Music" was the official debut of Badfinger, the album was to all intents and purposes an Iveys album and new guitarist Joey Molland did not perform on any of the songs. Faced with having no album to cash in on the success of a hit single, Apple compiled "Magic Christian Music" from tracks taken from The Iveys' "Maybe Tomorrow" album, the three songs that The Iveys had recorded for the soundtrack to the *Magic Christian* film and several other songs that the band had recorded in the summer and autumn of 1969.

Apple was in such a rush to release "Magic Christian Music" that they could not even arrange to have a picture taken of new Badfinger guitarist Joey Molland to put on the album cover. The album's liner notes, written by "Mal" state that "Badfinger are four" and list Molland as a band member, yet only the three remaining Iveys are pictured on the back cover. The album cover also neglected to give Paul

McCartney credit for the three songs he had produced, simply stating that the songs were from the soundtrack of the "Magic Christian" film.

Released at a time when many British albums still included 14 songs (as opposed to the 11 or 12 tracks that were issued on typical American albums), the UK edition of "Magic Christian Music" included two songs that were not featured on the American album – *Angelique*, a pleasant ballad from The Iveys' "Maybe Tomorrow" album, and *Give It A Try*, a group composition that The Iveys had submitted to Apple as a possible follow-up to the *Maybe Tomorrow* single but which had been rejected by Apple.

In addition to the successful records by Badfinger and Mary Hopkin, there was also a great deal of Beatles-related activity at Apple in the early months of 1970. Making up for the lacklustre public response to *Cold Turkey*, John Lennon reached the top ten in February with his third solo single, *Instant Karma*. Produced by the legendary American producer Phil Spector, *Instant Karma* also served as an informal production audition for Spector. Both Lennon and George Harrison – who Lennon had asked to play guitar on the *Instant Karma* session – were impressed enough with Spector's work to hire Spector to work on The Beatles' "Get Back" tapes, hoping that Spector would be able to make the rough performances captured on the tapes suitable for release.

Indeed, much of the early winter and spring of 1970 would be devoted to preparing the release of what would become the "Let It Be" film and album. Work on the "Let It Be" project was almost complete by late spring and on 1 April, Richard Hewson joined Phil Spector at Abbey Road Studios to record the string arrangements that Hewson had written for *The Long And Winding Road* and *I Me Mine*. But Hewson was not Spector's first choice for the project. On George Harrison's recommendation, Spector had originally selected John Barham to write and conduct the string parts. Unfortunately for the recently married Barham, the session was scheduled when he was to be away on his honeymoon so Spector had little choice but to give the job to Hewson.

With Apple Records scoring several non-Beatles hits and a new Beatles album and film scheduled for an April release, on the surface it appeared that all was well within The Beatles organization in the early months of 1970. The reality of the situation, however, was that there was serious in-fighting going on between the four owners of the company, or rather between Paul McCartney and the other three Beatles.

Still reeling from Allen Klein gaining control of Apple,

McCartney's next battle with the other Beatles came over their decision to have Spector produce the "Let It Be" album. Enraged by the orchestra and choir that Spector and Hewson had overdubbed onto his poignant ballad *The Long And Winding Road*, McCartney was adamant that Spector's version of the album should not be released. "Paul McCartney hated the strings on "Let It Be", remembers Pete Bennett, "and he didn't want Phil Spector producing the album. Paul complained to us, but we put it out anyhow. It wasn't even Klein's doing... we put it out because John Lennon wanted it out. You have to understand that Lennon was the Director of Apple Records. Lennon had the last say. The four of them owned the label, and for whatever reason, they made Lennon the president when they set up Apple."

McCartney's anger over "Let It Be" was compounded by the fact that he had been informed by Apple that the release date of his solo album, "McCartney", would have to be postponed so as not to draw sales away from the "Let It Be" album and "Sentimental Journey" – the Ringo Starr solo album that had already been scheduled for release in April or May.

Tensions were running visibly high between the four Beatles, yet almost everyone working at Apple was as surprised as the rest of the world when the 10 April issue of the *Daily Mail* broke the story that Paul McCartney was leaving The Beatles. "There was never any watershed day when they broke up," maintains Bill Oakes. "The depth of the ignorance about The Beatles actual personal situation was amazing to me... the fact that the Apple Records staff, the accountants and the promotions people, they had no idea that The Beatles weren't still living and sleeping in one bed. I remember after I had been there about a year, I brought up some small domestic thing and people were shocked. They still viewed The Beatles in some sort of time warp. I don't think that the people outside of myself and Peter Brown – the people working for Beatles and Co. – had any idea that this time bomb was ticking. They were all very affected when the Don Short story was published. They all thought they were going to be pink slipped the next day, which I thought was a bit naive. Peter Brown had to remind me that not everyone was privy to the inside world of The Beatles."

The *Daily Mail* story was based on information that came directly from Derek Taylor. However, the actual interview from which McCartney's quotes were taken was conducted by Oakes: "I remember the interview that Paul had me do which was then quoted around the world as 'Paul quits The Beatles.' Although Derek has been taking credit for it, I did that interview. Paul didn't want to talk to anybody, but he wanted to get it out in the air and he wanted the information available to everyone. So he asked me to write down 12 questions that I would consider key if I was a journalist. Then he gave me the answers and wanted them printed up and included with every promotional copy of the "McCartney" album. So I told Derek that we would have to handle it quite carefully as the answers were quite incendiary, so Derek said, 'Let me handle it,' but I told him, 'No, you don't get it. He wants this printed up and sent out to every journalist who is reviewing the album.'"

Quoting the "interview" that McCartney had done with Oakes, Taylor then proceeded to "leak" the information to Don Short of the *Daily Mail*. "All of a sudden it was 'Paul quits Beatles' when it really was not about him quitting The Beatles, it was about promoting his album," recalls Oakes. "Actually, each of them was saying they'd quit. It was sort of a self-fulfilling prophecy. By saying he was quitting The Beatles, he ended the group because none of them liked the idea that it was him who was quitting."

John Lennon, in fact, was furious that McCartney had trumped him by announcing that he was leaving The Beatles. As early as the fall of 1969, Lennon had been telling the other Beatles that he "wanted a divorce" and it was only at the urging of Allen Klein – who was in the middle of negotiating a new contract for The Beatles with Capitol Records – that Lennon had agreed to keep his intention to leave the group to himself until the new contract had been signed. Regardless of the circumstances, it was clear that The Beatles would not be working together again anytime in the near future.

Fittingly, it was Derek Taylor who was called on to offer Apple's official statement to the world. A brief press release issued on 10 April reflected the complicated nature of the split as well as Taylor's eternal optimism and reticence to believe that The Beatles had ended. Taylor wrote:

"Spring is here and Leeds play Chelsea tomorrow and Ringo and John and George and Paul are alive and well and full of hope.

The World is still spinning and so are we and so are you.
When the spinning stops – That'll be the time to worry, not before.

Until then, The Beatles are alive and well and the beat goes on, the beat goes on."

Today, the break-up of The Beatles is often seen as an end of an era, and as perhaps a fitting and convenient end to the sixties. And while

The Beatles were greatly mourned in many circles, at the time the group split in April 1970, they were generally viewed as simply a popular rock group that had decided to call it a day. Indeed, once "Let It Be" had been released and the immediate repercussions of McCartney's split with The Beatles had subsided, new idols were quickly found and the pop music machine marched on to a new tune.

Shortly after McCartney's announcement on 10 April that he was leaving The Beatles, fans were given the opportunity to see the group disintegrating before their very eyes when the *Let It Be* film was finally released in May. *Let It Be* captured The Beatles in the final stage of their musical partnership, still making music together, but seemingly without any genuine enthusiasm and often with a significant amount of tension clearly evident between the members of the group. The London premiere of the film also drove home the intensity of the split. Where once all four Beatles could be counted on to attend the premiere of a new Beatles film, not a single Beatle attended the 20 May premiere of *Let It Be*.

When The Beatles split, many people in the music industry assumed that Apple would collapse along with its owners. But Bill Oakes stresses that McCartney's announcement had little significant impact on Apple. "It really made no difference to me on a day-to-day basis... they were all still there... they still had records coming out... it really got sticky later in the year. I left at the start of 1971, by which time it was real cloak and dagger stuff. Initially it was quite funny. Paul used to write to me as 'Bill Oakes – An Abkco managed company' and he would use me to find out what Klein was doing at Apple. But it was not too attractive when all the lawyers started coming in."

Once "Let it Be", Ringo Starr's "Sentimental Journey" and Paul McCartney's solo album had been issued, Apple entered a relatively quiet period and there was little activity in Apple's London office during late spring and early summer of 1970. In March, Derek Taylor started a six-month sabbatical in order to work on a book project. He would come into London each Thursday to check on any new developments and to get his mail, but with each visit to Apple he became aware that there was precious little to do. While Taylor was on sabbatical, Apple press matters would be handled by his assistants Mavis Smith and Richard DiLello.

While the early summer of 1970 was a quiet time at Apple, the lack of activity was not due to any lack of effort on the part of the Apple recording artists. With Mal Evans producing, Badfinger had recorded three new songs in April, including a catchy, Beatlesesque rock song written by group leader Pete Ham called *No Matter What*. Mal Evans and Badfinger thought that the powerful *No Matter What* would make an excellent follow up to *Come And Get It*. An excited Evans brought the tapes back to Apple and played them to everyone in the office, but after the tapes had been listened to, word came back from the record department that the song wasn't commercial enough and that Apple would not issue Badfinger's new recording as a single. According to members of Badfinger, several members of Apple's management even suggested that Badfinger record a version of Ringo Starr's recently completed composition *It Don't Come Easy* as the follow-up to *Come And Get It*.

Jack Oliver believes that, "What probably happened with *No Matter What* was that the tape was brought in and listened to by Paul or John and that they didn't like it. That would happen sometimes. It was their label, and if they didn't like something, no matter how good we thought it was, if they didn't approve it, we couldn't put it out. I do remember trying to get Badfinger to record *It Don't Come Easy*, but I don't remember why."

With no new records being issued and the ex-Beatles lying low after McCartney's announcement that he had left the band, there was little excitement to be found in Apple's once bustling headquarters. In the eerily quiet Press Office, Richard DiLello and Carol Paddon were perfectly content to while away their days reading magazines, gazing out the window and generally enjoying the relative calm that had engulfed Apple. Acting Press Officer Mavis Smith, however, soon found the lack of activity unbearable and she left Apple in June 1970. The only real activity at Apple that summer was on the fifth floor of the Apple building where Neil Aspinall and two assistants were working on a follow up film to *Let It Be*. Provisionally entitled *The Long And Winding Road*, Aspinall had collected a massive archive of Beatles films with which to compile a definitive film history of The Beatles.

With the departure of Mavis Smith, the Press Office was left in the hands of Richard DiLello. Speaking to *Rolling Stone* in May 1970, DiLello admitted: "The day after Paul's statement was released it was bedlam. But for just that one day. Then it got quieter than it had been before... I guess it's just the summer doldrums. I got worried one day and called Jo Bergman at the Stones' office, but she said everything was quieter than usual in her office, too – that it's always like this at this time of year. Anthony Fawcett has left John and Yoko, but there haven't been any sackings. We'll all have jobs as long as we want them. The accountants will always be busy. They're not going to assassinate the building... I think it [The Beatles split] will go on for about a year, then there will be a reconciliation. It won't jump like it used to jump. We're not going to sign any new artists for a while, we want to hand pick them. But it's still a gig for The Beatles, you just get what they want."

In the same *Rolling Stone* article, Peter Brown elaborated on DiLello's statements. "We still have four employers... they still demand the same amount of attention. They're all releasing albums after all. Allen Klein's arrival caused much more of a bomb than Paul's announcement... people did leave then. It's a bit quieter. We don't have Mary Hopkin or Jackie Lomax now. But Doris Troy, Billy Preston, The Radha Krishna Temple will be recording... George is working on a solo album. And there will be another Beatles film. They are to be seen together again for the first time in a documentary being put together from the vast collection of film bits and pieces collected over the years and from around the world. It is being produced by former Beatles road manager Neil Aspinall, now head of Apple Films. The tentative title is *The Long And Winding Road* with release set for Christmas."

Since Doris Troy, Billy Preston, the Radha Krishna Temple and Badfinger were still in the studio working on new albums, Apple found itself with little product to issue or promote in the summer of 1970. In America, Apple released Mary Hopkin's almost year-old recording of *Que Sera Sera* in June. Despite it being Apple's only project, the single made little impact and it only managed to reach number 77 in the American charts. Other than Hopkin's single, Apple would release no new records until the autumn of 1970. Work on the new albums by Billy Preston and Badfinger was further delayed when George Harrison asked both Apple artists to assist him on the recording sessions for his debut solo album during the summer of 1970.

Ironically, several months after Richard DiLello's optimistic proclamation to *Rolling Stone* that the Apple staff would have jobs for as long as they wanted, Allen Klein closed down the Apple Press Office in July and fired DiLello and secretary Carol Paddon after they both made comments on the depressed state of Apple's affairs in an interview with an English magazine. The article generated a good deal of negative publicity for Klein so he used the opportunity to purge the Press Office and gain even more control of Apple's image in the press. After closing the in-house press office, Klein hired the more tradition-al Les Perrin Agency to handle Apple's publicity.

Several weeks after the dismissal of DiLello and Paddon, Derek Taylor would return to Apple full-time, but with most of the press inquiries now being fielded by the Les Perrin Agency, Taylor would have little to do with most of Apple's day-to-day publicity. As Taylor poignantly recalled in his 1973 book *As Time Goes By*: "When my office closed and I gave up writing this – I returned to a different Apple. My artifacts and posters and friends had gone and the room was as smooth as silk and dead. Really dead. I would sit with Neil in his room and we would both get drowsy by the fire and then go out for lunch."

Sitting alone in the now empty Press Office, Taylor probably took little notice when Apple finally started to show some signs of life in August 1970, when *Jacob's Ladder* – another George Harrison-produced single by Doris Troy – was released. Troy's single was followed in September by three new albums – Doris Troy's debut album, John Tavener's "The Whale" and Billy Preston's second album for Apple, "Encouraging Words".

Out of the three albums released by Apple that autumn, it was John Tavener's that would receive the most interest but attract the lowest sales. Tavener was certainly an unusual artist for Apple to have signed and his debut album "The Whale" would prove to be a very difficult album to market. While Apple – who had signed both Yoko Ono and the Radha Krishna Temple to the label – had never shied away from signing non-mainstream artists, Tavener was the first artist signed to the label whose music had nothing to do with pop whatsoever. That said, Tavener was something of a "pop star" within certain circles and at the age of twenty-four he had already received considerable acclaim as England's most promising young composer of contemporary classical music. Tavener was by no means a typically tweedy classical music academic. With his long hair and contemporary clothes, he had become something of a media darling. Yet despite having had several of his compositions performed on critically acclaimed BBC broadcasts, none of Tavener's work had been captured on album by the time he met John Lennon in the summer of 1969.

Tavener first met Lennon at a dinner party in Kensington, hosted by a wealthy American. Tavener recalls that despite the host's cook having prepared an elaborate meal, John and Yoko arrived in their white Rolls Royce carrying their own specially prepared macrobiotic food.

Dining on the floor of the American's luxurious home, Tavener played John and Yoko a tape of an opera he had recently composed, while Tavener himself was treated to tapes of John and Yoko's "experimental" recordings. Tavener remembers that although John and Yoko had no interest in the opera's religious message, they were both captivated by the actual sounds and effects on the recordings.

Tavener must have made quite an impression on Lennon, who called Tavener the very next day and asked the young composer to record for Apple. Days after his conversation with Lennon, Tavener was summoned to Savile Row to meet Lennon, Ringo Starr and Ron Kass. Starr and Kass were apparently as impressed with Tavener as Lennon had been and Tavener was soon signed to Apple Records.

By strange coincidence, around the same time that John Tavener first met Lennon, John Tavener's brother, Roger, had been pitching the idea of having John Tavener record for Apple to Ringo Starr. In the mid-sixties, Roger Tavener was known in England as "the swinging builder" and his construction company had been doing work for many of England's brightest young pop stars. The Beatles were among his many clients and he had done work for both Nems and Apple as well as in the homes of all four Beatles. Roger Tavener had been hired to renovate Ringo Starr's Highgate home and he spent almost two years working on the property during 1968 and 1969. Each day, Tavener would join Ringo and his wife Maureen for breakfast to discuss what he would be working on next. In the course of these breakfast discussions, Roger brought up the possibility of his brother John recording for Apple, and he brought Ringo a tape of an early BBC performance of "The Whale" for his consideration.

Once signed to Apple, John Tavener may have had the full backing of two of The Beatles, yet little progress was made on his Apple debut until early 1970. Tavener believes that Apple's difficulty with getting the album recorded was largely due to no one at Apple having any idea of how to set up a classical music recording session. Sensing this problem, Tavener brought his friend Nicholas Snowman to Apple, hoping that Apple would agree to let Snowman coordinate the recording of Tavener's album. Tavener remembers that when he took Snowman to Savile Row to meet Ringo Starr, Ringo did not seem up to getting involved in a long conversation about classic music. Instead, he expressed his admiration for Tavener's work, reiterated Apple's commitment to John Tavener, and then sent out for an order of chips and tomato sauce, sending Tavener and Snowman downstairs to meet Apple's record department.

But after discussing his plans with the record department staff, Tavener did not get the impression that anyone at Apple would be able to oversee properly the recording of an album of classical music. Though impressed with Apple's well-stocked drinks cabinet and the ice-buckets that were shaped and coloured to resemble giant apples, Tavener realized that no one at Apple had the slightest grasp or interest in classical music.

With little coaxing, Apple's record department was more than happy to hand over all responsibility for producing an album of Tavener's music to Nicholas Snowman. In what he today considers "one of the great deals of all time" Snowman negotiated a "colossal" management fee for the London Sinfonietta Orchestra, then selected a church in Islington in which to record the album, hired a technical crew and negotiated all of the necessary royalty deals.

Sessions for Tavener's album finally took place on 22, 23 and 24 July 1970. By the time Tavener had actually started recording for Apple, Lennon had taken to spending long stretches of time abroad and he had little day-to-day involvement with the label. In Lennon's absence, Ringo Starr assumed responsibility for Tavener at Apple, attending several of Tavener's performances as well as the recording sessions for the album. Starr even provided a brief vocal contribution to "The Whale". The album earned bountiful critical acclaim when released in September 1970, yet it was not a big seller, mainly because, as Derek Taylor would admit in a 1988 interview with *Record Collector*, "We didn't promote it; we really couldn't." Fortunately for Apple, the British media was already very interested in Tavener. In addition to having been featured in articles in *Vogue* and the *Daily Mirror*, Tavener was even the subject of a BBC Television special.

"The Whale" was certainly unlike any record that Apple, or almost any other British record label for that matter, had ever released. The first movement opens with the famed BBC news announcer Alvar Lidell reading a scientific analysis of whales as the music slowly builds behind him. Inspired by the biblical allegory "Jonah and the Whale" Tavener deftly wove symphonic passages, opera and spoken word into a strikingly original work that was arguably several years ahead of its time.

While it is not surprising that Apple had difficulty promoting a classical record like "The Whale", their failure to successfully promote either the Doris Troy or Billy Preston albums was less understandable. Although Apple purchased obligatory print advertisements for both albums in the British and American music magazines, neither album received much in the way of press or radio play, which was surprising given the quality of the albums as well as the high calibre of musicians involved with the projects.

"Encouraging Words" was produced by George Harrison. In addition to co-writing *Sing One For The Lord* and performing on Preston's funky remake of The Beatles' *I Got A Feeling*, Harrison also let Preston record several of his best new compositions – *My Sweet Lord* and *All Things Must Pass* – several months before Harrison was due to release his own versions on his solo album "All Things Must Pass".

Apple had even scheduled Preston's version of *My Sweet Lord* to be a British single and it was given the catalogue number Apple 29 and coupled with the non-album B-side entitled *As Long As I Got My Baby*. Only after someone at Apple realized that Preston's record might take away from the impact of Harrison's forthcoming *My Sweet Lord* single, did Apple cancel the release at the last moment. The album track *Little Girl* was substituted and was subsequently issued as a single in Europe and America. Released in America in February 1971 – only after George Harrison's rendition had started slipping from the charts – Preston's stirring version of *My Sweet Lord* made it no further than number 90. In the end, Apple did not even release a single from Preston's album in Britain, which certainly hurt the commercial prospects of "Encouraging Words".

The commercial failure of Doris Troy's album came as an even bigger surprise to Apple. Before signing to the label, Troy had established herself as an in-demand session vocalist and songwriter, and she had already scored several British and American hit singles in the mid-sixties. The lack of musician credits on Troy's album was equally puzzling. Troy's album featured an impressive list of players, including George Harrison, Ringo Starr, Eric Clapton, Billy Preston, Peter Frampton and Steven Stills, yet the cover made no mention of these musicians. At a time when "super-groups" were all the rage and an album could sell many copies just on the names of the famous musicians who played on a record, Apple's decision to put little more than a dark photo of Troy taken by Mal Evans and a list of song titles on the cover of the album was a questionable commercial move.

Jack Oliver, however, suggests that Apple did not list the names of any performers on the album in order to avoid any contractual entanglements with the record labels of the musicians involved, as well as The Beatles long-standing efforts to try to let Apple artists succeed on their own merits rather than on the strength of their Beatles connections.

Doris Troy remembers: "The way they explained it to me was that because we had so many guest artists on the record that by the time we got around to calling everybody in the States to get permission to have all these people on the album, we would have never got the album out and everybody would want points and all that... it was basically done to keep us from having to deal with all those different record companies, because at that time, it just wasn't done. Also, Apple didn't give it mass promotion because at the time there was some chaos at the label... but we got some action on it, but not as much as it could have been or should have been."

Both Billy Preston and Doris Troy were keenly aware that a listing of credits for session musicians would have helped sales of their albums. "That was another mistake," lamented Preston in a 1971 interview with *Rolling Stone*. "No credits or liners. Like on "...God Planned It", there was Doris Troy, Madeline Belle, Ritchie Havens, Eric Clapton, Ginger Baker and Keith Richards and on *My Sweet Lord* on "Encouraging Words" the Edwin Hawkins Singers sang, The Temptations' rhythm section played on a couple of tracks, Delaney and Bonnie's band played, Ringo and Klaus Voormann were on it. George got them all in."

On top of the illustrious cast of session musicians who were featured on Doris Troy's record, the album also contained some exceptional songwriting collaborations with Harrison, Stephen Stills, and Ringo Starr. Troy also wrote several songs with her Apple label mates Jackie Lomax and Billy Preston. One of the albums many highlights was a soulful ballad credited to Troy and Lomax called *You've Got To Be Strong*.

Having had little to do with Apple since leaving England in late 1970, Lomax was until recently unaware that Troy had received a writing credit for *You've Got To Be Strong*. Lomax recalls: "After Doris first came to Apple in the summer of 1969, I knew that she was having a bad time... I don't like to speak ill of people, but messing around with dope is really bad. She had a problem with that, and that's why I wrote *You've Got To Be Strong*... and she was being strong and she was really getting it together... she had a great voice. So I ran into Doris in the studio one day and told her I had a song that she might be interested in doing, so I went round to her place and just played it to her on guitar and she liked it, so she did it... she didn't write any part of the song. I had the complete song before she went into the studio... she did a nice job with it though."

One of Apple Record's more financially rewarding projects in the autumn of 1970 was their efforts to cash in on the James Taylor album, originally issued in 1968. After Taylor had scored an international hit with *Fire And Rain* in September 1970, Apple realized that Taylor's debut album was now the most valuable asset in the Apple catalogue. To help stimulate sales of the album in America, Apple re-released Taylor's *Carolina In My Mind*. With *Taking It In* replacing the single's original B-side, the single reached number 65 in the American charts. To coincide with the reissue of the single, Apple also put a new promotional effort behind James Taylor's album. Their efforts were rewarded when the album settled into the American hot 100 album charts from October 1970 to April 1971. In an effort to repeat the feat in Britain, Apple finally released *Carolina In My Mind* as a UK single in November, but, as before, the record failed to chart.

Taylor's single was followed in November by *Think About Your*

Children – a new Mary Hopkin single that Apple issued in both America and Britain in an effort to score a lucrative Christmas hit. The song is easily one of Hopkin's best but it failed to match the success of her previous efforts. Despite having been given significant promotion, the Mickie Most produced *Think About Your Children*, an uplifting pop-soul song written by former Apple artists Hot Chocolate, reached only number 19 in Britain and number 87 in America.

With Billy Preston and Doris Troy failing to capture the interest of the record-buying public, it was Badfinger who finally returned Apple to the charts. Having been patiently waiting for Apple to release their new single since April, Badfinger enlisted Mal Evans to help lobby the Apple management to release *No Matter What* as a single. Evans appeared to make little headway with his campaign to get *No Matter What* issued until Badfinger's Tom Evans played the song to Al Steckler, who immediately recognized that the song was a sure-fire hit.

While the Apple staff were aware that Badfinger had the potential to become a hit-making group, they were strangely reluctant to release *No Matter What* as the follow-up single to *Come And Get It*. Apple may well have been concerned that *No Matter What* sounded as if it were performed by a totally different band than the one that had recorded *Come And Get It* only a year earlier. Technically, they were, as *Come And Get It* had been recorded when Badfinger were still The Iveys. On *No Matter What*, Pete Ham's rich tenor vocal was quite different from Tom Evans' performance on *Come And Get It*. In place of *Come And Get It*'s simple piano, bass, and drums sound, *No Matter What* featured bold electric guitars, soaring three part harmonies and exceptionally powerful drumming from Mike Gibbins. The addition of Joey Molland to the Badfinger line-up had totally transformed the band, giving them an edge that they never had as The Iveys. By late 1970, Badfinger sounded very little like the band that had recorded *Come And Get It*, a point that was certainly not lost on Apple Records.

The members of Badfinger were certain that *No Matter What* would be a great single, but even they were genuinely surprised by just how well it sold. In a 1971 interview with *NME*, Pete Ham admitted: "There wasn't much promotion done on it I don't think, because there suddenly wasn't anyone at Apple to work on it, so it plodded on. Then out of the blue, it appeared in the charts."

Reflecting on how Apple operated in the early 1970s, Badfinger's Joey Molland confirms Ham's observations. "We'd go down to Apple once a week at least. We'd see Derek and stuff and maybe have a glass of scotch and sit around for half an hour. There was a lot of coming and going at Apple. When I first joined in 1969, we used to go down there quite a lot and see everybody at Christmas parties and all that stuff. But as the group got successful we'd be away on tour so things like Derek leaving and all that stuff happened when we were away. We'd get back from tour and all of the people had changed. It was hard to believe when Richard DiLello was leaving. That was a bit of a weird thing."

Later that month, Apple followed up *No Matter What* with Badfinger's "No Dice" album, which failed to chart in Britain but made the American top thirty. Produced by former Beatles engineer, Geoff Emerick, the album had been recorded at several London studios during July and August 1970. Although Apple Studios was still more than a full year away from being operational, Apple had already started to assemble a team of engineers and producers to work for Apple Studios. Emerick had been lured away from EMI to be studio manager and a staff producer for Apple. Looking for projects to give the Apple Studio staff, Apple had assigned Emerick to produce Badfinger's album.

Members of Badfinger clearly remember that Mal Evans had hoped to produce the album that became "No Dice". Despite Evans' lack of production experience, the group had been very pleased with his production of *No Matter What* and they were more than willing to record their album with Evans at the controls. Joey Molland recalls: "Mal seemed to be able to do whatever he wanted. He was always at the George Harrison sessions taking care of things. He was very positive and encouraging. He knew how to make a good record from being around The Beatles." Evans was all set to produce Badfinger's album until, during a June 1970 meeting at Apple, Badfinger manager Bill Collins told a bewildered audience of Derek Taylor, Mal Evans, Allen Klein, Badfinger's Tom Evans, Geoff Emerick and a few other Apple personnel that Mal Evans was not welcome to produce Badfinger and that Emerick would be producing the album instead.

Joey Molland explains: "It turns out that Collins was very jealous of Mal Evans and Collins manipulated the situation so that Mal wasn't involved. To this day, Collins is obsessed with the idea that Mal wanted to manage the band. I talked a lot with Mal and he never, ever mentioned anything about managing Badfinger."

While two songs that Mal Evans had produced for Badfinger in the spring of 1970 – *No Matter What* and Tom Evans' *Believe Me* – were ultimately included on "No Dice," the production of the remaining songs on the album was a joint effort between the group and Geoff Emerick. The twelve songs – which included the sublime power pop of *No Matter What*, heartfelt ballads like *Midnight Caller* and *Without You*, all-out rockers like *I Can't Take It* and even the countryesque

Blodwyn – showed that Badfinger had developed into a first-rate hard pop band that was able to play effortlessly many different styles of music.

The provocative "No Dice" album cover, featuring a scantily clad model pointing suggestively at the camera, was designed by ex-Apple employee Richard DiLello and graphic artist Gene Mahon, the man who had designed the Apple logo. Since DiLello had always been close to Badfinger, and the members of the group enjoyed his company, DiLello had little difficulty persuading Badfinger and Apple that he was the right man to design the cover of "No Dice." When DiLello had been fired by Klein, Derek Taylor had promised to assign DiLello Apple projects on a freelance basis and the Badfinger album cover seemed to be a perfect assignment for Apple's former "house hippie". In addition, Taylor had also hired DiLello to design the 1970 Apple Christmas card.

To promote "No Dice", Badfinger went to America for what would turn out to be a tour lasting nearly three months. Kicking off the tour in Grand Forks, North Dakota on 25 September, the group would remain in America until December. Met by audiences who were under the impression that Badfinger were The Beatles in disguise, that Joey Molland was Paul McCartney's brother, or that one of The Beatles would be appearing on stage with the group, the tour was well received, especially after *No Matter What* was released on 12 October.

In an effort to help drum up enthusiasm for Badfinger in America, George and Patti Harrison flew to the United States from England to introduce the group on the first night of Badfinger's three-night booking at Ungano's nightclub in New York City. *Circus* magazine reviewed the show, noting how the arrival of George and Pattie electrified the usually blasé New York City audience and press. *Circus* writer Janis Schacht reported that just before Badfinger began their set, Harrison stepped to the stage microphone and announced, "Hello everybody, thank you for coming tonight. We'd like to have you welcome one of Apple's bands: Badfinger!" Harrison then returned to his front row table, opened a briefcase containing a tape recorder and proceeded to tape Badfinger's entire performance, which did little to soothe the nerves of the band.

In addition to the New York debut of Badfinger, December 1970 was also significant for Apple because it marked the true beginning of the solo careers of George Harrison and John Lennon. Despite having been integral members of the most popular rock band ever, the two ex-Beatles were genuinely concerned that they would not be accepted as solo acts. Having seen the "McCartney" album go into the top ten earlier in the year, both Lennon and Harrison wanted their solo debuts to do as well or even better than McCartney's and they instructed Pete Bennett to devote as much time as possible to making their solo albums successful. Pete Bennett admits that there was a keen sense of competition between the ex-Beatles: "The Beatles didn't give a shit about the other Apple artists... the only one that George and Paul cared about was Badfinger. We couldn't promote all of the non-Beatle Apple albums, it took too much time to promote The Beatles themselves. They were concerned about themselves first. It was a lot of work promoting the records by the individual Beatles and I was still doing the Stones. Not only that, but if one of Paul's records hit the top ten, John would call me and say 'How come Paul's record is at number 10 and mine's at number 15,' and I would tell him, 'Alright John, we'll make your record number 5,' and then Paul would say how come his record is at number 5 and George Harrison would say my record isn't even on the chart... every week was another problem at Apple. There was a lot of competition between them."

In the end, neither Harrison nor Lennon had much reason for concern, as both of their solo albums made the top ten in the United States and Britain. Harrison's "All Things Must Pass" album and the *My Sweet Lord* single were particularly well received and for the following several years Harrison would be the most commercially and artistically successful of the ex-Beatles.

The release of John Lennon's "Plastic Ono Band" also coincided with the start of Yoko Ono's career as an Apple Records recording artist. Inaugurating a tradition that would extend for the next three years, Yoko Ono would release an album of her own music every time John Lennon put out an album. While her music was certainly ahead of its time and could have possibly even been considered remotely commercial towards the end of the seventies, in 1970, Ono's music was as far removed from the popular music scene as you could possibly get.

Over the course of her four-year recording career with Apple, Ono would be a considerable drain on Apple's finances. The four albums she would record for Apple between 1970 and 1973 were recorded in expensive recording studios with some of the best and most expensive session musicians available. Since Ono was John Lennon's wife, Apple also spent far more money promoting her records than was warranted by her commercial potential. "The reason why we put out Yoko singles," confesses Pete Bennett, "was just to keep her happy. I promoted her to pacify her. But Klein never pacified her. He told her she couldn't sing. He told her to her face that she didn't have 'the sound'."

Al Steckler readily agrees with Bennett that Klein had absolutely no idea of what to do with Ono. "I don't profess to really like Yoko's music... that kind of music," explains Steckler, "but I understand what she was trying to do. One of the biggest problems that Klein had... on a personal level... was that when John and Yoko were living in New York, they were doing many projects and were going through a huge amount of money. Klein and John really liked each other – they were very close. On one very rare occasion that he opened up to me, Klein came into my office late one night and asked, 'How do I tell a man that his wife is fucking away millions of his dollars? I'm his manager and I have to do this. I don't know what to do,' he said, but he never said anything to John. The general public and mainstream press treated her albums as a joke. It is what it is. They didn't sell all that well."

While all of Ono's Apple albums would chart in the lower reaches of the top 200, this was mostly due to aggressive marketing by Apple and interest from curious Beatles fans rather than any realistic commercial viability. Perhaps the greatest financial strain that Ono brought upon Apple was her and Lennon's insistence that Apple release singles from Ono's albums. While Ono's small following of artists, feminists and adventurous Beatles fans may have been willing to purchase her albums, there was little prospect of Ono's offbeat attempts at straight-forward rock and pop like *Mrs. Lennon* and *Mind Train* becoming successful singles. Due to Ono's position as wife of one of Apple's Directors and owners, however, Apple Records was obliged to buy advertisements, send out promo copies and promote records that would never recoup Apple's investment of time and money.

Jack Oliver still clearly remembers the discomfort he felt when John Lennon would come into his office with an acetate or tape of one of Yoko's creations. "John would sit me down and make me listen to all of Yoko's records. It wasn't saleable. I would sit there for an hour listening to it and John would say, 'What do you think?' Being politically correct, I would tell him that it was very nice, but not particularly commercial, to which he would always say, 'What the fuck do you know?' I told him that I didn't think that it would sell a lot of copies and he would tell me 'Well, it's your job to make sure it does, isn't it?'"

Perhaps because he had known Lennon for almost a decade, Tony Bramwell still has the distinct impression that Lennon was fully aware of where Yoko Ono's records stood in relation to the music of the time. "John used to snigger about Yoko's music behind her back," he recalls. "He knew it was impossible to sell... but I was always polite. I remember when he came to me with "Two Virgins", he was laughing, saying, 'You got to listen to this!' I think it appealed to him as a practical joke."

1970 - And Then There Were Three

Despite having a difficult-to-sell Yoko Ono album to push as one of their Christmas priorities, 1970 had been a relatively good year for Apple. The company had managed to maintain their momentum with hits by Mary Hopkin and Badfinger, despite the fact that most people in the music industry thought that Apple would not survive the break-up of The Beatles. That is not to say that The Beatles' split had no effect on Apple. Tellingly, there had been little new growth in 1970. All of the records released during the year had been from artists who had been signed in 1969 while Ron Kass had still been running Apple.

Still, it was clear that Apple had changed and there was no denying that it would never again be the kind of company it once was or what it had once hoped to be. Few, if any, at Apple felt the changes at the company as keenly as Derek Taylor. Sensing that Apple would never regain its initial energy and promise and with little to actually do in the way of publicity, Derek Taylor resigned as publicist for Apple Records on 31 December 1970.

For Taylor, the final symbol of the complete dissolution of the Apple dream came when Paul McCartney served John Lennon, George Harrison and Ringo Starr with court papers. Having made several attempts during 1970 to get out of The Beatles partnership, McCartney and the Eastmans (who were McCartney's legal advisors) realized that the only way to get out of The Beatles and Co. partnership agreement was to sue the other partners of The Beatles and Co. – John Lennon, George Harrison, Ringo Starr and Apple. Although McCartney was hesitant to take his three former friends to court, he was eventually convinced that he was left with no other option. In *Many Years From Now*, McCartney recalled discussing his desire to get out of The Beatles partnership and off Apple Records to George Harrison, only to have Harrison reply, "You'll stay on the fucking label. Hare Krishna."

Claiming that it was ridiculous to be legally bound to a group that no longer existed, McCartney's main objection to The Beatles and Co. partnership agreement was that all of the money that was earned by the solo projects of the ex-Beatles was to be put into Apple to be theoretically shared equally by all four Beatles. It is probable that McCartney found it unacceptable that Ringo Starr would earn as much money from McCartney's solo records as he himself would. McCartney's biggest point of contention, however, was that he was adamant that Allen Klein should not be involved with his career in any way. To that end, McCartney took Apple and the other three Beatles to court in order to have a receiver appointed to oversee the assets of Apple until all four ex-Beatles could come to an agreement on how to end their partnership. The court case would begin on 20 January 1971.

McCartney's overriding concern was to disassociate himself from Allen Klein. Pete Bennett explains: "Paul never really knew Klein, he never really started with Klein. Paul had heard about Klein and knew he was a crook. Paul had to put out his records through Apple, but he never had any interactions with Klein after 1969, just with me. I used to deal with John and Lee Eastman. I was their contact at Apple. They wanted nothing to do with Klein. I remember being in the Stage Deli in New York with Allen in 1972, and Lee Eastman, who had offices on 54th Street, walked in to pick up sandwiches and when he turned his head around to walk out, he saw us and he came up to us and said, 'Pete, how are you?' and then he turned to Klein and said, 'You, you're no good, you're shit,' and he walked out."

In a highly surprising move, Peter Brown handed in his resignation the same week as Derek Taylor, leaving Apple to join his former Nems associate Robert Stigwood at his soon-to-be-giant RSO organization. Bill Oakes recalls: "Peter Brown took me to a very elaborate lunch at Inigo Jones and didn't tell me why. He told me, 'Robert Stigwood has invited you and me to start up his new American company, which was working on "Jesus Christ Superstar"... you met Tim and Andrew [Rice and Lloyd Webber] when they came pitching "Superstar" to Apple...' Apple was the first place they came to, and Apple turned them down. I thought it would be great to go to New York and I also realized that by saying no I would be staying at Apple at a time that I could easily fall between the cracks. By then I was really not sure about staying at Apple. Without McCartney being there, it was really not clear what I would do there. I had to write out my resignation to John and George because they were the Directors of Apple. George was the one who didn't want to accept it, because he knew where I was going... he took me aside and said, 'You'll be going over there with all those fucking faggots. Between Peter Brown, Robert Stigwood and Nat Weiss, you'll be back in a couple of weeks man... you'll hate it because they'll all be chasing you around the desk.' George felt a bit betrayed because he didn't think I'd go off with Stigwood, who he hated because Stigwood kept sending Apple bills for Eric Clapton's services on George's records. Eric didn't know that Stigwood was billing George... George kept sending them back unpaid because he said that Eric was doing him a favour. The irony was that I did split after a few months in New York... I just got fed up with the daily grind... I just didn't like being there. I didn't get sodomized out of the city, but I quit."

Oakes worked only a few months at RSO before being asked by Paul McCartney to come to London to be the head of McCartney's new MPL organization. Oakes accepted the position, but after several months at MPL, returned to New York to become President of RSO Records where he would go on to supervise and compile the "Saturday Night Fever" soundtrack album, one of the best selling albums ever made.

Peter Brown remembers that McCartney had begged him not to resign because Brown and Oakes were McCartney's last sympathetic contacts at Apple. Indeed, with the sudden exodus of Derek Taylor, Peter Brown, Bill Oakes, and Jack Oliver – who would leave Apple during the last week of February 1971 – Apple bore little resemblance to the company that McCartney had helped launch only three years earlier.

The sudden departure of many of Apple's senior staff only helped fuel media reports that Apple was nearing its end and that The Beatles split was becoming an ugly, acrimonious affair. While the legal aspects of the dissolution of The Beatles and certain isolated incidents between one or more of the ex-Beatles did get rather nasty, there were also times when the four ex-Beatles carried on as if nothing had happened. George Peckham, himself a Liverpudlian and familiar with the camaraderie between the four Beatles, is adamant that the split was not as bad as it was portrayed in the papers.

"I remember being in New York with George Harrison mastering 'All Things Must Pass'", he recalls. "It was all in the papers about the troubles between John and Paul and the rest of the stuff, but I remember we went out to dinner and John was there and Paul was there and some other people and George turned to me and said, 'You know nothing do ya?' and I told him, 'As you say, I know nothing.' It was all friendly talk going on, but in the press the total reverse was going on... it was all about how much they hated each other's guts. All I could read between the lines was that they were going through a divorce... but it wasn't all that bad. But we were told to keep our gobs shut basically. Klein did instruct the entire Apple staff that we were to say nothing to the press. He would close the doors and let us have it. He'd really try to make us all feel really small... all we were doing was trying to give the best we could to the company. We'd work extra hours and we'd often be there until eight or nine at night... not putting down overtime, just getting the job completed and Klein would come to us the next day and ask what we were doing because we hadn't signed out until nine.

"I remember one night it was around eight and John called and asked if I was busy at the moment... I told him no, I was just finishing up... he asked if I wanted to come over to Abbey Road because he was making a record and he wanted me to play a bit of guitar... I got there and it turned out to be *Instant Karma* and I got to sing on it and play tambourine. The next day one of Klein's guys comes down and says, 'You were over at EMI last night... what were you doing?' and I told him I was working with John and it had nothing to do with him. He said, 'Well, were you being paid for those hours?' and told him no, I hadn't asked for a penny. Klein always had people nosing around trying to find out what you were doing. He had this guy at Apple – Terry Mellis – he was English and he had worked for Abkco in Britain when Klein managed the Stones. When I went with George over to the States I saw how he ran the Abkco office. He treated them with an iron rod and there was fear in the corridors. The only nice person over there was Apple's London receptionist Laurie McCaffrey, who went over to New York to work at Abkco."

6

1971 - It Don't Come Easy

Having released so many records towards the end of 1970, Apple appeared to be relatively quiet during the first few months of 1971. But while Apple may not have been putting out new records, there was a great deal of activity at 3 Savile Row. The staff were fully engaged in promoting the albums that had been issued in late 1970, and despite Derek Taylor's conclusion that the Apple era had truly ended, plans were being made to re-launch and re-configure Apple in the coming year.

Lennon, Harrison and Starr all seemed to want to give Apple a fresh start and they all agreed to do whatever they could to revitalize the label. Al Steckler remembers, "The first thing that I was asked to do was by George. He asked me to find out what artists wanted to stay with the label and who didn't. Basically he said 'Look, there were artists that we signed up... with all good intentions... but we really don't know if we have the time to nurture them as we should. It's been a year and a half – two years – and we really haven't done anything for them. It's not fair to them. Try to call each one and find out if they want to stay or if they want to leave, and if they want to leave, let them leave.' Basically, what I did, I went to Billy Preston in California and he said he wanted to stay for a while. I spoke to Mary who was in the studio working on the "Earth Song" album... they played the album for me and I fell in love with it. I told them I really believe in the album and I'll do whatever I can, so she stayed."

Allen Klein was also committed to rebuilding Apple and as part of the plan he developed to give Apple increased presence and effectiveness in the American market, he opened up an Apple office in California in February 1971. Curiously, Jack Oliver claims the he and the other members of Apple's British staff had no idea that Apple was opening an office in California. "I don't remember anything about setting up an Apple office in California, so it must have been one of Klein's projects," says Oliver.

Located close to the Capitol Records tower, the new Apple office was to serve as a liaison point with Capitol for distribution, promotion and sales issues. To run Apple in California, Klein hired former Capitol Vice President of Independent Labels Charlie Nuccio to act as General Manager and former Capitol National Promotion Manager Tom Takioshi to be Apple's National Promotion man. Having succeeded Ken Mansfield at Capitol when Mansfield went to MGM Records, Nuccio had already worked closely with Klein and Apple since 1970.

Opening a California office seemed to have relatively little impact on the other Apple offices as all of the creative and accounting work would still be handled out of Apple's New York and London offices. "The Apple office in California was set up to make Apple look good by having someone work there, to give them a bit of the presence... nothing else," recalls Pete Bennett. "We had Capitol and the Capitol sales force, we didn't need anyone else. Apple had good distribution with Capitol. Tom and Charlie were basically there to work on distribution, they didn't do any work with radio."

Charlie Nuccio admits: "The California office was Klein's idea. He wanted to establish an image for Apple outside of Capitol and he felt that it would be good for Apple if I just concentrated on the Apple line, so they offered me a position as General Manager for Apple US. We moved to an office on Sunset Boulevard, which we shared with Phil Spector. We just had four people there... me, Tom Takioshi and two girls. It was a very small office – two rooms in a three and a half, four room suite that we shared with Phil Spector. He had his own entrance. We didn't really need a force, because that was handled by Capitol. We just gave them our input and helped with what we could do on the side, and Pete Bennett did some more out of New York."

Unlike the London or New York offices, Apple's Sunset Strip office would rarely be graced with a visit by a Beatle. "Occasionally The Beatles would come in," recalls Nuccio. "Harrison would come in, Ringo occasionally. Mostly George Harrison. Harrison was more concerned about Apple than any of them. He brought more artists to Apple than the other three, so he was concerned with promoting the other artists on Apple, not just himself. We tried very hard to push all of the Apple acts. There was a lot of effort put behind Badfinger and also the Radha Krishna Temple album. The only time I did business with John Lennon was when I was in the New York office... I used to go out to New York once or twice a month. I never even met Paul McCartney when I was at Apple. I think Paul's problem was with Allen Klein. I got along very well with Allen Klein. I never had any problems with Allen. As a promoter and a manager I'd rate Allen Klein number one, he was fantastic. He was a hard deal maker... he made The Beatles a lot of money. He wasn't a record head, the everyday didn't interest him at all, he was on the next project already."

Establishing an American distribution and retail promotions office was a long-needed move on the part of Apple. Since 1968, getting adequate distribution and promotion for non-Beatles albums had been one of Apple's biggest problems. Although EMI and Capitol were always eager to work on Beatles albums, both companies seemed to have less enthusiasm for working on acts like Doris Troy or Billy Preston.

Being familiar with Capitol's set-up at the time, Charlie Nuccio explains: "Capitol was a giant label, they had The Beatles, The Beach Boys, Anne Murray... you can go on and on. At the time the Capitol salespeople were selling one on one to accounts. A salesman would go to a store with twenty new releases, one of which was the Radha Krishna Temple and the other was a Glen Campbell or a Beach Boys album and so on, so the Krishnas would get the least attention. Normally a dealer wouldn't say, give me that, I want that in my store. What I'm saying is that when an album like the Radha Krishna's came out, there was no reason for Capitol to push it. Capitol at that time had a very strong pop roster with a lot of chart items. I was Apple's liaison with Capitol really, trying to get the best image we could for Apple Records through that giant distribution system. There was no problem with a Beatles record or a John Lennon record, but when Apple started to build a catalogue, Capitol didn't understand the importance of that to Apple. So when Harrison wanted to do a Radha Krishna album, they were sort of second-class citizens when they went though the distribution centre at Capitol. But we would treat them as a prime album, a number one promotion so we had to instill that through the Capitol system... sometimes we did, sometimes we didn't. All the production was done in New York and we did the promotion and marketing."

Perhaps due to Klein not being involved with its day-to-day running, the California office seemed to lack the basic efficiency of Apple's New York and London operations. In an interview with *Rolling Stone*, Billy Preston's manager Robert Ellis recalled going into the Apple office in L.A. and asking one of the women in the office for two of Billy Preston's albums, to which she responded, "Billy who? Oh yes, I remember him." In general, Apple's L.A. operation was a relatively low-key affair. Charlie Nuccio remembers: "We had a few people coming into the office and dropping off tapes. We tried to discourage them, but we'd send them on. It wasn't like it was in London. In London, everyone knew where Savile Row was... it was a landmark... it was a Mecca for young kids who thought they had some talent. I can understand that. We didn't have that problem... we did have some with the local Krishnas when forty of them would come in and sit on the floor and want to know how their album was doing. It wasn't well known that we were an Apple Records office... we didn't have a sign out."

It was not long after Klein had set up the office in California that Jack Oliver resigned as manager of Apple Records in London. "I left Apple in the last week of February 1971 and came to L.A. on 1 March

1971," recalls Oliver. "I saw what was going on, I knew The Beatles were breaking up, and I just couldn't see where it was going to go. Peter Asher in L.A. had been calling me for three years since he left Apple, so finally, I relented and went to work with him at Peter Asher Management. Klein was always on my case but I wasn't worried because I had Paul's backing and that of the others as well. There was a list that Klein got when he came in of people that he wasn't allowed to fire and I was on that."

With Oliver's departure, the responsibility of running Apple fell largely on Al Steckler. Even before Oliver's resignation, more and more Apple business was being conducted from the Abkco office in New York City. Steckler remembers, "At one point Abkco had a floor and a half... The Beatles fan club was there downstairs. I had an assistant and this young man... Jeffrey Michleson... he came in off the street one day... he was dressed very outlandishly... and said he wanted to work for Apple. I didn't hire him then but he did eventually work with us on a job to job basis. But basically I ran the Apple label by myself. I didn't have anyone to help... I ran around like crazy. Anything that had to be done, I did. I coordinated all the releases and got designers to do the art. George and Ringo came in fairly often. Once George came into the office and said, 'I don't like how your office looks, let's get you some nice stuff,' so we went out and got this big Indian chair and a couch... Ringo got me one of those big egg chairs with speakers in it. When the guys would come up into the office, they would go in to see Klein first and then they'd come in to see me in my office and that's where they hung out. I would get tapes to listen to that I would listen to and audition... you can't believe how many we got... and I tried to listen to as many as I could. We used to get 15 to 20 tapes a day."

Steckler continues: "I was in a very difficult position at Apple. I was the only American to ever have an Apple business card... George wanted it that way. I got on very well with the artists, but I worked for Klein... I was an Abkco employee. Klein knew that my allegiance was to him, but when it came to artistic issues, I would always side with the artists if I could and the artists knew that as well. They also knew that I tried very hard to stay out of the negotiations... it worked pretty well. There where times when I had problems with Allen... especially when Phil Spector was involved... but the artists respected me, they knew they could come to me and they did."

To replace Jack Oliver and to give Steckler some support from the London office, Klein directed Bernard Brown – the genial Englishman who ran Apple Music Publishing – to also assume management of

Apple Records. Brown had originally come to Apple Publishing in 1969, when he was hired to replace Jean Griffiths as Copyright Manager. Having worked in the British music industry for many years, Brown was well-suited to be General Manager of Apple. But Brown's appointment was also a symbol of how far Apple had drifted from its original intentions. Well into his mid-forties when he assumed the position, Brown was typical of the old-school music industry professional from which Apple had originally set itself apart. Klein was attracted to Brown due to his extensive experience in the numbers-orientated side of the music industry. As for The Beatles, they had all had enough of the crazy atmosphere that had characterized Apple in 1968 and 1969, and George Harrison, Ringo Starr and John Lennon were simply hoping that Brown would help turn Apple into an efficient record company.

One of Brown's first projects would be seeing to the completion and release of Badfinger's follow-up to the "No Dice" album. On the eve of their second American tour in March 1971, Badfinger delivered the tapes of their proposed new album to Apple's Savile Row office. Given Badfinger's success in 1970, Apple was looking forward to releasing a follow-up to the "No Dice" album and they had already tentatively scheduled a Badfinger single and album for release in May.

But after listening to the album that Badfinger had recorded with Apple Studios staff producer Geoff Emerick, Apple management felt that the tapes were not particularly commercial and they declined to release them, just as they had previously done with *No Matter What*. Al Steckler believes that the primary problem was that Geoff Emerick – who co-produced the recordings with the band – was simply not up to the task of producing a commercial pop album. "Geoff had a very good ear as an engineer," he explains, "but I didn't think much about his abilities as a producer." Steckler points out that Badfinger had experienced the same problem with "No Dice," which was also produced by Emerick. "After I became involved with Apple and Badfinger, I heard the tapes of the album that would become "No Dice" and I though it was good, but that it wasn't commercial. There wasn't a single on it. So I didn't know what to do with the group. I think it was Tom Evans who told me, 'We have some other stuff that we recorded, would you like to hear it?' and I said sure, and we went back into the studio and he played me this stuff that Mal did and I heard all this great pop stuff... I told him that I heard two singles... maybe three."

Even though Apple had deemed that the album Badfinger delivered to the label was not strong enough to release, Apple was impressed with a stately Pete Ham ballad called *Name Of The Game*. Apple made tentative plans to issue *Name Of The Game* as Badfinger's next single and arranged for the group to finish the track at Bell Sound Studios in New York while they were on tour. Apple even hired noted session player Al Kooper to record additional keyboards on Badfinger's original version and a final mix was completed, but Apple ultimately declined to issue it as a single.

Listening to the album that Badfinger hoped to release as the follow-up to "No Dice", it is obvious that it contains no songs that were as effortlessly commercial as *No Matter What*. Instead, Badfinger had recorded an album that reflected their live sound at the time, ranging from the all-out rock of *No Good At All* and *Baby Please*, to the poignant acoustic pop of *Perfection*. Still, it is a very strong "rock" album and it was certainly as good as almost any record issued in 1971. Perhaps Badfinger had simply submitted the tape to Apple at the wrong time. Given that on Friday 12 March, Paul McCartney won the first round in the legal battle to dissolve The Beatles' partnership agreement, it is quite likely that the decision makers at Apple were simply unable to give Badfinger's new album a fair listen. In the 12 March decision, England's High Court ruled in McCartney's favour and appointed accountant James Spooner as the temporary receiver for The Beatles' business affairs. The appointment of a receiver had immediate implications to Apple's business, as it meant that all Apple expenses would now need to be cleared through the receiver.

Lennon, Harrison, Starr and Apple considered appealing against the High Court decision, but on Monday 27 April, they abandoned any such attempt. In addition to now having their finances overseen by an independent third party, Apple had also incurred legal costs estimated to be around £100,000.

With The Beatles now "officially estranged" and Klein firmly ensconced at the helm of Apple, Neil Aspinall found himself with very little to do at 3 Savile Row. Pete Bennett remembers: "Neil seemed to just be around. He was just there. No matter what Neil said, it didn't mean anything anyhow." In a 1996 interview with *Mojo*, Aspinall himself admitted: "It was traumatic for everybody, including me. I didn't have a clue what I was going to do. And in all that there was Allen Klein and lawsuits starting. I really started making movies and music for movies. I put together the music for [the David Essex film] *That'll Be The Day* then I was making a little movie out at George's place, but I never finished it."

Yet even as Paul McCartney was dragging Apple through the English court system in an attempt to free himself from what Apple had become, Apple was working to transform itself from the inside. In May 1971 Apple Electronics "officially" ceased operations when Alex Mardas formally resigned from the company. Since Mardas had not been seen at Apple since 1969, this gesture was more symbolic than practical. However, it did signal that Apple was making efforts to streamline its operations. Since its inception in 1968, Apple Electronics had not produced a single invention or product for commercial use. After clearing out the electronic equipment, Apple would use the Boston Place building that housed Apple Electronics to store its film and audio tape library. Although they would not appreciate it until many years later, Apple wisely kept Apple Electronics registered as a company.

One of the more significant developments at Apple in 1971 was the emergence of Ringo Starr as a successful solo artist. Written off by everyone as a musical has-been after the breakup of The Beatles, Ringo Starr found himself with a worldwide hit when his single *It Don't Come Easy* was released in May. Written by Starr (with some uncredited help from George Harrison), the single was produced by Harrison and featured the talents of Harrison, Steve Stills, Badfinger's Tom Evans and Pete Ham, and several other top musicians.

Apple's first new non-Beatles project of 1971 was the Ronnie Spector single *Try Some Buy Some*, which came out in April. The song was written by George Harrison who also produced the single in conjunction with Ronnie's husband Phil Spector. As could be expected, the single was gloriously produced, featuring trilling mandolins, an epic rhythm section and an impassioned vocal performance from Ronnie Spector. But even Phil Spector's "wall of sound" production could not compensate for Harrison's dark, dreary melody and obtuse lyrics that made references to meeting a mysterious "big fry". The single was heavily promoted and reached number 77 on the American charts, which was good enough for Apple to be interested in a second single and possible album. Although work was started on another Harrison composition entitled *You* and several other songs, the sessions were never completed and no further Ronnie Spector records appeared on Apple.

Ronnie Spector – who later professed to have had serious doubts about the commercial appeal of Harrison's grandiose and lyrically awkward ballad – claimed that Phil Spector had been hired as Apple's "unofficial" A&R manager under the condition that he secured Ronnie as an Apple artist. Al Steckler, however, emphatically states that Spector, "never had a position at Apple" although he admits that Spector did serve as an A&R consultant by default, given that he was working so closely with both Lennon and Harrison throughout 1970 and 1971.

Apple's next project was the long-delayed album by the Radha Krishna Temple, which was released in May. The album – packaged in a lavish gatefold sleeve that provided listeners with Krishna prayers and a list of the locations of temples around the world – also came with a mail-order insert offering Krishna merchandise. Both *Hare Krishna Mantra* and *Govinda* were featured on the album, as well as six additional recordings that Harrison had produced at various sessions throughout 1970.

Considering that the Radha Krishna Temple had scored successful singles in Britain, the album made little commercial impression in either Britain or America. Pete Bennett remembers that he didn't really have any idea how to promote the album. "I told George, 'We'll put it out, a lot of Krishnas might buy it... all these guys on the street corners.' I sent the record out to radio, but I really couldn't promote it. But it wasn't bad like Lennon's *Woman Is The Nigger Of The World*, but there still wasn't much we could do."

Al Steckler agrees that Apple had problems promoting the Radha Krishna Temple album. "I met the Krishnas in London," he remembers. "George was very into it and I told him that I would help him. But it was very hard to tell people like Charlie Nuccio and Pete Bennett that this was a record we felt really strongly about, so it was not an easy album to sell. I did my college radio mailings and hoped for the best. I think we sold 20,000 copies, and the single *Govinda* got a fair amount of radio play." While hardly a mainstream record, "Radha Krishna Temple" is a very good album. Perhaps if Apple had released the "Radha Krishna Temple" album a year earlier when *Govinda* was still in the charts, the album might have enjoyed greater commercial success.

Since new albums by Badfinger and Mary Hopkin were not scheduled to be released until later in the year, Apple spent a good portion of 1971 re-promoting the James Taylor album. Since leaving Apple, Taylor had become an internationally successful recording artist and Klein was determined to make any money he could from the album that Apple controlled. In June 1971, Apple once again reissued and re-promoted Taylor's 1968 debut album.

Also in June, Apple released a second album by John Tavener, called "Celtic Requiem". Unlike Tavener's first Apple album, "The Whale", "Celtic Requiem" was not released in the United States. As had been the case with "The Whale", "Celtic Requiem" was warmly received by the classical music fraternity, and it did sell respectably for a classical music release. While "Celtic Requiem" would be the last record that Tavener would record for Apple, he would return to work on another Apple project later that year.

To keep up the label's profile on the pop scene, Apple released Mary Hopkin's *Let My Name Be Sorrow* in June. The single was Hopkin's first to be produced by her new boyfriend, producer Tony Visconti, who had previously worked for Apple when he produced several tracks for The Iveys in 1968 and 1969. Hoping to stem Hopkin's declining commercial fortunes, Visconti attempted to resurrect the formula that had brought her so much success by hiring *Those Were The Days* arranger Richard Hewson to provide the musical arrangement for the single.

Hewson's diary notes that he met Visconti at Apple's office at eleven thirty on 19 May 1971, where Visconti expressed Hopkin's interest in having Hewson arrange her new single and her admiration for the work that Hewson had done on her previous hits, *Those Were The Days* and *Goodbye*. Hewson welcomed the opportunity to work with Hopkin again. Although he had recently accepted an offer from Paul McCartney to write and conduct an orchestral version of McCartney's "Ram" album, Hewson made the time to write a tasteful arrangement for *Let My Name Be Sorrow*. Hewson also conducted the orchestra on the session, which was held in George Martin's newly opened AIR Studios in London and which featured future Yes keyboardist Rick Wakeman as a session musician.

Unfortunately, Mary Hopkin's reunion with Richard Hewson proved to be less successful than Visconti had hoped and the single only reached number 46 on the UK charts. While both Hewson and Visconti had done admirable work on the recording, the overly dramatic, almost dirge-like *Let My Name Be Sorrow* was not half as good a song as either *Those Were The Days* or *Goodbye* so it was hardly surprising that the song was not embraced by British record buyers.

Although few people at Apple seemed overly concerned with Mary Hopkin's waning commercial appeal, Billy Preston's decision to leave Apple in the summer of 1971 did cause ripples of concern at the company. Despite his lack of hits, Preston's close ties to The Beatles would have ensured that he would always have a place on the Apple roster. Surprisingly, in mid-summer 1971, Billy Preston followed James Taylor's example and requested to be let out of his Apple contract. While George Harrison was reluctant to see Preston leave, he nevertheless made arrangements for Preston to be released from his contract with both Apple Records and Apple Music Publishing. Although Preston's release from his Apple commitments may seem to have been a magnanimous gesture on the part of Harrison and Apple, Pete Bennett suggests otherwise, noting that, "The Beatles thought that Billy was a great musician, but they never thought that he would ever be a star."

In a 1971 interview with *Rolling Stone*, Preston explained, "They had to get their thing together... how could they do anything for me if The Beatles' affairs were messed up? The same people who were supposed to be doing my things were theirs, and they had to look after them first. I just bowed out rather than try to be there and hassle them. It's better for them too, 'cause George did everything he could but the people in the office just sat around... It was comfortable at Apple at first until they started changing all the key people... like the President... and people left right in the middle of getting my product out, and people came in to start from scratch and it just never got out."

Once free from Apple, Preston quickly signed to A&M Records, where his next album went top ten and spawned several hit singles. Preston believed that it was A&M's superior organization and infrastructure that finally helped him break through as a recording artist. "When I was at Apple, you know, you could only record one day out of a week because Trident and all the other studios were always booked up." Despite Preston leaving Apple, Harrison would continue to work with him, inviting Preston to perform at The Concert for Bangla Desh as well as making a guest appearance on his first album for A&M, which came out in 1972.

Preston's decision to leave Apple meant that the company had lost one of its last remaining high-profile artists, yet Apple continued with its reorganization efforts as if nothing had happened. As Ringo Starr related in a July 1971 interview with *Melody Maker*: "The only thing they [Apple] are doing now is getting it all together. It's like pruning the tree, then you get the great flowers. If you have a big tree with a thousand million rose bushes, you get little roses. Prune it down and you get maybe ten fantastic roses, that's what's happening... The problem with Apple is that we're so involved, we can't sign anyone unless one of us is personally involved. Like George was involved with Jackie, Doris, Billy and who else, and he had to produce them. I've got involved... the only one I've got involved with is John Tavener, and I had to go round with him and get it together with him. You see, we haven't got anyone at the moment who can do it. Tony King will soon be able to. He'll have the right to get people who he thinks are good for the company. We've gotta start giving responsibility. Right now Apple isn't like that, which is why we're pruning it down so you can say, 'Right, that's your job, you like them, it's up to you.'"

Tony King had been the last employee to be hired by Peter Brown before he left Apple. Brown remembers that, "Tony King was hired in December 1970, just before I left. I gave Tony King the job. When I gave him the job, I felt guilty getting him to come to work knowing that I was leaving but I couldn't tell him I was leaving... I couldn't tell anyone. He came in to take care of publishing mainly... we brought Tony in to be the professional manager of Apple Publishing."

Tony King recalls: "I started at Apple in late 1970. I had been asked before, when they first started and Terry Doran was in charge. At the time I was working for George Martin and George Martin's offices were right across from the original Apple office in Baker Street. I was asked to go work for them then, but I refused, well I politely turned it down, because I sort of felt at the time that Apple seemed a little chaotic and my job with George seemed more secure. George Martin had an independent production company called AIR and I was doing record promotion for him and three other record producers he had in the company. George had just lured me away from Andrew Oldham and The Rolling Stones. There was Ron Richards who produced the Hollies, John Burgess who did Manfred Mann and Peter Sullivan who did Englebert Humperdink and Tom Jones, and they did other artists too. I used to promote any records that they made, so I had a nice job over there working with George and Co.

"I knew The Beatles when they first came to London," continues King. "I used to work for the Stones in '65, so I used to hang out with The Beatles when they went to nightclubs like the Ad Lib and the Scotch, so I was very friendly with them and Terry Doran and Neil and all those people around them. It became more business-like when Allen Klein came in. I was offered the job again in late 1970 and I took it more seriously because they had more serious people in there. I went to see Ringo, who I was very friendly with, and he said to me, 'Oh come on, take a chance, we got Bernard Brown here, we got Allen, it's much more business-like now, so take a shot,' and I did. Initially I was employed in the publishing end working for Bernard Brown. He was an older man, a sweet man, and I think Bernard provided a lot of stability at Apple. Anyway, I gradually moved into the record company. I started to do record promotion and A&R work. Peter Brown and Jack Oliver both left right after I arrived, but I didn't mind because Apple had changed – they were a much more professionally run outfit."

Apple had been in dire need of an A&R Manager ever since Peter Asher left in June of 1969. Though Phil Spector was perceived by many people in the music industry to be Apple's acting A&R manager, he was not an Apple employee and he did little more than sign his wife Ronnie Spector to Apple and produce recording sessions for Harrison and Lennon. Before the arrival of Tony King, Apple had not signed a single new act since Asher had left the company.

Badfinger's Joey Molland recalls: "We never got any A&R direction from Apple... until we got into a recording situation. Then, they were very supportive usually. For instance, George was very supportive of everyone's tunes. Mal was the same way. There were a lot of positive, gentle people around. We never gave Apple demos. We would do our sessions and leave and a few weeks down the line some mixes would be made for Apple."

In contrast to the widely-held perception in 1971 that Apple was ready to implode, both Harrison and Starr seemed to be firmly committed to making Apple a successful venture. Tony King confirms that Harrison and Starr were very interested in re-launching Apple. "In early 1971, there was a drive to encourage Apple to take on some more artists and to concentrate on the career of Badfinger," he recalls. "I think there was a concerted effort to make Badfinger bigger and also to encourage new artists. Ringo and George were the two behind that because by this time John had gone to America. George and Ringo were very optimistic about Apple. They were very hands-on and I think they wanted it to continue."

In his 1972 book *The Longest Cocktail Party*, Richard DiLello recalls speaking to Harrison in the summer of 1971 about the future of Apple. DiLello remembers that after he had mentioned to Harrison that he had recently completed a history book on Apple, Harrison replied: "Well, it's only just beginning."

Despite George Harrison's optimistic declaration, there were employees who were still finding it hard to fill their days. "When Tony King came in, I had been promoted to chief office boy, which meant that they sat me in the accounts office with two or three telephones and I ordered stationery once a week... that was it," chuckles Nigel Oliver.

While there may have been some idle employees at Apple, most were spending a good deal of time and effort trying to make Apple a commercially viable record label. At the same time, the company was also attempting to re-establish its slowly fading reputation as a record label with a conscience and a sense of altruism. During the summer of 1971, Apple released no less than three charity singles, including George Harrison's *Bangla Desh*, and several other singles from which any proceeds would go to help specific causes championed by ex-Beatles

The first charity single, released in July, was *God Save Us* by Bill Elliot and The Elastic Oz Band. Still at the height of his involvement with the counterculture movement in both Britain and and the United States, John Lennon had been enlisted to record a song to raise money for the legal defence fund for the English "underground" magazine *Oz* which was involved in a highly publicized obscenity trial.

God Save Us was written by John Lennon who produced the song at his home studio in Ascot with assistance from Phil Spector and Mal Evans. Since Lennon was under contract to EMI and EMI would thus be entitled to most of the money generated by sales of *God Save Us*, Lennon decided to get around his contractual obligations to EMI by having another vocalist sing on *God Save Us*. Lennon reasoned that if he did not sing on the record, EMI could not claim any rights to the recording, which meant that more money would go directly to *Oz*. For some reason, however, there was no problem with having Lennon sing on the bizarre B-side, *Do the Oz*. Based on a mutated blues guitar riff, the song featured Lennon extolling listeners to "Do the Oz", as Yoko Ono shrieked in the background.

Lennon's original idea was to have members of the *Oz* staff perform on the single. To augment the *Oz* contingent – including the well-known music journalist Charles Shaar Murray on rhythm guitar and Felix Dennis (who would go on to found the glossy men's magazine, *Maxim*) on percussion – Lennon brought in Ringo Starr and Klaus Voormann to act as rhythm section. Lennon sent a van to pick up the *Oz* staff from the then-scruffy neighbourhood of Notting Hill Gate to take them to Ascot.

To provide the lead vocal, the *Oz* staff brought along Magic Michael, a performer who was well-known on the benefit concert circuit (and who would go on to record for the punk label Stiff Records in 1977). Recorded in a single day, both Lennon and the staff of *Oz* were quite pleased with *God Save Us*. But when the *Oz* staff heard the finished product a few weeks later, they were shocked to hear that Magic Michael's voice had been replaced by that of a 20 year-old English singer named Bill Elliot.

Elliot had come to Apple's attention after his manager sent a tape of his group Halfbreed to Mal Evans in the hope of securing a deal with Apple for the band. Halfbreed were not given an Apple contract (although Evans would soon begin managing Halfbreed songwriter Robert Purvis), but Evans did get Elliot the job of singing lead on *God Save Us*. Speaking to *Melody Maker*, Elliot recalled that he became involved as a result of "peddling tapes and through Rob Hill [his manager]. John had a few contractual hassles and decided to have my voice on the Oz song." Although Elliot's involvement allowed Lennon to get around EMI owning *God Save Us*, Lennon hadn't considered that the voice of the previously-unknown Bill Elliot did not have the same commercial appeal as the voice of former Beatle John Lennon. Despite Apple's reasonable promotional efforts in both Britain and the United States, the single sold few copies and Apple did no further recordings with Elliot.

George Harrison, however, seemed to have been impressed with Bill Elliot. When Harrison started his Dark Horse label in 1974, the second act signed to the label was Splinter, a group that featured Elliot as lead vocalist. Elliot later recalled that he had been introduced to Harrison during the *God Save Us* recording sessions. Speaking to *NME*, Elliot noted that he had first met Harrison in a recording studio: "George was there doing a couple of mixes, I think he was in the studio with Badfinger at the time, and just came through to see what was going on."

The other two benefit singles to be released in the summer of 1971 were both George Harrison projects. In August, Apple released a three-track single of Indian music by Ravi Shankar called *Joi Bangla*. This single, along with George Harrison's *Bangla Desh* single which Apple had released the same month, was intended to raise money for the refugees of Bangladesh. Unfortunately for the refugees of Bangladesh and the beleaguered litigants at *Oz* magazine, few people purchased either the *Joi Bangla* or *God Save Us* records.

Harrison's impassioned, if somewhat clumsily worded *Bangla Desh* single, however, sold well enough to earn some much-needed money to aid the refugees of Bangladesh and to publicize their plight to Western nations. But the single was only part of a much larger gesture of support that Harrison was planning. On 1 August, Harrison performed two critically acclaimed benefit concerts at Madison Square Garden in New York City. Apple Films filmed the concerts and within days of the event, work was started on a concert film and album.

The members of Badfinger were among the many artists who joined Harrison on stage at Madison Square Garden. Prior to organizing the concert, George Harrison had spent several weeks in June producing tracks for Badfinger at Studio 2 of Abbey Road. Harrison initially became involved with producing Badfinger at the urging of Al Steckler, who explains, "When I first became involved with Apple, none of them [The Beatles] were very involved with the label. I did get George involved with Badfinger. I went to George and said 'Look we have a group, they're signed to us, they've had some pretty good success, you like them, they have some new songs and they need a producer. Do you have some time to take them into the studio?' He didn't have as much time as he wanted, so I got Todd Rundgren to finish the album. But I don't think that George produced Badfinger because they were on Apple, but because he liked the group."

In addition to assuming production duties and helping Badfinger arrange several songs, Harrison also played on the sessions, contributing his distinctive slide guitar playing to *Day After Day*, a potential new single written by Pete Ham. After completing work on only four tracks, however, Harrison suspended the sessions with Badfinger in order to devote all his time to preparations for the concert.

The members of Badfinger were naturally disappointed when Harrison stopped working on their album, but they understood the importance of the Bangladesh project to Harrison. Their disappointment was further tempered after Harrison invited the group to perform several of their own songs during the concert. Unfortunately for Badfinger, Bob Dylan agreed to perform at the last minute. Instead of being given the opportunity to get some high-profile publicity by performing their music at the two sold-out shows, Badfinger reprised their roles from the "All Things Must Pass" sessions, providing percussion and acoustic guitar backing for performances by Harrison, Ringo Starr, Leon Russell and Billy Preston. Yet despite the disappointment of not performing any of their own music, the members of Badfinger considered it an honour to even be on stage, and Harrison did bring Badfinger guitarist Pete Ham into the spotlight to join him on a moving acoustic version of *Here Comes The Sun*.

After the concert, Badfinger returned to England to resume recording their album. With Harrison preoccupied with mixing the tapes of the Bangladesh concert with Phil Spector, they needed to find a new producer. Apple ultimately selected 23 year-old American musician Todd Rundgren to finish Badfinger's album. "I guess at first, my involvement with Badfinger just started as a series of rumours," Rundgren recalled in an interview with *Melody Maker*. "Finally, one day somebody from Apple called me up and said they thought it might be a good idea if I went to England and did some work with them. I went to England and worked with them a couple of days, and then we decided that we'd finish the album together. I met George about a couple of days after I started recording with them and he said that he had these four tracks. He gave me the tapes and said do whatever I want with them. So I took the tapes and recorded things on them and remixed them myself. One of them [*Day After Day*] turned out to be a single. Somebody just didn't pay attention and said that George Harrison produced it, when he had actually given up the production of the act. He had turned the tapes over to me and said 'I'm not doing this project anymore – you finish it.' So actually, the entire album is my production even though George Harrison is credited in four places. I'm sure he's aware of this as much as anybody. It was more of an administrative mistake than anything."

While Todd Rundgren finished Badfinger's album in several different studios around London, Apple finally opened the new 16-track studio located in the basement of the Apple office. A party to celebrate the opening of the studio was held in the evening of 30 September 1971 with guests including recent Apple signings Lon and Derrek Van Eaton, Badfinger and George Harrison. To Harrison, the opening of the studio was apparently a bittersweet experience. In an interview he gave to a journalist at the grand opening, Harrison noted that: "It's a bit sad now that Apple is in the position all four of us planned three years ago. I just wish Paul would use the studio if he wants to. It's silly not to."

McCartney would set foot in the Apple studio, but only on a handful of occasions, which meant that he was denying himself the opportunity to use the studio that he had helped pay for and which came to be regarded as one of the finest in Europe. Before the end of 1971, both the Van Eaton brothers and an American, all-woman group called Fanny recorded albums at Apple Studios.

The studio had been under planning and construction since the "Get Back" fiasco in January 1969 and by the time it was completed, Apple had spent an estimated $1,500,000 on the project. Extensive work was required to build the studio in the basement and since the autumn of 1970, the exterior of Apple's Savile Row headquarters had been obscured by scaffolding.

Building the studio had been a monumental undertaking. Since being appointed studio manager, Geoff Emerick had played a very active role in its creation. George Peckham still maintains, "Soundwise it was a very good studio indeed, you had good engineers, good equipment, you couldn't have asked for more. It was small, but you could fit an orchestra in there. The studio was constantly booked." Unlike many of the independent recording studios that had sprung up around London in the late sixties, Apple's Studio measured a relatively snug 30ft x 45ft with an 11ft ceiling and a 12ft x 22ft control room. Apple's cutting room was even busier than the studio. Since 1969, Apple's cutting room had been cutting masters for albums by the Stones, The Who, The Zombies, Cat Stevens and many other artists.

The first act to record in Apple Studios would be Lon and Derrek Van Eaton, whom Apple had signed to a five-year contract on 15 September 1971. Derrek Van Eaton remembers that he and his brother were very surprised to be signed to Apple. "After our first group Jacob's Creek split up, Lon and I got together and made demo tapes in our house in Trenton and sent them to every record label we could think of. A couple of weeks after we sent out the tapes, we got a call from George Harrison. We had already had a couple of bites from small labels in New York and Philadelphia when George called us up and asked if we wanted to do an album on Apple. We got on Apple just by sending them a demo tape. We didn't even send them a picture. Klaus Voormann, who was with George Harrison when George first listened to the tape thought we were black." It was Al Steckler who received the tape that was sent to the New York office, and he confirms that Apple was very excited by the Van Eaton brothers. "I fell in love with the tape," he explains, "and I played it for George who loved it. John happened to be in the office the same day and George grabbed him and said, 'Listen to this.' John loved it too and they said, 'Sign them up.'"

Derrek Van Eaton remembers that their association with Apple happened very quickly. "We met George when he came to New York to do Bangladesh. We went to the Bangladesh concert, then they took us over to England. We were in England for around three months and we would stay at George's place at Friar Park just about every weekend while we were there. Our first night in England, Apple put us up in this place that was pretty dumpy right by Heathrow Airport. We asked them if it was possible to put us in a different place, so they put us up in one of Ringo's places up in Mayfair, which was real nice and we stayed there until we left England."

Despite his schedule being totally consumed with work on the Bangladesh album and film, George Harrison was able to find a few days to produce a single for Lon and Derrek Van Eaton. Two weeks after they had signed to Apple, Harrison took the duo into Abbey Road Studios where they were joined by Ringo Starr and several other musicians to record a song called *Sweet Music*. Derrek Van Eaton believes, "The reason that George ended up producing *Sweet Music* was that it was the song on the demo that he had first heard and he liked a lot. Also, it was the same approach he was using in those days, four acoustic guitars, the harmonium, two drummers – the same sound he was using on his own albums."

With Harrison unable to devote any further time to working with Lon and Derrek Van Eaton, Klaus Voormann was given the job of producing the album. Derrek Van Eaton feels that, "Klaus came in as a producer because Klaus was with George when George first heard the demo. Klaus was really into it, so George told him that he could produce it. I don't think Klaus had any previous production experience. It was more of a joint production effort with us, outside of when George

165

was producing. When George was there it was his stuff – he did it. He was a lot stronger personality. George dropped in a lot during the sessions that Klaus produced. We even ended up using the demo of *Warm Woman* on the record, because we couldn't recreate it in the studio the way we wanted to do it. We had everybody try to do it – Ringo played drums on one version – but it didn't come across with the same feel, so we just tried to doctor up the demo to make it sound good enough. While we were working on our album, we also met Richard Perry when he came to Apple Studios to work on sessions for [former Righteous Brother] Bobby Hatfield and Harry Nilsson. We didn't finish the album until we got back to New York. We got back from England a few days before Christmas 1971. After Christmas we did some more recording in New York, another 6 or 8 cuts then we mixed it all in New York and decided what to put on the album."

One of the outtakes from the Apple Studios recording sessions was a track called *The Sea*, a collaboration between the Van Eaton brothers and fellow Apple artist John Tavener. In a 1972 interview with the *Daily Express*, Tavener recalled how Ringo Starr had asked him to take time off from the opera he was working on so that he could contribute, "a bit for some pop record they're producing – just something for the middle, different from the rest. Ringo just said, 'You write whatever you want to write.'" While *The Sea* remains unreleased, both Lon and Derrek Van Eaton claim that the results were quite striking and they hope that the song – as well as the ten or so other unreleased songs they recorded in London – will eventually be released by Apple.

Many of Apple's British staff were surprised by how much time George Harrison was giving Lon and Derrek Van Eaton. To give an unknown act close to three months in a top line studio was an almost unheard of occurrence in the early seventies. Curiously, the most vivid memory that many former Apple staff have of the Van Eaton recording sessions is the artistic temperament displayed by the confident young Americans. Having been brought in by George Harrison to work on arrangements, John Barham recalls: "I remember working on the Lon and Derrek Van Eaton album. I did a couple of sessions for them. One of the guys... the slightly younger one, the prettier looking one, was a bit abrasive. I got the feeling that he resented me as an arranger. I think he wanted to do it."

George Peckham agrees with Barham's assessment. "We spent a few bob on Lon and Derrek Van Eaton... they were in the studios for ages. Everyone was saying that they made great album tracks, but they had a problem coming up with a single, but it was nice gentle music. I think George got a bit fed up with them... everybody at Apple did...

they were going on and on and they were acting like superstars, look-ing down on all of us." Regardless of the friction that the group gener-ated with Apple's staff, Harrison remained firmly committed to seeing that the album was done right and that no expense was spared.

On top of overseeing the Van Eaton and Bangladesh projects, Harrison was also involved with producing a proposed single for The Beatles' old Liverpool friend, Cilla Black. John Barham remembers: "Around the same time as the Lon and Derrek Van Eaton album, George wrote a song for Cilla Black called *I'll Still Love You*. It's a nice song, but it never came out. It was a complete track with Cilla's vocals... I was there when she did it. I put strings on it and we record-ed it at Apple."

Harrison was not the only ex-Beatle to be working on multiple proj-ects in 1971. In addition to collaborating on a wide range of "art" proj-ects with Yoko Ono, John Lennon had recorded his second solo album, "Imagine," which was issued in the United States on 7 September and in the United Kingdom on 8 October. Unlike the emotionally raw "Plastic Ono Band" album, "Imagine" featured some of Lennon's most melodic work, particularly the stately title track, which became a major hit when issued as an American single on 11 October. It cannot be said, however, that there are no raw edges on "Imagine." At the time of the album's release, the most talked about song on "Imagine" was *How Do You Sleep*, a scathing, vicious attack on Paul McCartney that was presumably motivated by McCartney's recent court victory over the other three Beatles and the hurt feelings that remained from the group's still recent split.

Unlike Harrison and Lennon, Ringo Starr made relatively little music in 1971. Instead, he appeared to be focusing on films, accepting roles in *Blindman* (which also featured Allen Klein and Mal Evans making cameos as bandits) and the Frank Zappa film, *200 Motels*. Starr also developed an interest in producing movies, and he took the lead in resurrecting Apple Films. Tony Bramwell, however, claims: "Apple Films was just Ringo's hobby... there was nobody actually working there." Still, under the guidance of Ringo Starr, Apple Films would soon start preliminary work on a film about Marc Bolan called *Born To Boogie* and a feature length documentary on Ravi Shankar called *Raga* in mid-1971.

Another Apple Films project contemplated that year was The Beatles documentary that Neil Aspinall had been working on since 1969. By mid-1971, Neil Aspinall had finished work on what was now known at Apple as *The Long And Winding Road* and the film was mooted as a possible follow-up to The Beatles' *Let It Be* film.

Unfortunately, as Aspinall recalled in an interview with *Mojo*, "The Beatles had split up by then, so there was really no chance of anything happening with it. I sent them a copy of it each, which they all quite liked, then I put it on the shelf. And it stayed on the shelf from 1971 till '89, about twenty years!"

Given that Apple's owners were now tied up in highly visible public squabbles, the company itself seemed to be doing surprisingly well. Considered to be doomed by the music industry as little as a year earlier, Apple was once again buzzing with activity in late 1971. With Apple's finally-completed studio the talk of the London music scene, and with several new artists having been signed to the label, it looked as if Apple may have found a new lease of life.

In addition to the official Apple projects, Allen Klein had also started to utilize Apple as a vehicle for his personal endeavours. Since Klein would not launch his own label, Abkco Records, until early in 1972, he had started to use the American record division of Apple to release the soundtrack albums of several unsuccessful films that were produced by his new film company, Abkco Films. The first Abkco Films soundtrack to be released on Apple was "Come Together", issued in September 1971. Also released in September by Apple's American division was Yoko Ono's first solo single, *Mrs. Lennon*. The haunting piano based ballad – a highlight from Ono's forthcoming double album "Fly" – would be released in Britain in October.

While Yoko Ono's debut as a singles artist left many music industry insiders wondering what Apple was thinking, Ono's single was almost a mainstream release when compared to an album that New York City beat poet Allen Ginsberg had recorded for Apple in November. After being given what he considered to be a verbal contract from a very enthusiastic John Lennon, Ginsberg went into New York's Record Plant Studios to record an album for Apple that was to have been called "Holy Soul and Jelly Roll". Backed by a band that included Bob Dylan, Ginsberg recorded a full album of poetry and songs. Apple, however, declined to release the album, leaving Ginsberg with a hefty studio bill that he had paid for out of his own pocket. The recordings would not be released until 1994, when they were included on the Ginsberg box set, "Holy Soul Jelly Roll: Poems and Songs 1949-1993".

The final months of 1971 also saw the return of Mary Hopkin. Having released only singles since her debut album was issued in February 1969, Hopkin's second album, "Earth Song Ocean Song", finally found its way into the shops in October. Produced by Tony Visconti, the album abandoned the upbeat pop feel of her debut album and subsequent singles, replacing the carefree pop stylings of her early work with a highly contemporary acoustic folk sound. "Earth Song" featured musical contributions from some of England's finest folk musicians, including Ralph McTell, Danny Thompson and Strawbs guitarist Dave Cousins, as well as some strong compositions from McTell and Cat Stevens. Although the album was not a commercial hit, it received excellent reviews and earned Hopkin some well-deserved critical respect.

Apple's Al Steckler remembers Hopkin's "Earth Song" as being: "probably one of the most difficult Apple albums to promote, because her image was so pop. There was a huge distinction between pop AM stations and FM stations in those days. So the FM stations wouldn't touch her because she was an AM artist and the AM stations wouldn't play her because there was no pop single there. Being aware of the importance of college radio, I did some mailing to college radio, but Pete Bennett didn't understand that market at all. Pete was a real, old time record promo man. He didn't understand the changes that were going on... he didn't understand the importance of the college market... he didn't even really understand the importance of the FM stations. So I just went to Klein and told him, 'I want to do a mailing to college stations and I wanted 500 copies of each album to do mailings,' and Klein said, 'Fine, just do it.' Whatever success the album had was due to that.

"I don't think that Capitol really believed in "Earth Song." It wasn't a distribution problem as much as a problem that Capitol had with Apple. We were really one of the first independent labels... Capitol resented us. They resented the fact that we started doing our own advertising. We started doing our own advertising because we didn't like the ads they were doing for us... we were just another cog in their wheel, which is understandable. When a Beatles record came out of course it was important, but anything else... Capitol had nothing to do with Apple other than to press and distribute the records. Tom and Charlie were hired away from Capitol by Klein to make sure that Capitol was doing the job they were supposed to do. We did the advertising ourselves, all the records were cut in New York, we told them when we wanted to release the records, we did the artwork in New York. There were always people at a lower level at Capitol who were trying to cut costs and be heroes. Like on the "Bangla Desh" album – we wanted to print it on a certain high quality orange paper but Capitol wanted to print it on cheap orange stock, those kind of things... but we didn't want it... it was our label."

In December, Apple ended 1971 by issuing several soundtrack albums. The first, "Raga", was an Apple Films project. The film itself was a 96-minute documentary about Ravi Shankar that had premiered on Monday 22 November at the Carnegie Hall Cinema in New York City. Both George and Pattie Harrison and John Lennon and Yoko Ono attended the premiere. George Harrison, who appeared in a sequence of the film, was also credited with producing the accomplished Indian music that comprised the soundtrack album. For reasons unknown, "Raga" was only released in America.

The second soundtrack album Apple released that month was that of another Abkco film called *El Topo*. Like "Come Together", "El Topo" was only released in the United States. Fortunately for Apple, it was also the last Abkco soundtrack that it would have to release. John Barham, a frequent arranger and guest musician on many of Apple's early projects, had returned to Apple to contribute to "El Topo".

Unlike *Come Together*, a would-be mainstream film that faded into oblivion shortly after its release, *El Topo* was a controversial, critically respected film that had received a fair amount of attention from the underground media. A surreal, twisted movie, both the film and the soundtrack album have since acquired a sizeable cult following. John Barham remembers: "I got the 'El Topo' work through John Lennon, who I knew through George. I first met John at the 'Sgt. Pepper' sessions at Abbey Road. George had asked me to come down to hear his recording of *Within Without You*. When I got there, John was coming down from an LSD trip and I remember when I was introduced to him, he almost jumped out of his chair... he recovered very quickly though and he was very charming. So when Allen Klein wanted to record the soundtrack to *El Topo*, Al Steckler mentioned to John Lennon that he wanted to record it in London, which I guess was cheaper, and so John recommended me to do it. I got a phone call from Al Steckler in New York saying, 'You don't know me, but John mentioned you,' and he flew me over to New York, which in a way was unnecessary, to see a private screening of the film and to sign a contract. I went over on a Thursday and on the Saturday ten days following we had to record it at Island Studios. I wrote two or three addition pieces to fill it out. We did the album in two sessions over the weekend. It was a very interesting album. It had a Latin style and it was hard to get the English musicians to play like that. Al Steckler produced the recordings... he was a really nice guy."

Al Steckler recalls that John Lennon was particularly enthusiastic about *El Topo*. "It was an independent film that was shown at this theatre in the Village every Friday and Saturday night at midnight," explains Steckler. "John saw it, flipped out, and went to Klein and said 'I want it... I want you to buy the film,' and Klein did. He bought the movie to launch on a national basis and we released the soundtrack on Apple, but it was too far out."

The soundtrack albums "Raga" and "El Topo" sold as expected, but paled in comparison to the sales of Badfinger's new album, "Straight Up", the jewel in the crown of Apple's December release schedule. For the American market, the album had been preceded by the single *Day After Day*, which had quickly risen to the top ten. Although "Straight Up" would not follow *Day After Day* into the top ten, it sold extremely well in America where it reached number 31 of the *Billboard* album charts. Once again, Apple hired Richard DiLello to take pictures for the publicity stills and the album cover. Like "No Dice", the album jacket was designed by DiLello and Gene Mahon.

In December, Apple also made one last vain attempt to resuscitate Mary Hopkin's career. Unlike "Straight Up", "Earth Song Ocean Song" had barely dented the charts in either Britain or the United States. Surprised by the universal indifference to Mary Hopkin's superb new album, Apple attempted to generate some interest in "Earth Song Ocean Song" by releasing the stirring track *Water, Paper And Clay* as an international single in December. The single was certainly one of the most commercial songs that Hopkin had recorded for some time, yet the record failed to chart in any country and it appeared that Apple would not be able to re-establish Mary Hopkin as a commercial success.

But with Badfinger riding high in the charts and with the recently reopened Apple Studios booked for months to come, there was a new sense of optimism at Apple. But that optimism was apparently not enough to keep Tony Bramwell – Apple's Promotion Manager since 1968 and one of the few remaining senior staff members to have been with Apple since the launch of the company – from resigning from Apple to join his former Apple boss Ron Kass at Hillary Music Publishing. "I left on New Years Eve, 1971," recalls Bramwell. "I was bored. There was nothing going on, so I left. It wasn't because of Klein. When Allen Klein came to Apple I wasn't affected at all. I always got along very well with Klein... I still do. He couldn't get rid of me... he got rid of everyone else but John said he couldn't get rid off me, so he had to live with me."

Of all the Apple staff, it was Bramwell who was best known to London's pop music community, as his position required him to interact frequently with BBC radio personalities and the music journalists who played a critical role in promoting any record. Also well-known on the London party circuit and for dating fashion models like Julie Edge, Bramwell was arguably Apple's last connection to what had once been swinging London.

Bramwell certainly made quite an impression on his Apple colleagues. "Tony Bramwell came up from the record department on the ground floor to Peter Brown's office quite often," remembers Bill Oakes. "He'd love hanging around and looking through my mail to see if there were any spare invitations hanging around. He would also love to have a few words with the fabs if any of them would come in. It seemed to me he placed more emphasis on that than most of the other workers at Apple... they really took it in their stride... they weren't terribly impressed and they weren't too interested in scoring brownie points with the lads... but for Tony it was a big vanity thing for him. He was always big on getting his hair done. He used to worship Paul and try to dress like him actually. He did the Apple promotion and I used to think how difficult could it be to promote a Beatles record? Also, with the other Apple stuff, how hard could it be when you could always say you won't get the new Beatles record if you don't play White Trash or whatever. But I suppose he was a bit of a legend in his own lunchtime as they used to say."

After Bramwell left the company, Apple A&R man Tony King was assigned the task of handling promotion duties for Apple Records and Publishing. King remembers: "For most of 1971 I was working in Publishing except that I seemed to be doing more and more work for the record company. Then I sort of split from Bernard and I was the boss of my own department where I was reporting directly to George and Ringo. I was made General Manager of Promotions/A&R. Chris Stone was my assistant and he did the promotions after Bramwell left. Chris was an English promotions man who worked for another English company and I poached him. He stayed at Apple until the end."

7

1972 - "They seem to be getting it together really well"

By 1972, Apple was generally no longer perceived to be the anarchic hippie haven that it had been regarded as in the late sixties. In fact, the company had evolved into what was, by the standards of the day, a fairly traditional small record label. Even though busloads of tourists still regularly stopped at Savile Row to snap pictures and try to catch a fleeting glimpse of an ex-Beatle or two, most left with little more than a photo of the building and the satisfaction of having seen where The Beatles did their business. For those who showed up at Apple's door to see if Apple was really as wild as they had read in old issues of music magazines, the reality of Apple circa 1972 must have been quite a disappointment. No longer could they witness Apple office boys dragging bags of stolen roof lead into the street, nor did they have to contend with the territorial "Apple scuffs", who were now seen only fleetingly outside 3 Savile Row. One former scruff, Margo Stevens, had even been given a job at Apple by Tony King.

Much had changed since 1968, and 1972 would prove to be a pivotal year for the company. In many ways, it was almost a renaissance year for the Apple organization.

The Apple Records label was the most visible division of the company in 1972, scoring a big hit with Badfinger and releasing new records by several promising new artists. With the departure of Tony Bramwell, the responsibility for running Apple Records in the UK had passed to Tony King and Bernard Brown. "It was a true joint effort," recalls King fondly. Bernard Brown – having proved himself to Klein through his successful management of Apple Music Publishing – was given the title of General Manager of Records and Publishing. Under Brown's leadership, Apple was soon more active than it had been since 1969 and the company quickly became a very efficient place of business. The year began auspiciously in America with Badfinger's "Straight Up" album reaching number 31 and the *Day After Day* single reaching the top ten of the American charts. *Day After Day* did so well that it became Apple's second non-Beatles gold record in America. In Britain, Apple ushered in the New Year with the January release of *Day After Day*, which was followed by the "Straight Up" album in February. Although *Day After Day* climbed to number 10 on the UK charts, the album failed to register on the charts, despite having been given a promotional push by Apple.

Apple's big success story of 1972, however, was Apple Music Publishing. Thanks to Badfinger's Pete Ham and Tom Evans, Apple Publishing would enjoy a golden year in 1972, though not from the sales of Badfinger records alone, but from a song that Ham and Evans had composed in 1969 while the group were still known as The Iveys.

American singer Harry Nilsson had first heard *Without You* – the brooding ballad that closed the first side of Badfinger's "No Dice" album – at a party in 1971. The next day, he called his hosts from the previous evening to find out the name of the record with "You" in the title. Nilsson initially thought it was a John Lennon song, but after being unable to find it on any Beatles album, he (incorrectly) concluded the song was by Grapefruit.

It was eventually determined that the song was *Without You* from Badfinger's "No Dice" album. When Nilsson finally located a copy of the album and gave the song a closer listen, he thought Badfinger's rendition was somewhat lacklustre, but felt that the song had the potential to be a big hit. Nilsson took the song to his producer, Richard Perry, who reworked Badfinger's subdued arrangement into a dramatic, impassioned love song that became a massive international hit. Thanks to Nilsson's hit version of *Without You* – and the countless cover versions and muzak renditions that followed in the wake of the Nilsson hit – the song became a huge earner for Apple Music Publishing.

In addition to the royalties from *Without You* and from the sales and radio play of Badfinger's albums and hit singles, Apple Publishing also owned the UK publishing of American singer-songwriter Kenny Rankin, whose 1968 composition *Peaceful* was significant hit when recorded by Helen Reddy in 1972.

Apple's good fortune in the early months of 1972 proved that the company could be successful independently of The Beatles. The problem, however, was that most of Apple's non-Beatles success was due to Badfinger. Given Apple's lightweight artist roster and the fact that little new music was issued by the ex-Beatles in 1972, Apple relied heavily on Badfinger to keep the label's momentum going. Fortunately for Apple, Badfinger were a very prolific band. Even before "Straight Up" had been released in the UK, the industrious group had already started work on what they hoped would be their next album.

Regrouping after the Christmas holiday, Badfinger had gone into Apple Studios with producer Todd Rundgren on 17 January to start work on a follow-up album to "Straight Up". Given that most of the group claimed to not have enjoyed working with Rundgren on "Straight Up" (they felt that Rundgren seemed to have little respect for their musical abilities – a common complaint amongst Rundgren's production clients) he was certainly an odd choice for producer. During the four sessions at Apple, Badfinger completed two songs – *The Winner* and *I Can Love You* before Rundgren pulled out of the project due to an ongoing dispute with Apple over the production credits for *Day After Day*.

With Badfinger due to begin their third American tour in February, sessions for the new album were reluctantly put on hold as the band instead concentrated on preparing for the tour. Joey Molland remembers that Badfinger were not particularly pleased to be recording at Apple Studios and that the group hoped that they would be able to resume recording at a different studio when they returned from their tour. "Apple Studios wasn't a great place to record," he explains. "It was much more comfortable to record at Olympic Studios or Abbey Road. The Apple Studio was a tiny basement room… it was L shaped and fifteen feet wide but it wasn't right for us. We did *Piano Red* and *Timeless* there." With little progress having been made on the new album, Badfinger left England for an extensive tour that would keep them out of a recording studio for several months.

The tour opened in Boston on 3 February and, with the band arguably at the peak of their powers, it was a great success. The highlight was certainly the band's triumphant performance at Carnegie Hall in New York City. The group were given a tremendous reception by the audience and the show attracted rave reviews by the usually reserved New York City music press. During the show, Al Steckler stepped out on stage to present the group with a gold record award for *Day After Day*. Despite the fact that the actual gold record award presented to Badfinger that night was not *Day After Day*, but rather another gold record hastily snatched off the wall at Abkco (Steckler remembers that the actual award for *Day After Day* had not arrived at Apple, so he used the first gold record he could find) it was a nice touch that helped make it a very special evening for Badfinger. Former Apple employee Richard DiLello had even been hired to take photographs of the show. The only thing missing from the event was Allen Klein. Although several seats had been reserved for Klein, the manager of Apple did not bother to attend this prestigious New York City performance by one of the best-selling acts on the Apple Records label.

Badfinger were to score another US hit a few weeks into their tour when Apple issued *Baby Blue* as a single on 6 March. The song – a soaring, bittersweet power pop gem written by Pete Ham – was a massive hit on American radio and it eventually climbed to number 14 on the American singles chart. *Baby Blue* was the second track taken from the "Straight Up" album, earning Badfinger the distinction of being the only Apple artist at that time, apart from George Harrison, to have two hit singles taken from one album.

The decision to release *Baby Blue* as an American single was made by Al Steckler, who was confident that the song would make an excellent follow-up to *Day After Day*. Steckler's only reservation about issuing the single was that he felt the mix did not do full justice to the song.

Steckler remembers that he initially attempted to get Todd Rundgren to do a remix, but when he was unable to secure Rundgren's services, he elected to remix the song himself. The resulting single mix, as overseen by Steckler, was a dramatic improvement over the original, replacing the dull thud of the drums on the introduction with a crisp, echoed drum sound that greatly enhanced the vitality of the song. Steckler's mix also brought a brighter sound to the guitars, giving the track a jangling quality that would later characterize the power pop movement of the late seventies.

Given how successful the song had been in America, it seemed obvious that *Baby Blue* should have been issued as a single in the UK, yet for reasons no longer remembered by either Badfinger or Steckler, this never happened.

Despite Badfinger's prolific output and relentless work schedule, Apple knew that they needed to sign more artists if the company were to succeed beyond simply being an imprint for albums by the ex-Beatles and by Badfinger. By 1972, the label's artist roster had completely turned over, leaving only Badfinger and Mary Hopkin left from the fold of 1968. Unlike Badfinger, however, Mary Hopkin had not managed to sustain her initial success, and in March she declined to renew her Apple contract.

Hopkin had been Apple's one true international star and she was strongly identified with both The Beatles and Apple. Since 1970, she had been attempting to reshape her image from that of the wholesome pop singer of *Those Were The Days* into that of a more serious folk singer. Apple supported her efforts, yet Hopkin slowly came to the realization that perhaps it was time for her to move on. By the spring of 1972, there were very few people left at 3 Savile Row who were at Apple when Hopkin's *Those Were The Days* had seduced the world, and Hopkin's relationship with the label had been reduced to little more than her management dropping off tapes and Apple issuing those tapes as records. The music press naturally tried to frame Hopkin's departure as an end of an era for Apple, but Apple simply wished her well and then went back to work developing the careers of the

1972 - "They seem to be getting it together really well"

ex-Beatles, Badfinger and a new generation of Apple artists.

Apple Records and Publishing were not the only Apple divisions to get a new lease of life in 1972. Throughout the year Apple also put substantial resources into re-launching Apple Films. Having essentially been dormant since Dennis O'Dell was let go in 1969, Ringo Starr had reactivated Apple Films to produce a movie featuring his friend Marc Bolan. In 1971 and 1972, Bolan and his band, T-Rex, were perhaps the biggest pop act in England and Starr was fascinated by the fan hysteria that he was now free to observe from the vantage point of a spectator. The film *Born To Boogie* was filmed in March and April and it would mark Starr's debut as a film director.

Starr was also responsible for signing British singer Chris Hodge to the Apple label. In May 1972, Apple released Hodge's *We're On Our Way* as the young singer's debut Apple single. Like Lon and Derrek Van Eaton, Chris Hodge's signing was almost straight out of Apple's original 1968 script for finding and developing new talent. Today, Chris Hodge is still amazed by how easy it seemed to get a deal with Apple. "I was born in 1949 and was 22 when I signed to Apple," he explains. "I was living in Rome for three years working as a fashion photographer, writing poems and songs. When I left Italy, I came back to London and signed a music publishing deal with Robert Mellin Publishing – they gave me money to record some demos. After I got back from Rome, I tried all the record companies and I kept getting turned down because they weren't into UFOs. So one day in early 1972, I phoned up Apple and spoke to Apple's A&R man, Tony King. We had a nice chat and I told him I'd written a killer song about UFOs and he said come on in. So, I met him and I played him my tape. I left my tape at Apple, and Tony played my music to Ringo, who then wanted to meet me personally.

"I remember when I came to Savile Row to meet Ringo, he was lying on a couch and he had jeans on with a big rip at the knee," continues Hodge. "He said, 'Hey man, do you want to release your demo?' I said I wanted to do some changes to it. I wanted to polish it up and add an orchestra and a choir. He was ready to go with the demo. But Ringo really liked it so they put me in the Apple Studio at Savile Row to record a new version. When they heard the first version of the demo, they realized that some of the lyrics had to be changed, because I said in the lyrics, 'the Karma is gonna be heavy on all the Mafia men; the Karma's gonna be heavy on all the Ku Klux Klan.' They told me I couldn't say that, so I had to take those lyrics out. I had told Ringo that I wanted to do it with a choir and a large orchestra and Ringo gave me a free hand and said, 'Just change those lyrics around a little bit and

177

then go do what you want to do,' so then I recorded the track along with *Supersoul*, which actually did better in Europe than *We're On Our Way*.

"When I finally got the deal with Apple, I stumbled across Tony Cox [former member of the sixties pop band, The Young Idea] and he ended up producing *We're On Our Way*. Apparently Apple changed his mix in New York – done by friends of Phil Spector's people in New York. They asked us if we approved, and we said go with it, it sounded good. One of the biggest mistakes of my career was that I never came to America. I never went to Apple's New York office. Apple's publicity in America was immense. They bought full-page ads in *Billboard* and *Cashbox*. For some reason Europe favoured the B-side, *Supersoul* and Apple promoted *Supersoul* in England. There was one DJ in England that had *Supersoul* as the intro to his radio show."

Tony King remembers that Chris Hodge quickly became a regular visitor to the Apple offices. "Chris Hodge was such a nightmare," recalls King with a laugh. "He was a very, very gregarious, outgoing person. He charmed his way into Apple and he came in wearing his silver boots with stars on... he used to wear lots of satin jackets and things. He played me the song and I sort of liked it. I played it to Ringo and he liked it too, so we signed him. Chris was a bit of a headache though... he just never stopped bugging me, but I guess that was his enthusiasm. He came in all the time! I think he got on everybody's nerves after a while... he was just a bit too persistent. I was shocked when *We're On Our Way* became a hit. It was very gratifying. Al Steckler called me up to tell me it was in the American charts and I was thrilled. Ringo was really pleased, as it was Ringo who was behind Chris Hodge. George was very much behind the Sundown Playboys and Lon and Derrek."

We're On Our Way was certainly much more of a "pop" record than most other Apple releases. Though totally overproduced, *We're On Our Way* was – in its own odd way – a great, silly pop record that was one of the most commercial records that the company had ever issued.

Given their poor track record for breaking new acts, Apple was shocked to see *We're On Our Way* reach number 43 on the American charts. Presumably because there was not too much Beatles music to promote at the time *We're On Our Way* was released, Pete Bennett was able to devote at least some of his time to promoting Hodge's record. Hoping to emulate the success that Hodge enjoyed in America, the single was released in the UK in June, although it failed to get the same enthusiastic reception as it had in America. Still, encouraged by America's positive response to *We're On Our Way*, Apple sent Hodge into the studio to work on new material.

Hodge remembers: "After *We're On Our Way* and *Supersoul*, I cut a lot of other different tracks in Apple Studios, because I was planning to do an album, but what happened was that the Apple corporation finally started to collapse. One of the tracks was called *The Year 2000* which was never released by Apple because they thought the lyrics were too heavy... it talks about, 'All revolution boys are dead, laser shots through their heads in the year 2000.' UFO activity and Stonehenge seemed to be a running theme in my writing at the time. I recorded around four or five other tracks that I was playing around with to use on an album. Another track was *Karma Is Going To Get You* with a giant orchestra of cellos and a big American Indian drum that I brought in. Tony Cox was still involved. I was doing some crazy stuff in those days. I recorded my second single, *Goodbye Sweet Lorraine* at Apple Studios too. I remember that all the plug sockets were gold, and the floors were rainbow colours, they had all this soft rainbow lighting in there... it was unbelievable."

The Apple of 1972, with its new recording studio, a manageable artist roster, and professional, highly regarded staff members such as Tony King and Bernard Brown on the payroll, had changed almost beyond recognition from its original incarnation. In fact, Apple appeared to have almost completely rebounded from the problems that had initially plagued the young company. Had Paul McCartney been still involved – other than in his role as owner in exile – he would have certainly been pleased.

Speaking to *NME* in May 1972, Badfinger guitarist Joey Molland admitted that the Apple offices had changed greatly from the 1969-1970 era: "You'd never feel really comfortable. I never did when we went in there. It was like that from my first day until Apple sort of dis-integrated and this new place opened up. I like it a lot more now. The bigness of it has gone. They're just trying to be a good record company now. They seem to be getting it together really well."

As part of their efforts to "get it together", Apple also attempted to earn back some of the money that had been invested in Billy Preston between 1969 and 1970. Having sat back and watched in amazement as Billy Preston scored several massive hits for A&M Records in 1971, Apple re-promoted Preston's "That's The Way God Planned It" album in the summer of 1972 and from June to August, Preston's generally overlooked Apple debut enjoyed renewed sales and spent several months in the American Hot 100 album charts.

One of the more arduous projects undertaken by Apple during the summer of 1972 was packing the entire contents of the Savile Row building into boxes and moving the company into a temporary office in order to enable renovations to be made to the Apple building. The renovations – which began the first week of July – were allegedly necessary to keep the entire building from collapsing. "Savile Row was unsafe to be in after a while," recalls Tony King, still amazed by how close the building came to literally falling to pieces. "I remember we had a Christmas party at Savile Row and the next day the architects came and said, 'We wish you had told us you were having a Christmas party because the whole building could have collapsed.' That could have ruined the whole party!"

While some of the structural problems at 3 Savile Row could be attributed to the advanced age of the building, most of the more serious problems were traced directly to Magic Alex and Apple Electronics. It transpired that during the construction of the original recording studio in late 1968 and early 1969, Apple Electronics had apparently removed important structural supports from the basement, which ultimately threatened the stability of the entire building.

In order for the engineers to properly renovate the building, Apple was required to completely empty the upper floors. Apple apparently decided that as long as they were going to be doing extensive construction on the Savile Row building, they might as well also use it as an opportunity to expand the Apple Studio facilities.

To accommodate all of the business that Apple Studios was attracting, Apple drew up plans to build a film editing suite and a second mixing studio in one of the upper floors. While the Apple recording studio would remain open during the renovation, all of the other Apple departments moved to temporary offices at 54 St. James Street.

Originally believing that the renovations to the Savile Row building would take only twelve to eighteen months, Apple seemed to have put little thought into finding an appropriate temporary office. While the St. James Street location was conveniently located very close to Savile Row, Apple's new office had previously been a car showroom and the space was hardly a traditional office setting for a record company. When the Apple staff moved in, they simply put up curtains in most of the large windows of the former showroom and resumed their business activities. In addition to the large, wide-open first floor office, Apple also had use of the upper four floors of the building. Tony King remembers: "Apple had the whole building. The upstairs floor was Ringo's office, my office was in the front where the cars are now, and then there was a basement. We had the basement, ground floor and first floor. It was a weird building, I don't know why they picked it."

Though the upper floors of the Savile Row building became eerily quiet after the staff exodus, both George Harrison and Ringo Starr spent a good part of 1972 in the basement studio, recording what would respectively become their "Living In The Material World" and "Ringo" albums. In spite of the chaos generated by the move, Apple Studios remained in operation throughout the summer of 1972. The same week that workmen were moving furniture and shipping boxes out of the upstairs offices, in the basement, Apple Studios producer Phil McDonald was recording an album for English singer Linda Lewis. McDonald had joined Apple in November 1971 as a senior balance engineer. Like many of the Apple Studio staff, McDonald had started his career at EMI Studios and at the age of twenty-five he had already engineered sessions for The Beatles, Roy Harper, The Shadows, as well as solo sessions by all four of the ex-Beatles.

The renovations at 3 Savile Row began immediately after Apple moved to St. James Street. However, all work on the building appeared to stop soon after the upper floors of the building's interior had been totally gutted. From their vantage point in the Apple Studio, both George Peckham and Nigel Oliver were bemused by what was going on above them. Nigel Oliver remembers: "It was surreal, because after 1972, you could go up the studio stairs to what had been the offices and there was just sky... all the floors had been knocked out. All the artists had to go up to the first floor to use the toilet and there was nothing there, just the walls and the bog. When the building was knocked down inside and only the studio was left at Savile Row, we weren't really aware of what was going on with the rest of Apple. I went over to St. James once in a while, but when Apple moved there, the studio and the record company became very separate. It became a sort of them and us situation... Apple Records at St. James Street was still Abkco dominated, and we went back to being more of a studio, and George and Ringo used to come in and it used to be like it was before Klein."

1972 was certainly a busy year for Apple, yet there was a conspicuous lack of musical activity on the part of any of the four ex-Beatles. The only ex-Beatle to release an album that year was John Lennon, who released the rather unspectacular "Sometime In New York City" that summer. Pete Bennett remembers that he had a significant disagreement with Lennon about the commercial potential of "Sometime In New York City" and especially the album's single, *Woman Is The Nigger Of The World*.

"John Lennon came to me with *Woman Is The Nigger Of The World* and he and Yoko wanted to put it out in America very badly," Bennett remembers. "They thought it was a number one record. I told him I hated it – I thought it was a piece of shit and I told him that I wouldn't promote it. So John says to me, 'Well, you're our promotions man, you have to listen to us, we pay you... I'm the President of Apple.' I said, 'John, I don't care what the story is. I don't want the record – I'm not going to promote it. If I don't like it I won't promote it.' So John says, 'I'll tell you what – I'll promote it, and if I make this record number one, that means you're not the number one promotions man in the business.' I said, 'John, you got a deal... but if the record doesn't happen, I want you to kiss my butt and double my salary and expenses.' So he says, 'You got a deal... but I'm gonna make it number one.' But without John knowing, I checked out all the radio stations and they said they weren't going to play it.

"So John called all of the stations himself and he tried to do a promo job," explains Bennett. "He was so happy and he came back to me and said, 'We still got that bet,' and I said 'John, god bless you, we still have that bet and you better kiss my butt if you lose, and if you win, you can tell me, "Peter, you're shit," and if you don't want me to work with you anymore, that's it.' 'Well, you're gonna lose,' he told me, because he had called Chicago, he called San Francisco and he talked to the Program Directors and they were so nice to him, they took interviews with him. The thing was, the stations put him on tape, and while they played the record in the studio, they never put it on the air. What happened was that a few idiots played it on FM, but at that time FM was nothing, it couldn't sell two records and all the top stations wouldn't play it. Apple sent out 30,000 records and about 15,000 came back. The highest it went on the chart was like 68. And he did kiss my butt. He bowed to me and Yoko said, 'You see, we have to listen to Peter.'"

Unlike George Harrison – who used Apple as a means to help develop worthy new artists and to sharpen his skills as a record producer – Lennon never had much creative input at Apple and his commercial instincts were often overshadowed by his tendency to become obsessive, and lose his objectivity, when it came to particular projects that he held near to his heart. Lennon was officially the President of Apple Records and had been to some extent involved with Apple's business decisions since 1968. However, it was not until 1972 that Lennon started to take an active role in finding and producing talent for Apple.

Lennon had always been interested in Apple, but mainly as an outlet for releasing albums by himself or Yoko Ono. From 1969-1971, Lennon could often be found at 3 Savile Row, either working on his own projects, or, once The Beatles had split up, attending to Apple business. Back in 1969, Lennon even had a promo picture created that showed his face and the caption – "I am at 3 Savile Row most days." Though Lennon would never again set foot in Apple's London office (or England for that matter), after he left for New York City on 3 September 1971, he would continue to be actively involved with Apple business.

Once Lennon had set up camp in New York City, he became a regular visitor to Apple's New York office and soon signed several New York artists to the Apple label. Unlike the artists that George Harrison brought to Apple, however, Lennon seemed to sign acts to Apple more as a personal favour to the artist involved, rather than as a viable commercial proposition. While Harrison discovered and produced several of Apple's better selling artists, Lennon seemed to have a knack for signing Apple's least successful and, in the case of Yoko Ono, most expensive artists.

The first act that Lennon signed to Apple was a New York City-based rock band, Elephant's Memory – a hard-hitting, denim and leather clad group that had been active on the New York scene for several years. Lennon first came into contact with the band during his search for a backing band to work with while he and Ono were in the United States. Having settled into an apartment in New York's bohemian, yet trendy West Village neighbourhood, Lennon and Ono were anxious to start playing live shows and recording music. Drummer and founding member of Elephant's Memory Rick Frank remembers: "The hook-up with John Lennon was quite coincidental. We did a very high energy radio show for WLIR in Long Island. It was a really good tape and it was simulcast. Lennon heard it, or it was brought to his attention. He was looking for a band that could reproduce the sound of his last album, with sax and hard rock guitar, because every time he wanted to record, he would have to bring in Eric Clapton or Ringo Starr or Jim Keltner. So when he heard our tape he said, 'That's the sound I want.'

"So, Lennon got in touch with us through Jerry Rubin, and Rubin came to see me at my apartment on Bank Street," explains Frank. "He put us in touch with Lennon, who asked me to bring over some photos and informational material. Within a day, I was in a studio auditioning for him on drums... he had me play on material that had no drum tracks recorded... I walked into the Record Plant and I saw an engineer we had worked with, so I connected with him right away. I was never a Beatles fan, so the awe-struck aspect of it... it was there, but it was not like I had some fanatical desire to meet John Lennon, or his lovely wife. But I connected with Lennon and he asked me to put drums on these songs. The rest of the band was at this little 8-track studio in the Village called Magnographics. In the spring of 1972, Elephant's

Memory were at a very confused point. We were either going to sign with this black music label, or we were going to break up. The band didn't believe that I was really going to meet John Lennon. I didn't brag about it – I just told the band that I was going to a very important business meeting and that their careers might depend on it, so why don't you hang out and rehearse a little. I kept them waiting for around four hours... John was very casual. After we played and recorded we went to a tea house, had some tea and talked things over while the band was still waiting there for me in the studio. I finally called the band at the studio and they thought I was bullshitting them. So Yoko, John, Phil Spector and I met up with the rest of the band and we started jamming within minutes."

Elephant's Memory's first project with Lennon was to back him on the recording sessions for what would become the "Some Time In New York City" album. It was during these sessions that Lennon expressed an interest in producing an album for Elephant's Memory. The band's deal with Lennon stated that Elephant's Memory were free to sign to any label they wanted. However, Lennon suggested that if Elephant's Memory were to sign with a label other than Apple, it could create contractual problems that would ultimately jeopardize Elephant's Memory doing any more work with Lennon and Ono. Frank remembers that the band agonized about signing to Apple.

"We were signed to Apple," remembers Frank, "but we had the right to play shows on our own, plus we had a relationship with John where he would give us money under the table because we weren't getting enough from Apple. When we signed to Apple, we were on salary and it was taxable and all that... John gave us cash. Apple didn't pay us a hell of a lot, but John made up for it, so we were OK. I ended up negotiating the deal myself. We were signed to managers Lieber and Krebbs – they managed Aerosmith and the New York Dolls too – and they figured they had a right to be in on the Apple deal, but having been in the business since 1967, I knew all the answers, so I did it myself. But I didn't know much about legal matters, so I hired John Eastman as our attorney and he helped negotiate the deal. Eastman was suing The Beatles for Paul, but Eastman and Lennon didn't care – there was no conflict of interest. As John said, 'The more the merrier.'

"So we signed a multi album deal with Apple with a commitment to do the double album for John, several singles for John and Yoko, a double album for Yoko," continues Frank. "In return, John and Yoko would produce an album for Elephant's Memory. It was a great deal, except for that the business of Apple was folding and they were slowly going under. I only met Allen Klein once, and it was a scary experience. This was when May Pang worked at Abkco and she still had nothing to do with John at the time. I knew her very well from other circles. So May helped take care of business for us. There weren't that many people working for Apple, just Al Steckler and Dan Richter, who was helping out around Apple. We were also signed to do a tour with John and Yoko, but due to Lennon's immigration problems he wasn't allowed to work in America."

As Frank noted, by the time Elephant's Memory had signed to Apple, they were seasoned music industry veterans. Formed as a jazz-influenced rock group in 1967, Elephant's Memory had already gone through several line-up changes, had recorded albums for Buddah and Metromedia Records, and had even appeared on the "Midnight Cowboy" soundtrack album. Although Elephant's Memory were often considered to be a "bubble gum" band through their initial association with the Buddah label, the group had actually developed into a dynamic hard rock-outfit by the time they met Lennon. Invigorated by playing with such rock-orientated musicians, Lennon was brimming with plans and enthusiasm in the spring of 1972.

Elephant's Memory were not the only New York City rock artists to capture Lennon's attention. Lennon also signed David Peel, a "street singer" who had previously released several albums on Elektra Records. David Peel remembers: "I met John Lennon on a Friday in the spring of 1972. I met him on St. Mark's Place at a hippy clothes store called Limbo. I had a friend named Howard Smith who brought John and Yoko to see me perform in Washington Square Park on Sunday. They liked my song *The Pope Smokes Dope*. Then there was another time when I told Jerry Rubin that I wanted to audition a song for John Lennon. I wrote a song about them called *The Ballad Of New York City – John Lennon And Yoko Ono*. I went to their house on Bank Street and they liked the song of course... it was about them. Then John and Yoko signed me to Apple."

Soon after issuing an Apple contract to his latest discovery, Lennon took Peel into Record Plant Studios in New York City and produced a full album of Peel's ragged, enthusiastic street rock. The completed album – provocatively titled "The Pope Smokes Dope" – was issued in the United States in April 1972. Presumably due to the controversial nature of the title and the music, Peel's album was never given a European release. Lennon actively helped to promote the album in the United States, yet despite his involvement with the record and the fact that Peel was already partly established in the music industry, the album sold poorly – suggesting perhaps that "the people" were not interested in Peel's would-be street rock anthems like *I'm A Runaway*,

Those Were The Days

Everybody's Smoking Marijuana and *I'm Gonna Start Another Riot.*

Peel agrees that his Apple album was not particularly well received and claims that it was almost impossible to find the album in the stores. He also is quite certain that Lennon and Ono were the only people at Apple who thought that his album was even worthy of release. "I met George Harrison at Apple and I shook his hand. He looked at my pictures and then he turned around and left. The other Beatles didn't like me but John didn't care – they didn't like Yoko either. They didn't like me singing about dope and pot and revolution. I was too radical for their image. Paul McCartney thought I was a troublemaker. As a matter of fact, I was given a quote from Paul McCartney. In 1972 McCartney played on a song called *God Bless California* on ESP Records and I did a song on the same record, *To Err Is Human*, and he told Leslie Fradkin, the band director, 'I never thought that I would see the day that I was on the same record as David Peel.' I don't know what Paul thought about my music, but I got his attention."

While John Lennon seemed to be entertained by Peel's antics, Rick Frank of Elephant's Memory has a less charitable view of his radical label mate: "David Peel is a joke. He was a symbol of something that might have been if things had been the way John wanted... the ultimate hippie trip. David Peel was constantly asking us to play drums on records and he was always in the wings. We had to physically restrain him from appearing with us a lot. David Peel and the Lower East Side was embarrassing... we usually brushed him off."

Undaunted by the cool commercial and critical reaction to "The Pope Smokes Dope", Lennon dived headfirst into a new project, which was producing an album for Elephant's Memory. Rick Frank remembers, "John Lennon was great in the studio... he was a lot of fun and very, very committed to an ongoing production value. There was a lot of jet-setting while we were recording our album, which John though was funny for a while... but it wasn't in our best interest. We went to dinner at Jackie Onasis' house one night, and Rosie Greer came down to see Lennon and it cut into our recording time. It was not something that John wanted to get too involved with and I felt the same because we were losing our impetus. We were losing the ability to have John Lennon as a producer because we were going to dinner with Jackie O. So we finally cut some cords and made sure everyone left us alone while we finished our album.

"The sessions were endless," continues Frank. "John wanted to release certain songs as singles that we didn't want. He really related to this song *Black Sheep Blues* and he sang double lead on it. We recorded a lot of songs that didn't come out. It was confusing because

1972 - "They seem to be getting it together really well"

John and Yoko had a drug problem and they were trying to cure it alternatively. They saved us from a major drug problem by keeping it apart from the studio and apart from the scene. We were more of a drinking band; we were never really into hard drugs. John was trying to tidy up his heroin problem and work very hard on our album. John was a very appreciative guy, and he appreciated how hard we worked on Yoko's album trying to make it sound good – and that was very hard because she had a difficult voice and was a difficult person to work with. With Yoko we had an agreement that we were going to back each other to the hilt... I did interviews saying all these glamorous things about her."

The self-titled album that Elephant's Memory recorded for Apple came out in the United States in September 1972 and it was released in Britain in November. Unfortunately for Apple and Elephant's Memory, the album received positive reviews but only average sales. The album – which featured everything from rocking boogie numbers like *Liberation Special*, to gentle, melodic ballads like *Wind Ridge*, certainly deserved to do better.

Rick Frank believes that the commercial failure of the Elephant's Memory album on Apple was due to Allen Klein's attitude towards any Apple Records artists who were not former Beatles. "When our Apple record finally came out, it didn't happen because Allen Klein only worked for The Beatles... he didn't push anything else. We needed promotion, our managers Lieber and Krebbs had failed us. In fact, they were going to sue us to get in on the Apple deal. And here I was doing all the work of a manager, and John was too. I'm not going to slight his efforts, he was really our manager. He did all the work helping to package our record. It was a very expensive album. John was very proud of the album, he wanted to get a single out and wanted to get us on the road. Elephant's Memory needed the support of Apple to do promotional stuff, tie-ins with radio stations and they weren't doing it. Allen Klein was not willing to spend money on outside projects besides the Lennons. John raised hell with Klein, but it didn't do any good. Klein was the kind of guy who was extremely paranoid – he sat in a bullet proof sealed-off office with a shotgun next to him. When I met Klein I was a pretty rough guy at the time and he scared us. We only went up to Apple when we needed to."

Al Steckler on the other hand feels that Elephant's Memory were not victims of Klein's indifference, but rather that Apple simply had trouble promoting acts like Lon and Derrek Van Eaton and Elephant's Memory. "Pete Bennett couldn't promote an album like Lon and Derrek Van Eaton. He was a top 40 guy and it was not that kind of album. Elephant's Memory was the same thing. Elephant's Memory was a project that no one was interested in other than John. They were a pretty good bar band, but nothing more than that."

The Elephant's Memory album was not the only new product that Apple issued in September. Late in the month, radio programmers and obscure record aficionados were treated to *Saturday Night Special*, a single by an American group called The Sundown Playboys. Released in the UK in November, the single consisted of two authentic Cajun songs, performed by a part-time band from Lake Charles, Louisiana. The band comprised several oil refinery workers, a grocer, a truck driver and a 17 year-old high school student named Pat Savant on accordion. Featuring two rousing Cajun stomps sung in Cajun French, the *Saturday Night Special* single was a wonderful record that had no realistic chance of becoming a hit – yet Apple promoted it to the full extent of its abilities.

To this day, Tony King remains effusive with his praise for The Sundown Playboys. "I loved The Sundown Playboys... it was my favourite of all the things I did for Apple. I got this strange little 45 from Pat Savant, I played it and it was wild... it sounded so fresh and real. I played it to Ringo and George and they loved it and I told them I'd really love to put this out on Apple, and they said, 'Let's do it.' So I called up Pat Savant and told him we'd like to put it out on Apple and he couldn't believe it – he was seventeen years old. I think the oldest member of the band was sixty-five or something! I did a really good press release for it and it got loads of play in Britain. It was a turntable hit, but it didn't sell. People liked listening to it, but they didn't want to spend money on it. It was played all over the place. It really brought Cajun music to people's attention. It was such a wild sounding record that I decided to do a 78. It was kind of magic that song."

Pat Savant, who was a high-school senior when he was signed to Apple, has especially vivid memories of his time as an Apple Records recording artist. "I started with the band in June 1971 and in December 1971 we got together the finances to have the two songs released as a single on the Swallow Records label. We recorded the single in December of 1971 at the Swallow Studio and it came out in the first part of January 1972. At the time we made our record, there were a lot of groups out on the Apple label, I think Mary Hopkin and Badfinger... I loved Badfinger's music. So around March or April I was just wondering out loud to a friend in a record shop, 'You know, I wonder what they would think about our music,' so I sent a copy of the single we did on the Swallow label and an explanatory letter to Apple's London office. Two weeks to the day that I sent our record to Apple, I heard back from Tony King, Apple A&R Manager, and the letter he sent me was to the effect that Apple was interested in the group and were we going to record any new material?

"So we sent them some information, the history of the group, brief bios of the band members and so forth. They were particularly interested in *Saturday Night Special* so they wanted more copies of the Swallow record, which we sent them. So this went back and forth until we signed a contract in August of 1972. The first letter I got from Apple was from Tony King, but after that I started hearing from his assistant Margo Stevens. So we went to Floyd Swallow and asked him to come in on this. Of course he wanted his percentage, but we knew that he had dealt with the big companies. The first time Apple issued us a contract, they wanted to pay us based on 90% of sales, but Floyd got them up to 100% and they re-did the contract. Apple signed us to a single deal and wanted an option on all our material for five years. The contract was that if they didn't want to release a song we had the right to release it locally or on some other label. I remember I had to have my father sign for me because I was under age. I signed it and he had to sign his name under my signature. So after he finished the contract, Floyd Swallow sent off the master tape to Al Steckler in Apple in New York and it was released in September 1972. Apple also bought the UK publishing rights to *Saturday Night Special* which was originally published by Swallow's Flat Town Music.

"After we did *Saturday Night Special* Apple wanted some more material and we did something with a country and western flavour, a song called *Back Home In Louisianne* and we sent that to them along with some other material," recalls Savant, "but they didn't seem all that interested. I guess the sales weren't as good as Ringo Starr or some of the other records they had done before. I also think that Apple started going downhill around then."

While the band's Apple record was not a big-seller, Savant feels that being on Apple opened a lot of doors for The Sundown Playboys. Despite the fact that Paul McCartney and John Lennon had recently released such thoroughly average albums as "Wild Life" and "Sometime In New York City," anything even remotely associated with a former Beatle and the Apple label still had an almost magical allure in 1972.

"The local reaction to *Saturday Night Special* was unbelievable," remembers Savant. "We had a local radio station KLOU that called itself "the rock of Lake Charles" and they would play nothing but top forty material. When we did *Saturday Night Special* for Swallow, our guitarist Daryl Higgenbothem and I went to the radio station to talk to the Program Director and see if he would play our record on the rock station. He looked at our single and told us something to pacify us at the time, but it was never played. So a few months later, Daryl and I took another ride over to the radio station and the Program Director remembered us. We asked him 'Do you have any new Apple Records?' and he said 'Well we have some records that just came in but I haven't had the chance to look at them yet.' He still had the old copy of our Swallow single and he looked through the stack of new records and there was our Apple record. He said 'I can't believe this, this is the same record on Apple?' Then they really got behind the record. We had pretty good record sales locally.

"I never met anyone from Apple. I talked to Chris Stone in Apple's London office on the phone, but that was it. Apple did this nice full-page ad for us in *Billboard*. I went to this record shop and the owner of this record shop handed me a copy of the *Billboard* ad and said 'Here, take it.' It was a really nice time for us. At that time Danny and I were kind of oddballs because our music was kind of the music of the older generation. There wasn't that many young people playing Cajun music at the time... we were far and few between back then. If nothing else, being on Apple made the people of my generation realize that maybe what was in the top forty was not the last word in music... maybe people somewhere else look at things differently, and that's what the people at Apple apparently thought. If nothing else, the Apple single did that."

The release of The Sundown Playboys' single neatly coincided with Apple's "Back to Mono" campaign. Though Tony King no longer recalls the motives behind this campaign, it was probably initiated to create advance publicity for Apple's planned reissue of Phil Spector's 1963 Christmas album. It wasn't much of a campaign, however, as "Back to Mono" consisted of little more than a "Back to Mono" pin that Apple distributed as a promotional item and issuing The Sundown Playboys' *Saturday Night Special* single only in mono. As an attention getting promotional item, Apple also had a limited number of 78rpm copies of The Sundown Playboys' single pressed up to distribute to important members of the press.

Savant recalls: "Apple sent us each copies of the 78 and the British version of the single with a small hole in the centre. They also sent us a kit with promo material about the band. I remember they had this 'Back to Mono' campaign going at the time and they also sent each of us this 'Back to Mono' badge."

In addition to The Sundown Playboys record, when Apple issued Elephant's Memory's *Liberation Special* single in November, it was also issued only in mono. Apple would wind up their "Back To Mono" campaign with the international release of "The Phil Spector Christmas Album" in December 1972.

The release of adventurous records such as those by The Sundown Playboys and Chris Hodge led many in the music industry to believe that Apple was back in business and poised to become a viable record label. With Badfinger making substantial money for both Apple Records and Publishing, and Apple Studios now one of the busiest disc cutting and recording operations in Europe, it appeared that Apple was turning around and transforming itself into a well-run and even profitable business. For a brief moment, Apple was looking so promising that in February 1972 Allen Klein had initiated talks with Lennon, Harrison and Starr about the possibility of Abkco buying Apple. David Peel remembers how he and a few other people, "knew that Allen Klein wanted to buy Apple and we thought that it was very un-revolutionary for someone like that to control Apple. So we told John that it would be a very bad idea to sell to Allen Klein and his people."

It will never be known if Lennon heeded Peel's advice, but due to the complicated issues involved with Apple's ownership and ongoing litigation with Paul McCartney, no deal was ever struck.

The renewed success and sudden burst of activity in 1972 boded well for the company, but any plans that Apple may have had of becoming a full-blown record label came crashing to a halt when Badfinger unexpectedly signed to Warner Brothers Records on 21 September 1972. What made Badfinger's decision to leave so surprising was that Badfinger were arguably the only Apple act who were generally pleased with how they were treated by Apple.

With their Apple Music Publishing contract due to expire in October 1973, and their Apple Records contract set to expire in July 1973, Badfinger's management had been attempting to renegotiate a new contract with Apple since the summer of 1972. The members of Badfinger had always assumed that they would re-sign with Apple and they had indeed instructed their management to negotiate a new deal.

Speaking to *DISCoveries* magazine in 1991, Joey Molland explained why Badfinger left Apple: "We tried to negotiate with Allen Klein... we wanted to stay with Apple. We wouldn't have wanted to stay with them if they had been screwing us around. Klein was in control, though now at Abkco in New York City. We went to see him... we wanted a sixteen-track tape machine and a mixing console... What was ridiculous about the whole thing was that we had enough money in Chemical Bank in New York that we could've bought fifteen 16-track machines. But our business manager didn't want to spend the money. He wanted to keep it for himself... We left Apple because Klein wouldn't

Those Were The Days

negotiate with us at all. We were the biggest band on Apple bar none. We were selling more records than John Lennon... we were the biggest selling act on the label and we were doing it quite regularly for them. I'm not trying to be egotistical. We didn't really make those kind of demands – I can say that now looking back on it, because it's a fact. But we went to Allen Klein and said, 'Look, we want to build a little studio. We'll buy ourselves a house, and we want to build a 16-track studio... will you give us the money?' It was about fifty grand, it was nothing. We made fifty grand in two weeks... And he [Klein] said, 'No. And from now on you're going to pay your own recording costs.' Klein would not negotiate with us, even though we were making money for the company."

On top of wanting Badfinger to start paying their own recording costs, Klein also demanded that Badfinger take a royalty cut as well. Their original Apple contract, written in Apple's idealistic early days, gave Badfinger a very fair artist royalty of 5% of the retail selling price of their albums, with Apple picking up the group's recording costs and all the costs of promoting their records.

Most traditional recording contracts of the time gave an act an artist royalty of between 2% and 10%. However, an artist would not receive these royalties until all of the recording and marketing costs had been recouped by the record company. Faced with Klein's demands, Badfinger's management team, Bill Collins and Stan Polley, started to speak to other labels. Badfinger ultimately signed a contract with Warner Brothers Records and Music Publishing.

Tony King believes that Badfinger leaving Apple for Warner Brothers was indeed the beginning of the end of Apple. "Badfinger were thought of very highly by the people at Apple," he recalls. "They were Apple's stars. I don't know why Badfinger didn't do better in the UK – perhaps they were a little bit too 'Beatley'. We did alright with the singles, but we did better with their albums in America."

King admits: "When Badfinger left Apple for Warners, everybody was a little bit hurt, because it was a very personal thing between Badfinger and Apple. Everybody had put themselves out a lot on behalf of Badfinger, and in a way Badfinger had ridden to success on the back of The Beatles, so it was natural that we were upset. But at the end of the day, when someone waves a big fat cheque at you, off you go. After Badfinger left, people started to lose interest in Apple and it started winding down. The trouble is when you're an artist like George and Ringo and you have artists on your label, they take up a lot of time. In a funny kind of way, you have to be a businessman to deal with artists, it's no use you being an artist dealing with other artists because they want a lot of time and you want a lot of time. George was really attentive to all the artists he worked with, but I think there's a limit for everybody. He still had to go off and make his own records and do his own tours... you're not always available to work with the artists."

Like King, Al Steckler feels that when Badfinger left Apple, "it was a big nail in the coffin. George was not happy about it, but none of them ever did anything to keep them on Apple. Their manager was looking for big bucks and Apple just didn't do that... and Badfinger got something like a two million dollar advance from WB for something like six albums. After they signed, Bill Collins came up one day with Peter Ham and told me what the advance was and I figured it out for them. When you deducted the costs of the albums that they had to pay for, deducted Polley's cut [Stan Polley, Badfinger's American business manager] and split the money between Collins and the four guys in the group, it came out to nothing... like $60,000 apiece per album. They really though they were millionaires. They looked at each other and realized that I was right and that it was too late to do anything about it. Peter just had this horrible look on his face. That was the last time I saw Peter. They had a deal with Apple that was unheard of at the time. Apple would pay for all studio costs and the band would get paid from record one. Most record deals at the time made the artists recoup all the costs for the album before they got paid. It was a very, very fair deal."

As Steckler noted, George Harrison was particularly upset when he found out that Badfinger were leaving Apple. In an interview with *Beatlefan*, Joey Molland claimed that Harrison angrily confronted Badfinger manager Bill Collins, asking him, "Why the fuck didn't you tell us, you guys fucked us, after we did all that work for you." Collins told Harrison that the reason Badfinger left Apple was that Badfinger had been unable to talk to Harrison directly and that Klein was unwilling to work out a deal. Like the members of Badfinger, Harrison had assumed that Badfinger would simply re-sign to Apple, and he seemed to be unaware of Klein's actions.

Badfinger's Joey Molland remembers that it was a difficult decision to leave Apple. "We didn't come in and announce that we were leaving the company. It was all done in third person. There was never a time when we were in Apple and said, 'That's it, we're leaving.' The decisions were made by businessmen – by Stan Polley, Bill Collins and Allen Klein. The deal with Warner Brothers was a spectacular record deal. Allen Klein on the other hand wanted to give us nothing. Klein was managing The Beatles – he didn't care about us. There was no one bigger than The Beatles. I think he might have liked us as another badge on his lapel, but The Beatles overshadowed everything for Allen Klein."

With still a year to go on their Apple Records and Publishing contracts, signing to Warner Brothers in the autumn of 1972 could have made for a very uncomfortable environment for Badfinger at Apple, but Molland insists: "We never got a bad vibe from anybody when we left. I think maybe they were a bit puzzled. But when everybody looks back, there really wasn't any other way for Badfinger to react in the situation. We didn't have any options. It wasn't like we could go to Neil and he could sign us. That just wasn't going to happen. Once they handed over the company to Klein – it didn't matter that it was Klein, it could have been anybody – but once the company was handed over to someone else in the business sense, then all of the original relationships that the group had with Apple went out the window."

In the end, the most likely reason that Apple lost Badfinger to Warner Brothers was that Klein had simply botched the deal by misjudging the resolve of the group's management and underestimating the interest that Badfinger had from other labels. Klein gave Badfinger a take it or leave it ultimatum, and Badfinger's management called his bluff. In late 1972, Klein was still working hard to make Apple profitable for The Beatles and he might have simply been attempting to manage costs by getting Badfinger to re-sign to Apple for even less than they were getting under their current deal. It is equally possible that Klein, with less than a year to go on his management contract with Apple, was sensing that his contract would not be renewed and that he intentionally drove Badfinger away from Apple in order to ensure that the label would not succeed without him.

By late 1972, it was not only the Apple artists and staff who were exasperated with having to deal with Allen Klein. Several Apple staff members from this period recall that George Harrison and Ringo Starr also appeared to be growing tired of Klein and Abkco. George Peckham remembers: "Right before Christmas 1972, Nigel Oliver and I went upstairs into Neil Aspinall's old office and designed an 'Abkco Brown Nose of the Year Award'. We always used to catch Malcolm Davies trying to be an Abkco company man, so we thought we'd go after him and also John Mills [Apple Studios engineer]. We made these badges with Abkco on it and put 'Brown Nose of the Year Award' around the edges. We also made this presentation box... we called it a Grummy award.

"So at the Christmas party the whole office was there and we awarded John Mills a Grummy award... it had a plaque on it for not making a fool of himself in public," recalls Peckham. "John Mills threw it in the Thames later that night. It was a great party... Donovan, George Harrison and Nilsson were there. Later that night, I was putting these brown nose badges on Malcolm Davies' back and George caught me. I thought 'Oh shit, I've been caught,' but George pulled one off of Malcolm's back and said, 'Come here, give us some of these, they're great,' and he and Terry Doran put them all over their jackets. Just then, one of Klein's guys, Terry Mellis, comes over and says, 'I don't think this is funny at all,' and George gave him this look and told him 'They're bloody marvelous!'"

Apple would release several more records in the closing months of 1972. Mary Hopkin's once idyllic association with Apple came to an end in November 1972 when Apple released "Those Were The Days," a Mary Hopkin best-of collection. Apple was confident that this album, which contained all of Hopkin's non-LP hits, would be a big hit for the 1972 Christmas season but it failed to chart in either Britain or America. In conjunction with the American release of "Those Were The Days," Apple issued Hopkin's two-year old recording of *Knock Knock, Who's There* as her final Apple single. The song reached number 92 – Hopkin's final appearance on the American pop charts.

Apple did enjoy an unexpected surprise with their December 1972 reissue of the "Phil Spector Christmas Album." The album, which featured Christmas songs recorded by The Ronettes, Darlene Love and other acts, had originally been issued on Spector's Phillies label in 1963 but had been out of print since Spector had shut down Phillies Records in 1966. Al Steckler remembers that, "'The Phil Spector Christmas Album' did very well for us. I brought that album to Apple. I used to go out to the office in California and I saw Phil a lot. One day I said to him 'Phil, it's a shame that the Christmas album isn't out, can we have it for Apple?' and he said 'Sure!' It was as simple as that. I went to Klein and said we wanted to put it out and Klein worked it out with Phil."

To make the album more attractive to the modern music consumer (the original album cover showed the artists – all dressed in suits and dresses – popping out of oversized gift boxes), Apple engaged John Kosh to design a new cover. Kosh remembers Spector to be one of his most unusual subjects. "We shot the Phil Spector Christmas cover in New York. We started in London and I remember I had to meet Phil in the bathroom of his hotel because he was worried about snipers. He was extremely paranoid. He was convinced that someone was trying to assassinate him so we actually had to meet sitting on the bathroom floor. But he was very well behaved at the session."

Since first being hired by Apple in 1969 to work on the book that was included with the initial copies of the "Let It Be" album, Kosh had become Apple's favourite designer. As of September 1970, when Apple contracted Kosh to design the cover to Ringo's "Beaucoups of Blues" album, almost every subsequent Apple album – with the notable exception of the Badfinger albums – had a cover designed by Kosh. He was also responsible for designing most of Apple's press advertisements, including the elaborate eight-page advertisement that Apple took out in the 1972 *Billboard Music Annual*.

For the reissue of the "Phil Spector Christmas Album", Kosh designed a colourful sleeve that was more in line with the times. The album sold well in the United States and especially well in Britain, where it reached number 21 in the charts. This was Apple's highest charting UK album since Mary Hopkin went to number 3 with "Postcard" in 1969.

Like Apple Records, Apple Films also did some brisk business in Britain during Christmas 1972 with their T-Rex film *Born To Boogie*. Released in December, just in time for the school holidays, the film was very popular with Bolan's legion of young fans. While *Born To Boogie* features several exciting music sequences, the overall film is a bit of a mess. Ringo Starr's first outing as a film director was some-what reminiscent of *Magical Mystery Tour*, as it eschewed a coherent story line in favour of disjointed fantasy sequences such as a magic tea party and perplexing scenes of Ringo wearing an animal costume, behaving strangely.

It was the music – which included excellent live footage of T-Rex in concert and a jam session in Apple Studios featuring T-Rex, Ringo Starr and Elton John – that ultimately made *Born To Boogie* a success. Although the film failed to garner much in the way of critical praise, it made money for Apple and it gave Ringo Starr a creative outlet at a time when it was still unclear whether he would be able to sustain a successful solo music career.

8
1973 - The Dream Is Over

Even with the unforeseen exodus of Badfinger and Mary Hopkin in 1972, Apple still appeared to be an active record label in the early months of 1973. George Harrison – the only Beatle other than Ringo Starr who remained interested in the original Apple concept of finding and developing new talent – even considered buying Apple from the other Beatles and re-launching the label. But after Apple lost Badfinger, Harrison realized that he would be better off starting a label from scratch and began making plans to launch an entirely new label of his own.

For the time being, however, Apple continued to issue new records. Apple even signed one final artist in 1973. Early in the year, American singer-guitarist John Beland was touring England as a member of Johnny Tillotson's band, performing on a package tour that featured Tillotson, Bobby Vee and Del Shannon. Beland came to Apple's attention through a demo tape submitted to Tony King. "I recorded this tune out in L.A. called *Banjo Man* and it was kind of like a *New York Mining Disaster* Bee Gees kind of tune. I used a lot of Beatles effects on the drums and it was very sort of Beatles/Bee Geeish," recalls Beland. "Midway through the demo sessions I took the rough tracks with me to England. While we were on tour in England, Johnny [Tillotson] said he really liked what I cut and he said, 'I have this friend over at Apple Records who used to do publicity for me and his name is Tony King. Let me set up an appointment and you can go into London on a day off and see Tony and play him your stuff.' So on my day off I went down to Apple and walked in. I remember that the office was very white and there were a lot of gold records up all over the place. There was beautiful furniture up there in Tony's office but from the outside it was just another little building. I also remember that I was nervous and freaking out because it was The Beatles' label.

"So I went up and played the tape to Tony and he really liked it, so I left him the tape and that was the end of that, and I went back to Birmingham to do the rest of the tour. Then early one morning I got a call and I hear this heavy English accent saying, 'John, it's Ringo here,' and I thought it was one of the guys from our English band pulling my leg, so I said, 'Yeah, uh huh,' and he laughed. Then he said, 'Wake up mate, this is Ringo,' and I made some comment like 'Tell John and George that I said hello,' and he says, 'Wake up mate, it *is* Ringo.' When I realized it was him my hands started to shake because it was the real deal. He said, 'Tony gave me your tape and I really like it. Why don't you come on down and we can talk about you joining the Apple family.' I called my manager Downey [Morton Downey Jr. – who would later become a notorious television talk show host in America in the late eighties] and told him to get over here because The Beatles wanted to sign me to Apple Records. But instead of being happy for me he was real mad because he had already verbally agreed to a deal with Scepter Records. So he got on the plane and the next day Tillotson, Downey and I went down to Apple and signed a deal. It was a really fair deal. There was no advance, strictly recording the album and putting it out. I could go to any EMI studio where I wanted to record and they would pay for it. They seemed to be very pro artist. They had no problem at all with me producing and arranging the whole album. So we signed the deal, we got some pictures taken and then we went out to a private club where The Beatles used to go to. It was a funny label. You didn't expect to be heard one day and actually signed two days later. It happened so fast that I thought someone had spun me through a revolving rock and roll door."

Apple's first release for 1973 in America was a new single by Ringo Starr's other protégé, Chris Hodge, who issued *Goodbye Sweet Lorraine* in January. Presumably because Hodge's *We're On Our Way* had attracted little interest in Britain, the record was only released in the United States and a few European countries. Unlike *We're On Our Way*, however, *Goodbye Sweet Lorraine* failed to garner any significant airplay or sales in America.

Chris Hodge believes that Apple didn't really get behind *Goodbye Sweet Lorraine*, but he also now admits that *Goodbye Sweet Lorraine* was probably not the best follow-up to *We're On Our Way*. "I had a double single deal with Apple," he explains. "They were going to give me an LP deal, but then everything started falling apart at Apple. I should have followed up *We're On Our Way* with another hard rocker and *Goodbye Sweet Lorraine* was more like a laid-back Eagles song, but more spacey of course. But I was 22 and had no manager or anyone to direct me. No one at Apple gave me any real guidance.

"The only people I ever dealt with were Tony King and Ringo Starr and that was it," continues Hodge. "I never met any of the other Apple artists. George, Ringo and Allen Klein signed my contract, I think you needed two Beatles to sign an artist. I popped into Savile Row every once in a while to see Ringo, have some coffee and shoot the shit. I remember Ringo telling me, 'Hey man you got a hit single with a bullet,' and I said, 'If it ain't in the top ten it doesn't mean shit to me,' and he couldn't believe I was so naive. For some reason, I figured that it had to be in the charts. Ringo said, 'No, this is great for a first single.'

All I could think was why wasn't it in the top ten."

The first album to be issued by Apple in 1973 was a two-record set by Ravi Shankar called "Live in 1972". "When the mentor of Ravi Shankar and Ali Akbar Kahn died," explains Al Steckler, "the two of them decided that they wanted to play together as a tribute. I heard about it so I called George and told him that I wanted to record it and he thought it was a great idea and told me to do it. So we recorded it live and George mixed it. That's how things happened. And it sold pretty well, around 40,000 copies. It's a beautiful record."

In Britain, Apple finally got around to releasing Lon and Derrek Van Eaton's "Brother" album in February 1973. The album was followed by the March release of the duo's first UK single, *Warm Woman*. Derrek Van Eaton admits that he has no idea why Apple chose to wait almost a year to release their album in the UK, nor why Apple picked *Warm Woman* to be the British single. *Warm Woman* had been taken from the original demo tape that the Van Eaton brothers had submitted to Apple. It had been recorded in a home studio and as a result, had a lo-fi, murky sound that would have precluded the song from being played on any radio station. Derrek Van Eaton remembers: "Klaus Voormann had wanted *Sun Song* to be the single from the start and there was talk of putting it out, but that never happened."

Shortly after Apple released "Brother" in Britain, it became apparent to the Van Eaton brothers that their future with Apple was at best an uncertain proposition. Derrek Van Eaton recalls: "I remember we had gone ahead and finished "Brother" and George came up to us and said that the Apple thing was breaking up. He said that it wasn't any good and that they wouldn't be able to put the promotion into it anymore. He said, 'I'm going to talk to Richard Perry about you guys because I don't think it's fair that we didn't promote the album like we should have,' and that's how we ended up with Richard. We had been back in New Jersey since coming back from England in December 1971... we never did go back to England after that. After George informed Richard Perry that Apple wasn't going to be able to promote our album, Richard sent us some money and said he'd get something going for us out in L.A. So we drove across the country and the night we drove into L.A. we went right to the studio and played on the session for Ringo's *Photograph* after we had been driving all day."

The collapse of Apple Records essentially came on 31 March 1973, which was the day that Abkco's management contract with The Beatles and Apple expired. As of 1 April, John Lennon, George Harrison and Ringo Starr opted to have their individual managers and Apple assume management of their respective business affairs.

When the Abkco contract was not renewed, Apple found itself having to quickly vacate their office in Abkco's headquarters at 1700 Broadway. May Pang remembers: "We took out Apple and all the paperwork from the Abkco offices and we brought it over to the Dakota and that's where we left it. We never set up another proper Apple office until Tony King went out to L.A." Temporarily without an American office, the displaced Apple Records label listed the New York address of Capitol Records – 1360 Avenue of the Americas – as the new address of Apple Records.

With the Abkco deal expired, Apple's L.A. office was also shut down. "We closed the L.A. Apple office when The Beatles split with Klein," recalls Charlie Nuccio. "I think we kept it open for two or three months as Abkco, but there wasn't enough to sustain it. When Allen was out of the management of the three ex-Beatles, that was the end of the relationship. I never even discussed the possibility of keeping the office open with Apple in London... the contract was over. We knew it was coming. Allen was trying to make it work, he tried to renew it, but I guess they didn't."

Once Klein's contract had expired, little time was wasted in getting Klein's people out of Apple's London office. Tony King recollects: "I sort of remember that Peter Howard and Terry Mellis had to go. And I remember that was a bit of a thing. But because I liked Terry, Peter and Allen, I wasn't one of the gloating committee... there were a certain number of people in the office that didn't mind seeing the back of them, but I wasn't one of them. They were all very good to me. I still have a very good relationship with Allen. Allen is still my friend. Peter and Terry didn't get along with the people in the office, but I liked them."

Reflecting on Allen Klein's stint as manager of The Beatles, Pete Bennett concludes: "It was a good thing, in that they got me to promote them. It was lucky for them because I was in the middle between them and Klein, but I don't think their association with Klein was a good thing for them. In my opinion, Klein was deadwood – it was luck. I think he got himself a fortune without doing anything. They wanted their records to be broken and Klein told them, 'I got Pete Bennett, I got the accounting, and I'll run the whole label and the publishing for 20%.' In 1972, they decided that they wanted to have me run Apple. I said, 'Look, I couldn't do that to Klein, and we'll see what we can do.' They found out that Klein wasn't the guy for them. They found out that Klein wasn't worth 20% – he wasn't even worth 5%. They wanted the promotion, that's all they wanted. They didn't need Klein for that. You don't need an Allen Klein to negotiate a deal for Apple Records with

Capitol. But at the time they signed with Klein, John didn't want to go with the Eastmans because of Paul and the fights that they were having. The Beatles could get any accountant they wanted. That's how John and Lee Eastman explained it to them. The Beatles would have been better off going with Lee Eastman and John Eastman, because they would have had a legal office, an accountant and me to do promotions. I wasn't tied to Klein. They could have hired me independently."

Peter Brown concurs with Bennett's belief that The Beatles and Apple would have been much better off with Lee Eastman. "It would have been a good idea, because the Eastmans have proved now over the years, particularly John Eastman... to have been very successful dealing with artists like Billy Joel, David Bowie... and being a very low-key and reliable attorney, accountant, etc. I think going with the Eastmans would have been a very successful route for The Beatles if they had gone that way. However, there was a problem in that Lee Eastman was a much more dominating figure than his son, John... John Eastman is much quieter about the way he does things, so Lee Eastman was a bit of a problem. But the real problem would have been the fact that Lee Eastman was Paul's father-in-law and the balance would not have been as good as it was. Paul was always the most noticeable of The Beatles and he had the most drive and energy. Also, Paul had built Apple and by the late sixties Paul had become the frontrunner within The Beatles, although John, George and Ringo still regarded The Beatles as John's band."

Reflecting on The Beatles' split with Allen Klein, Tony King claims: "I can't honestly say why the three of them split from Klein. I was so caught up with just doing my job that I didn't get involved with the big problems. Don't forget that by this time all of them had managers. Ringo had Hillary Gerrard, George had Dennis O'Brien and John was really looking after himself with Yoko, but he did have Harold Seider [Allen Klein's ex-attorney]. So everybody had their own representatives so it kind of fragmented off at that time and Klein was given the elbow. 20% was a lot, but at the same time, he renegotiated their contract with EMI. I think the problem with Allen is that he does a good job for people he represents but he does a really good job for himself too."

Al Steckler, who was perhaps the only person who saw the split from the perspective of both Apple and Abkco, notes that throughout 1972 and 1973, "the relationship was slightly eroding... though not with any really visible incidents. Klein had his own agenda, which wasn't always their agenda. I really think what happened was that when the contract was due to be up, George really believed that he could get the group back together. He was more unhappy with Klein than John. I don't really know to what extent Ringo was involved and how important a role he played. I don't think he played a big role. I think in those days, everything had to do with McCartney, John and George. John was struggling with his career, George was starting to struggle with his career. George seriously thought about getting The Beatles back together and I think George realized that he couldn't do that with Allen in the picture. What I recall having heard was that he called Ringo a day or two before the contract was up and said to Ringo, in essence, 'If we're ever going to get together as a group we can't re-sign with Abkco, so let's just not do it.' So Ringo called Klein and that was then end of it. John was very unhappy about the split with Klein. He and Klein had a very good relationship."

Steckler remembers that Klein reacted quickly to the news that Apple would not be renewing his contract, demanding that Apple immediately vacate the Abkco office on 1700 Broadway. "It all had to be out," recalls Steckler. "They had like a week to move out. When it was over, it was over."

Breaking ties with Abkco more or less signalled the end of Apple as an active record label. By April 1973, the only artists that were still under contract were Yoko Ono, Ravi Shankar, Elephant's Memory, David Peel, Chris Hodge, John Beland and Lon and Derrek Van Eton, although George Harrison had already made it clear to Lon and Derrek Van Eaton that they were free to find a new record deal.

Now free of Allen Klein, The Beatles once again turned to Neil Aspinall to take control of Apple. In an interview in *Mojo*, Aspinall explained: "What happened was that John, George and Ringo asked me if I'd run Apple. I said 'OK, but as long as it's OK with Paul,' because I wasn't going to get into any three-on-one situation. I'd always been with the four of them. So I rung up Paul and said, 'Hey, the other three have asked me to do it, is that OK with you?' He said 'Sure, that's fine,' so I was back. I'm working for the four of them... their individual battles might be going on between their individual advisors, if you like, but I was neutral to that."

Apple's first post-Abkco release in the UK was Ravi Shankar's "Live in 1972" double album, which was issued in April 1973. In Britain, the expensive two record set sold even less than it had done in America. So few copies were manufactured that it is now one of the rarest of all of the albums issued by Apple in the United Kingdom.

Both David Peel and Elephant's Memory recorded more material for Apple in early 1973, but no further recordings by either artist were ever issued by Apple. "We did a song called *Amerika* for the sound-track to the film *Please Stand By*, recalls Peel. "Yoko wanted Apple to put out *Amerika* as a single, but because of the problems with Apple, it didn't happen."

On 28 March, 1973, Elephant's Memory went into Media Sound Studios in New York with producer Marty Thau to record a proposed new single for Apple. Even though Apple assigned the resulting song, *Everglade Woman*, a catalogue number and pressed up test copies of the single, it was never released. Still linked to Apple, Elephant's Memory then decided to go over to England to play some shows to support their Apple album.

Rick Frank recalls how, "After the Apple album came out, we did a tour of England... we played the Cavern in Liverpool. We ended up in Wales where we did a spec album at Rockfield Studios in Wales. It ended up coming out on Polydor. Apple gave us no support when we were over there. We had no manager and John was our only manager, and he couldn't leave the country... so it was very difficult to communicate all the things we needed to communicate with Apple. Polydor eventually paid for the recording. Apple never even bothered to drop us... we were actually signed to John and Yoko... so we were free to sign to any label we wanted. I was sort of aware of Apple's problems when we got involved with them, but I was trying to play the optimistic side. But here we were playing with former Beatle John Lennon and we had to make the most of it. And I pushed that aspect of it all the way even though I was very angry at times and I had a problem with Klein, because everyone did who was on Apple at the time... It scared me because this guy didn't want anyone on the label besides the Lennons and Paul."

But the problems that Elephant's Memory and David Peel experienced with Apple may not have only been due to Allen Klein's indifference to any artist who was not an ex-Beatle. May Pang suggests that John Lennon may have simply lost interest in Elephant's Memory and David Peel. "John liked David Peel in the beginning," she recalls, "He thought he was different and very New York. But when John's own political album came out, which was "Sometime In New York City," he couldn't handle that he didn't get a good review. So he withdrew and he didn't record anything for a long time. He was depressed... part of his ego couldn't handle it. So after that he didn't want to hear about the politics. Even Elephant's Memory was too radical for him after a while. John also got upset at David for saying that nothing was done for him. John did a lot for him at Apple. John saw him on TV one day talking about how Apple didn't help him so John got really annoyed and never wanted to speak to him again."

While Elephant's Memory and David Peel were in New York City trying to get some support from Apple, across the ocean Badfinger and former Beatles engineer Chris Thomas went into Manor Studios in Oxford in April to complete the last album that Badfinger owed Apple under their original contract. One of the new songs recorded at the Manor was a Pete Ham composition entitled *Apple Of My Eye*, a bittersweet ballad that perfectly summed up the end of the Apple era and Badfinger's association with the label. According to his friends and band mates, Pete Ham was genuinely sad to leave Apple, as he cherished the family atmosphere he felt at Apple.

Joey Molland explained in a 1991 interview with *Discoveries*: "The words were, 'I'm sorry but it's time for us to go (sic), inside my heart I really want to stay,' and it was really true. We didn't want to go anywhere. Apple treated us well. They paid us on time, they didn't screw us for money. They used all the weight they could to break us, spent loads of money in America promoting the band, with full-page ads, posters and billboards."

Once Badfinger had completed their final Apple album, there was little label-related activity in the Apple office. After none of Apple's early 1973 releases enjoyed any real success, the label started winding down operations. With the exception of Yoko Ono and Ravi Shankar, all of the Apple artists would be released from their contracts by the end of the year.

Unlike the other non-Beatles artists on Apple, Yoko Ono would continue to release records on the label throughout 1973. In Britain, Yoko Ono's *Death Of Samantha* was released in May, but as had all of Ono's previous singles, it failed to stir up any commercial interest.

Pete Bennett maintains: "Apple could have been a full-scale label, but there was too much work with The Beatles. You have to understand what it was like to have four recording artists who owned the label... if they saw new artists breaking like mad and their records weren't breaking, they'd say fuck the other artists. So Apple was never gonna happen. We could have signed a lot of people, but they didn't want to – they didn't give a shit. They had the resources to do it. They never expressed any concerns to me about the other artists not happening. The only one was George who asked me to see if I could get Badfinger a hit, and he sat down with me to discuss Lon and Derrek Van Eaton... but that album didn't have it, but they were nice guys."

May Pang agrees that the former Beatles were generally too involved with their own music and careers to be much concerned with the other artists on Apple. She remembers a discussion she had with

John Lennon about Badfinger, when she told him: "'Don't you realize that we have *Without You*? That's an Apple Publishing song,' and he was like, 'It is?' John was oblivious to a lot of this stuff. For all of them, when they were involved with themselves, they were involved with themselves. The four owners were not going to turn around and say that I'm really interested on a day-to-day basis in somebody else. George Harrison was involved to a certain degree. When he had his first solo album coming out he was very protective about it. After that release he did a lot of production for the other artists like Badfinger and Ravi Shankar so he spent a lot of time at the Apple offices at Savile Row."

The fall-out that enveloped Apple after the collapse of Apple Records eventually also filtered down to Apple Studios. Once it became clear that something was amiss at Apple, many key Apple Studio staff members started to leave the company. In mid-1973, both Geoff Emerick and George Peckham resigned. George Peckham recalls: "The studio staff was pretty stable. Once you started, everyone wanted to stay. There was no reason not to. The Apple Studio had a staff of around twenty... there were a lot of junior tape ops and trainee engineers. I finally left in 1973. I felt I was working very hard but getting nowhere fast. I wanted to update equipment and things like that... and nothing was being done. I was still upset about the "Let It Be" album... on the bloody "Let It Be" album... it says engineer Malcolm Davies... he never even touched the tapes. I did all the edits, all the acetates and the masters and it has his name on it! I said to Malcolm, 'What the fuck is this?' He was like, 'I don't know, it must have been Phil who put that on there.' It made me laugh because Mal was round the pub all the time getting pissed with the lads, and I was busy working away on the records. All that work and then someone else got the credit for the job I did... all these little secrets between Malcolm and Paul... so I decided to go elsewhere."

The departure of Geoff Emerick and George Peckham presumably should have meant an increased work-load for the remaining Apple Studio staff. However, Nigel Oliver remembers that by mid-1973, there was often very little to do at the studio. "After George Peckham left, I was left there with just Malcolm Davies... and he had to cut everything and he didn't like that at all. I used to drop acid and take drugs during sessions. When I started at Apple I was very anti-drug, and Apple used to send me out in a taxi to buy dope for John Lennon. It was a maintenance engineer at Apple, Paul Leighton, who turned me on to drugs. I took acid because I thought, 'Well, The Beatles took it – I should take it.'

"I had done three years as an office boy upstairs," remembers Oliver, "and then I went into the studio around 1972. I set up the tape library with Malcolm Davies. But for the two years after Geoff Emerick left in 1973, Phil McDonald didn't like me very much, so I didn't get any sessions. I just sat in the tape library and did nothing – there was nothing to do. There were three engineers – John Mills, Geoff Emerick and Phil McDonald – and three tape operators, but there was only one studio, so only one pair could be working at any time, the other pair would be doing nothing. The engineers wouldn't have to come in, but the tape operators would have to be there. And we'd just sit around and take LSD and smoke dope and do nothing. It was wild. I had another job for part of the time in a shirt factory because there was absolutely nothing to do. I left in September 1974 because it was just so boring in the end. I had worked for The Beatles for six years."

Ultimately, a decision appeared to have been made by Neil Aspinall and the ex-Beatles to wind down operations and to pull out of any non-Beatles related business. Once this course of action was decided upon, the only Apple project left to complete was the release of Badfinger's final Apple album. Given the success of Badfinger's "Straight Up" album in 1972, Apple expected the new Badfinger album to be a big money-maker for the label. Badfinger's manager Stan Polley and his attorney Walter Hoffer met Neil Aspinall and Bernard Brown on 9 May and tentatively agreed to issue Badfinger's new album, entitled "Ass", in the summer of 1973.

There were several significant legal issues, however, that would complicate plans to issue "Ass" that summer. Due to the fact that Joey Molland had never actually signed a contract with Apple Music Publishing and that Badfinger's business manager Stan Polley was trying to use this issue to bargain for concessions from Apple, it was difficult to establish a definitive release. Since Apple Publishing did not "officially" own the rights to Molland's new songs (Molland had previously assigned Apple Music Publishing the rights to his songs on an album to album basis), Apple needed to be granted the rights to Molland's songs before they could issue a new Badfinger album.

Complicating the negotiations was the fact that Apple was overdue in paying Badfinger £20,000 in back royalties. Due to a receiver having been appointed to oversee Apple's finances as a result of Paul McCartney's 1971 lawsuit, any Apple expenditure – including paying royalties to Apple artists – had to be cleared by the court-appointed receiver. Getting the receiver to release large sums of money was a time consuming effort.

1973 - The Dream Is Over

Apple had every intention of paying Badfinger's royalties, but they were having difficulty getting the funds released from the receiver. During the 9 May meeting with Apple's Brown and Aspinall, Polley negotiated a deal where Molland's songs would be assigned to Apple Publishing if Badfinger's royalties were paid out immediately and if Apple let Badfinger out of their Apple Records and Publishing contracts in May as opposed to the respective July and October termination dates of Badfinger's original agreement with Apple. Aspinall and Brown allegedly agreed to this deal and to a tentative summer release date for "Ass", but they also told Polley that formal approval of the deal would have to come from either John Lennon or George Harrison.

Badfinger's Joey Molland believes that Apple may have even tried to sell the "Ass" album to Warner Brothers. As he noted in an interview with *Good Day Sunshine*, "I think Apple tried to sell us to Warners... I've got an acetate... it's got an Apple on it. It says Badfinger "Ass" and then it says at the top of it Warner Brothers. So, I think a deal was started to be made there. I think Apple made some acetates and sent them to Warners 'cause they knew that Warners was sniffing and Klein wasn't negotiating... maybe they decided, 'What the hell, why don't we just sell the Badfinger product off to Warners and you know, wash our hands of it.' I think maybe that's what happened there. Of course it was never released on Warners... it was released on Apple... at exactly the same time as our first Warners record."

Even though Apple now had little to do with non-Beatles artists such as Badfinger, Tony King claims that Apple remained as busy as ever. "There was always something going on, especially from '73 to '75 because there was all these solo albums: there was "Goodnight Vienna", there was "Ringo", there was "Mind Games", there was the "Rock And Roll" album, there was "Walls And Bridges", there was "Living In The Material World". There was lots and lots going on, especially with John. John kept me really busy. Once I went to America I was always busy doing stuff for John."

Since Apple had lost its L.A. office and staff when the company broke ties with Klein in the spring of 1973, Tony King often found himself having to go to L.A. to oversee Apple business at Capitol. "I moved to America in 1974," he explains. "I had gone over to America in the spring of 1973 to help Capitol put the art together for the "Ringo" album. Capitol was having a lot of problems with getting the artwork together, so they asked if someone from Apple could come out to California to help, so I went out. I was working out of the Capitol tower for three or four weeks and I was just about to go home when John called me up and said, 'I'm coming to L.A. tomorrow, can you hang on because I got an album... and I'd like you to help me put it out.' By this time he had left Yoko and was living with May. He came out with May Pang and brought with him the "Mind Games" album.

"So I started working on the "Mind Games" album – the promotion, fixing John up to do interviews with *Record World* and *Billboard*, getting him out to meet people... getting him to do stuff I thought he should be doing because he hadn't been doing these things. While he had been with Yoko he had been involved with all these semi-subversive activities, which had not given him a great reputation in America. He said to me at the time, 'Look, I've got this album, what do you think I should do?' I said, 'Honestly, you've just got to go out and make a few friends because you've lost a bit of support because you've been involved with things of a controversial nature.' So he said, 'Fine, you organize it, I'll do it,' and he did. At the same time, John started to make an album in Los Angles... the "Rock And Roll" album... and then things got a bit mad. There was a lot of lunacy going on."

King remembers: "One night when we were at the Whiskey A Go Go, John turned to me and told me that he wanted me to come and work in America. I said 'Oh really?' and he said, 'Yeah, I'd like you to come over here and be Apple's person in America. George and Ringo have people in London, but I don't have anybody over here, so I'd like you to come over.' I told him I'd have to think about it. I was kind of undecided about it... but then in the end he kind of persuaded me. At Christmas in 1973, I went to Ringo and George and told them about John's wishes and they were OK with it. I had a lot of fuss and bother getting myself over to America because Capitol was a bit resistant to me being over there all the time and they said, 'We'll only agree to do it if all four Beatles agree,' thinking it would never happen because of Paul's separation from the other three. But I went to Paul and asked if he would help me out with this. He said, 'Yeah, I won't sign anything myself, but I'll get my manager to do it.' So I went out to work for Apple at the Capitol tower in July of 1974."

While Apple's record division may have been scaling back operations in 1973 and 1974, Apple Films – still under the guidance of Ringo Starr – had continued to operate. Throughout 1973, Apple Films had been working on completing several films, including *Son Of Dracula* and *Little Malcolm And His Struggle Against The Eunuchs*.

Little Malcolm was George Harrison's first attempt at being an executive producer of a film. (Harrison would enjoy great success as a film producer in the 1980s and 1990s with his production company, Handmade Films.) The film – starring English actor John Hurt – featured the song *Lonely Man*, written by Mal Evans and Bobby Purvis, a guitarist and songwriter who had come to Evans' attention after Purvis sent a demo tape to Apple in 1971. Purvis later formed a group called Splinter with Bill Elliot, the singer that Apple had hired to provide the lead vocal on John Lennon's *God Save Us* benefit single for *Oz* magazine.

When Elliot and Purvis formed Splinter in August 1972, Mal Evans helped manage the group and it was through Evans that Splinter first came to Harrison's attention. Harrison had been looking for a song to use for the soundtrack of the *Little Malcolm* film and he agreed with Evans that the Splinter song *Lonely Man* would work well. Harrison – aided by Badfinger's Pete Ham – recorded a rough version of *Lonely Man* with Splinter at Apple Studios that was later used for the film's soundtrack.

As Harrison explained to the press when Splinter's debut album was released on Harrison's Dark Horse label in 1974: "While making the film *Little Malcolm And His Struggle Against The Eunuchs*, Big Malcolm Evans materialized with the ideal group song required for a certain part of said film and, thinking it was a potential hit that may help to get the film noticed by the controllers of the film industry, I thought I would try to produce a hit single by Splinter." *Lonely Man* never did become a hit (it was never even issued as a single), although a new Harrison-produced version of the song was a highlight of Splinter's 1975 album, "Harder to Live".

Son Of Dracula was a far more elaborate production than *Little Malcolm*. The feature-length film starred Harry Nilsson (who had no previous acting experience) as a vampire who no longer wanted to be a vampire. In an effort to help get Beatles fans into the theatres, Ringo Starr – who was the film's producer – took a supporting role as Merlin the magician. Keith Moon and Led Zeppelin's John Bonham were also given bit parts in the film. Starr, who is said to have disliked having the responsibility associated with producing a movie, allegedly had great difficulty completing the film. Harry Nilsson later claimed that copious alcohol consumption on and off the set greatly slowed progress on the film, although he noted that he, Ringo Starr and Mal Evans took great pleasure in going out to London clubs at night while still in costume.

With the exception of the Apple Films projects, by the end of 1973 Apple had wound up most of its non-Beatles activities and was now ready to focus on getting several ongoing Beatles-related business issues settled. In November 1973, Apple began its first suit against Allen Klein for "mismanagement". Named as plaintiffs in the suit against Allen Klein were John Lennon, George Harrison and Ringo

Starr as well as the British companies Apple Publishing; Apple Films; Subafilms; Harrisongs; Startling Music; Python Music; Singsong Music; and Ono Music. The American companies involved in the suit were Apple Records Inc. of New York; Apple Records Inc. of California; Apple Music Publishing Co Inc.; Apple Films Inc.; and Apple Music Inc.

In between initiating a lawsuit against Allen Klein and fending off threatened legal action from Badfinger's management, Apple released its final Yoko Ono album "Feeling The Space" and its accompanying single *Run Run Run* in November 1973. Although John Lennon was now living in L.A. with May Pang, he was still apparently very committed to Yoko Ono and her "art". Many of Apple's remaining staff assumed that once Lennon had shifted his affections to May Pang, that would be the end of Yoko Ono's career as an Apple Records artist. It came as quite a surprise that not only was Apple issuing Ono's "Feeling the Space" album, but that they were also giving it quite a push in the American market.

Tony King explains: "John absolutely adored Yoko. He respected her and thought she was a great lady. When he split up with Yoko, he said to me, 'I want you to go to the Dakota when you are in New York and I want you to meet Yoko, she's a great lady.' It was a great love. She's a rather remarkable person. If John laughed at Yoko, it would have been in a sweet rather than malicious way. John used to laugh at her a lot. When I first got to know her, I used to say to John 'God, she's such a funny character,' and he'd say, 'I know, tell me about it.' They were fabulous together. John had a nice time with May too, but Yoko was his great love."

Shortly after issuing Ono's "Feeling The Space", Apple's American operation finally released Badfinger's "Ass" album on 26 November 1973. "Ass" was the final non-Beatles album to be issued on the Apple label in America. Badfinger's new single *Apple Of My Eye* would be released a few weeks later on 17 December.

Ever since the initial meeting between Neil Aspinall, Bernard Brown and Badfinger manager Stan Polley in March, the release of "Ass" had been delayed due to intense wrangling on the part of Badfinger's management. Having been originally scheduled for release in America during the first week of September 1973, the album was pushed back until November after Polley boldly requested that Apple assign the rights to the "Ass" album to Warner Brothers. Polley was allegedly frustrated by not being able to get at the Badfinger royalties that Apple was holding, yet the only reason that Apple was holding on to Badfinger's royalties was that it was difficult for Apple to get the receiver to clear the payment. Apple attorney David Braun had informed Polley of this problem and even suggested that Apple could take out a loan to pay Badfinger, but Polley was unwilling to give Apple the time needed to get a loan together.

Apple and Capitol finally grew tired of Polley's wrangling and issued "Ass" without officially securing the mechanical licence rights to Joey Molland's songs. To protect themselves legally, Apple simply credited the songs to "Badfinger" instead of the individual writers. Since Badfinger were under contact to Apple Publishing, it would now be difficult for Polley to sue Apple. Polley, however, was not deterred by Apple's clever move and the company that he controlled, Badfinger Enterprises, sued Apple in New York City District Court on 5 December for copyright infringement.

Ultimately, all the legal action was of little consequence after "Ass" failed to get into the top 100 of the American charts. The relative commercial failure of "Ass" was especially surprising considering that the last Badfinger album that Apple had released a mere year and a half earlier had made the top forty and had spawned several hit singles. But with little incentive to further develop Badfinger's career and no longer having access to a seasoned promotions staff, Apple did little to promote the "Ass" album. Without Pete Bennett in their corner, Apple found out that it was very hard to get records played on American radio. And by the time Apple made that discovery, it no longer really mattered.

In retrospect, the poor commercial performance of "Ass" was not surprising. It had been almost two years since Badfinger had had a hit in America and few pop groups from that era were able to return to the charts after a two-year absence. "Ass" was also a very different record than the previous Badfinger albums. On "Ass", the majority of the songs were written by Joey Molland, rather than Pete Ham, who had composed all of Badfinger's hits except for *Come And Get It*. While "Ass" was a good album, it was clearly not as commercial as either "No Dice" or "Straight Up". Due to rivalries within the group, there were only two Pete Ham songs featured on the album, and even Ham's *Apple Of My Eye* – arguably the finest song on "Ass" – was not in the same league as Badfinger hits like *No Matter What* and *Day After Day*. In fact, the most distinctive feature of "Ass" was its cover, which at first glance appeared to represent a bitter attack on Apple.

The striking cover painting depicts a donkey wearing headphones looking up at a giant hand extending a gleaming carrot from out of the clouds. Joey Molland refutes that the group had any intention to slight Apple, insisting that the cover was their view of the music business in general. "We were the donkey," he explains. "The group was the ass being tempted. It wasn't about Apple or Warner Brothers – it was about the business. There was never any intention to brand Apple as some sort of business assholes. It wasn't a malicious feeling. We were very pleased to be associated with Apple and loved the people there dearly. Apple wasn't a bad thing at all. It was a great thing. At the bottom of it all, everybody wanted Apple to be a perfectly normal place of business and they got damn close to achieving that."

The release of Badfinger's "Ass" album marked the end of Apple's existence as a record label and all of the other remaining Apple acts were officially cut free from Apple that December. Chris Hodge clearly remembers how, "On my birthday, 22 December 1973, I got a letter from Apple saying that The Beatles' company was making changes or coming to a close and that they were going to release me from the second part of my contract and that I was free to find another record deal. I was surprised, because I had no idea that Apple was in trouble." Released from his Apple contract, Hodge went on to record singles for both RCA and DJM Records, before emigrating to America to work in the film industry.

John Beland, who had been signed to Apple only months earlier, claims that he was never informed by either Ringo Starr or Tony King that there were problems at Apple. Upon completing the tour of England with Johnny Tillotson's band, Beland recalls that he immediately returned to America to start recording his debut album for Apple. "I went back to America with my contract in my hand and I did the string session for *Banjo Man*... it was an Apple session," he recalls. "And then Downey called me and said that he had got a telegram from Tony King saying that because of litigation, everything at Apple was frozen. I was devastated... I had told all my friends in Hollywood. Apple said they would put out the album once the litigation was over or we could have our contract back and take the tracks with us, which is just what we did. I had no idea that Apple was in trouble. Downey was able to go back to New York and salvage his deal with Scepter who eventually released the album."

9
1974 - 1975:
All Things Must Pass

By 1974, Apple Records and its fifteen person staff was basically acting as a management, album production and accounting office for Lennon, Harrison and Starr. Acknowledging that Apple's time had passed, George Harrison announced the formation of his own label, Dark Horse, in May 1974. One of Dark Horse's first releases would be Ravi Shankar's "Shankar Family And Friends" – an album that Harrison had produced in April 1973, and initially planned for release on Apple.

Former Apple artist Bill Elliot's band Splinter was also signed to Dark Horse and their George Harrison produced album "The Place I Love" would be released on Harrison's new label in September. Curiously, Splinter's album did not include *Lonely Man*, the Mal Evans composition that Splinter recorded for the Apple Film *Little Malcolm*. While Splinter's album was not a big commercial success, it did spawn a top 20 British single, *Costafine Town*, a gentle, melodic pop song that evoked the work of the then-successful pop band, America.

By early 1974, the curtain was also finally coming down on Apple Films, whose *Son Of Dracula* was premiered in Atlanta, Georgia on 19 April. The film was a critical and commercial disaster and Apple Films became once again dormant after *Son Of Dracula* failed to gain national distribution. The soundtrack album – which was issued on the "Rapple" label (presumably a joint venture between Apple and Nilsson's label, RCA) – was also a commercial flop.

The other Apple Films project, *Little Malcolm*, fared even worse than *Son Of Dracula*. After being shown at several international film festivals and garnering significant critical praise, the film seemed to vanish from the face of the earth and it has not appeared in cinemas or on video since 1974.

In March, Apple Records issued its final non-Beatles releases in Britain, which were Badfinger's "Ass" album and the *Apple Of My Eye* single. Seven years after The Iveys had helped launch Apple, it was fitting that they had the honour of being the final artists – excluding the ex-Beatles – to release a record on the Apple label. But even during the best of times, Badfinger's records had not sold particularly well in Britain. Now given almost no promotion by Apple, neither record was able to make a dent on the British charts and Apple Records effectively disappeared once the Badfinger records had been shipped to the record shops.

The lack of any tangible promotion on the part of Apple may have been due in part to the ongoing suit against Apple by Badfinger's management. Ironically, Badfinger's claim against Apple would be resolved in June when the court ordered that Joey Molland was indeed bound by Badfinger's 1968 Apple Music Publishing contract. The court also ruled that Apple was required to pay Badfinger their back royalties within two weeks of the settlement, which gave Apple's receiver a justifiable reason to release the frozen funds.

With the resolution of the Badfinger litigation, Neil Aspinall assumed that Apple would now be free from having to deal with any non-Beatles business, but he was surprised to receive a call from Badfinger members Tom Evans and Joey Molland shortly after the settlement. Molland and Evans told Aspinall that Badfinger had started to suspect that their manager, Stan Polley, was embezzling money from the group.

Evans and Molland were concerned that the Apple royalties that Aspinall had recently paid were in danger of being stolen by Polley. Due to Badfinger's tangled business affairs, the group would be powerless to stop the loss of their royalties unless they were able to keep Polley away from the money. Desperate to avoid losing any more money to their management, Molland and Evans pleaded with Aspinall to have Apple hold on to Badfinger's publishing and record royalties until the group was free from their manager. A sympathetic Aspinall agreed to their request and Apple cancelled the cheque and awaited further instruction from Badfinger.

While the release of Badfinger's "Ass" appeared to mark the end of Apple as a label for anything other than records by the ex-Beatles, Apple Records did contemplate several new record projects in 1974. The first was a planned double album compilation that would feature highlights from Apple's first five years. Though a track listing was compiled, no album was ever released. The second project was a fifth Apple album by Yoko Ono. Ono did indeed record a fifth album for Apple at the Record Plant Studios in New York City in 1974, but the album was not issued until 1992, when it appeared as part of a Yoko Ono box set.

With Bernard Brown and Tony King able to handle any work associated with the solo albums that the ex-Beatles still issued on Apple, Neil Aspinall was able to devote a good deal of his time to trying to broker a deal that would end The Beatles' partnership. Once Lennon, Harrison, Starr and Apple had terminated their relationship with Allen

Klein, Paul McCartney's lawyers were finally able to make some progress in negotiating an agreement that would end the partnership. Since 1971, all of the royalties that were earned by the four ex-Beatles were put into a joint account that was managed by the court-appointed receiver. Their royalties would continue to be put into that account until the ex-Beatles were able to come to a mutually acceptable agreement.

An agreement was finally reached in November and McCartney, Harrison and Lennon were scheduled to meet – either on 19 or 20 December – at a hotel in New York City after a George Harrison concert at Madison Square Garden. (Starr was trying to avoid being served with court papers by Allen Klein, so he arranged to sign the agreement in London.) When the time came to get together to sign the agreement, however, John Lennon apparently had second thoughts at the last moment and failed to show up. May Pang remembers that Lennon, "got so freaked out he locked himself in the room. I called up Yoko and asked her, 'What should I do?' Finally, he opened the door and he was in tears... he was in bits. He was afraid that he would be responsible for paying so much money in taxes to the United States. A lot of people don't realize that they were paper rich and cash poor. John was nervous to be liable for one or two million dollars worth of tax... he was freaked out. He didn't want to be left poor."

While the agreement was considered to be fair to all parties, it would require Lennon – who had lived in the United States since 1971 – to personally pay approximately one million dollars in taxes to the United States. Another issue was that in the course of the three years that Lennon and Yoko Ono had lived in America, they had charged close to two million dollars worth of personal expenses to Apple. The other Beatles rightly thought it unfair for them to have to pay for those expenses, especially those incurred from recording Yoko Ono solo albums. While Lennon acknowledged the expenses, he found it difficult to agree to getting less out of the settlement than his three former partners. In her book, *Loving John*, May Pang also suggests that Lennon's reluctance to sign the agreement may have also had something to do with Lennon's realization that signing the agreement would mean the official end of The Beatles – and more significantly, that Paul McCartney had won once again.

Lennon did meet with Lee Eastman a few days later to try to make some changes to the agreement, but little came of the discussions and there would be no agreement signed in 1974.

By early 1975, the Apple staff knew that it was only a matter of time before the company would cease to exist. While Apple was still involved with coordinating the releases of solo albums by the former Beatles, no new non-Beatles music was coming out of Apple and there was less to do with each passing week. When Dee Meehan (who had joined Apple Publishing as a secretary in 1967 when Apple was still at Baker Street) left the company to have a baby, Neil Aspinall was left as the sole remaining staff member to have been with Apple since its inception in 1967.

Since the down-sized Apple had plenty of unused space in its massive office at 54 St. James Street, Ringo Starr had started operating a new record label, Ring'O Records, out of the Apple offices. Following Harrison's lead, Starr had elected to start an entirely new label, rather than try to revive Apple Records.

No one at Apple really had any idea of what was going to happen in the coming months, although the end of the company seemed to come one step closer when, in January 1975, John Lennon finally signed the agreement to end The Beatles' partnership. May Pang believes that it was Paul McCartney who finally convinced Lennon to sign the agreement. "When John didn't sign the agreement, Paul called up and said, 'OK, we're brothers, I'm here, what is it that we can do to work this out?' Paul jumped in."

Lennon's signature on the agreement may have meant that the ex-Beatles were legally free from the Apple partnership and were no longer required to put their individual royalties into a shared Apple account, but they still remained co-owners of Apple, which would – for the time being – remain open to administer their joint interests and to work on resolving several lawsuits that all four ex-Beatles had an interest in settling.

In the wake of the legal dissolution of The Beatles' partnership, Apple lingered for a few more months before the announcement was made on 6 May that Apple Records was ceasing operations. Neil Aspinall planned to retain a small staff of some half a dozen employees to assist with accounting and legal work, but apart from that small group of business affairs staff, all of the remaining Apple employees were let go by the end of the month.

Bernard Brown, Apple's General Manager of Records and Publishing, left the company at the end of May, explaining to *Billboard*: "To me and other people, this was inevitable. Now that The Beatles have gone their own way and have their own set-ups, what future was there for Apple? There was no point in keeping the organization going at its present level."

Tony King remembers that as late as 1975, the general public still considered Apple to be an ongoing concern. "We used to get an endless amount of tapes. I remember once when we did this thing in the newspaper about looking for new artists that we had so many people coming around to the building and so many phone calls that the switchboard girl lost her voice after three days. This was around 1970 and 1971. Towards the end we would still get tapes and such, but nothing ever came of it. To be honest, Apple was all a bit amateurish. I don't know if the music business at the time was as business-like as it is today. It was more of a family affair at that time. It was part business and part family and people were signed because people liked them and stuff like that. It would be quite different if it was around today. I mean nobody would sign The Sundown Playboys today... they would say what a joke, there's no album behind it... it was done on a whim. That's what the joy of it all was and that's what Apple represented. And when Apple closed its doors, it was the last of all that really. It was rather a wonderful thing. I must say I'm rather proud of my association with Apple and I'm particularly proud of The Sundown Playboys. I was very proud to be involved with putting out something that was completely out of the ordinary and bringing people's attention to a sort of music that people hadn't heard of over here. It was a real thrill and I think Apple at that time represented that to a lot of people. It couldn't exist like that now."

While it was a sound business decision for Apple to shut down its record division, the decision to close down Apple Studios was more surprising. Since 1972, Apple Studios had been constantly busy and had developed a strong, highly respected staff, even after the departure of key personnel in 1973. Apple Studios was making money for Apple, yet in the end, Apple simply cancelled any remaining projects that had booked studio time, locked the doors, and walked away from 3 Savile Row. After announcing the shutdown, Apple seemed to have no immediate plans for the future of the studio. Interviewed in *Billboard*, Studio Manager Malcolm Davies admitted: "It's going into mothballs as far as I know... and I only hope that the facilities and the reputation that we built up do not go to waste."

Given that the punk revolution would sweep through the British music scene in little more than a year, it was fitting that the final act to record an album at Apple Studios was Kilburn and the Highroads. The "Kilburns" were a "pub rock" band led by Ian Dury, who would later top the British charts as a solo artist with songs like *Sex And Drugs And Rock And Roll* and *Hit Me With Your Rhythm Stick*. Although the album that they recorded with producer Tony Ashton for the Warner Brothers subsidiary Raft Records was completed, it was not released until after Ian Dury became a star in 1978.

Badfinger had also been among the final acts to record at Apple Studios, returning to 3 Savile Row in December 1974 to record a third album for Warner Brothers. Despite there being a feeling at Apple that Badfinger had deserted the label, few of Apple's staff blamed them for leaving and they were pleased to hear that Badfinger were recording at Savile Row. Even after the group had left Apple for Warner Brothers, most of the Apple staff remained quite fond of Badfinger and it came as a horrible shock to everyone at Apple when Badfinger leader Pete Ham committed suicide in April.

May Pang, who spent a week in Apple's London office in April, met Pete Ham and Tom Evans a few days before Ham's death. "I was always Badfinger's biggest supporter because they were good people," she recalls. "So I called them up when I was in London. I remember that Tommy said, 'Oh my God, I can't believe you would talk to us,' and I said, 'Why? We're friends,' and he replied, 'Well, you know, you're kind of famous.' I felt that they had a very low self-esteem just by saying that to me. So I offered to take them out to dinner. I asked them to please meet me at Apple, and that was the first time they had set foot in Apple since they split. Laurie McCaffrey said to me later that she didn't realize that it was Pete who came with Tommy... they looked different, especially Pete. Their look of worry changed their look. Everyone was surprised to see them. I guess I was the only one who brought them in. I know that Tommy and Pete enjoyed the visit and everyone who knew them was genuinely happy to see them."

Paul McCartney, who received news of Ham's suicide while he was in L.A. finishing his "Venus and Mars" album claimed that, "It upset me because he was so good. It was one of those horrible things where you think, 'What if... what if I called him a week ago? Would that maybe have stopped him doing it?' You always wonder."

Having already released two unsuccessful Badfinger albums and now involved in their own management-related litigation with Badfinger, Warner Brothers decided not to release the album Badfinger recorded at Apple Studios. Their decision not to release "Head First" was surprising, given that Badfinger had many allies at Warner Brothers. Since 1970, Warner Brothers' London office had become home for many former Apple employees and artists. Soon after leaving Apple, Derek Taylor became Director of Special Projects at Warners. Ron Kass later joined Taylor, coming over to be Manager of the Warners London office. In addition to Badfinger, both James Taylor and Jackie Lomax were also signed to the Warner Brothers label.

Despite the fact that the albums that Badfinger and Kilburn and the Highroads had recorded at Apple Studios would remain unreleased for many years, there was never any shortage of artists wanting to record there. Apple Studios could have remained a lucrative investment for the ex-Beatles, but given the complex legal problems that haunted the former Beatles and Apple, Apple presumably thought it best to be involved with as few activities as possible so they made no plans to re-open or even sell the studio.

Tony King feels that there came a point when the ex-Beatles simply wanted to be free of Apple. "I think John was quite relieved when Apple was shut down," he says. "I think that everyone was quite relieved at the time. I don't remember anyone being particularly upset about it. It was a bit of a headache that was got rid of. By the time Apple closed its doors I was only involved with Ringo and George. When Apple closed their doors I got paid off... they gave me my Mercedes and some money... and then I went to work for Elton John at Rocket Records. Apple to me was the turning point in my career... it was a fabulous time for me. I loved working for Apple. Probably some of the happiest years of my life were spent working at Apple."

Since the downsized Apple organization no longer needed a large office, the company moved across the street to a smaller office at 29-30 St. James Street. Occupying a simple front office on the second floor of the unassuming building, Aspinall and the remaining Apple staff put their past behind them and focused on looking after the affairs of Lennon, Harrison and Starr and re-structuring the Apple organization to operate in a world without Beatles.

Though Apple Records had "officially" ceased operations, Apple would continue to coordinate the production and promotion of solo albums by Lennon, Harrison and Starr until the expiry of The Beatles' contract with EMI and Capitol. Since the ex-Beatles were signed to EMI until February 1976, the Apple imprint would be kept alive until that time.

In October 1975, Apple released a John Lennon greatest hits collection called "Shaved Fish" and George Harrison's "Extra Texture" album. "Extra Texture" was the last album of new music to be released on the Apple label. Having worked so hard to keep Apple viable in the early 1970s, Harrison seemed to be the only Beatle to give much attention to Apple's passing. To signify the end of Apple, the label on Harrison's album featured an Apple that had been eaten to the core.

In addition to those two albums, Apple also finally released John Lennon's *Imagine* as a single in Britain, where it effortlessly found its way into the top 10. In December, Ringo Starr's "Blast From The Past" – a belated greatest hits collection – became the final album to be released on the Apple label.

10
Apple After Apple

Once Apple closed the office on 54 St. James Street, the company seemed to be quickly forgotten by both the music press and the majority of British record buyers. When two final Apple singles were issued in the UK in early 1976, both records received little press coverage and few copies of either record were sold. The first single, released in January, was Ringo Starr's *Oh My My* – a three-year old, disco-friendly track taken from his 1973 "Ringo" album. It was soon followed by George Harrison's *This Guitar Can't Keep From Crying*, a gloomy song lifted from Harrison's poorly-received "Extra Texture" album. Given scant promotion by either Apple or EMI, the singles did little more than mark the fact that the Apple label had indeed reached the end of the line. From that point on, all future pressings of Beatles albums and the solo records by the ex-Beatles that had originally appeared with Apple labels reverted to Parlophone/EMI in the UK and Capitol in the United States. More significantly, Apple's entire catalogue of non-Beatles recordings was deleted around this time. Although Apple's business affairs had become increasingly tangled since splitting with Klein in 1973, it was an unusual and arguably quite unnecessary step for Apple to delete its entire catalogue. It is likely that the Apple albums of James Taylor, Billy Preston and Badfinger probably would have continued to sell respectable quantities if Apple had bothered to work out a deal with Capitol/EMI to keep them in print.

To outside observers, it appeared that Apple simply wanted to get totally out of the music business. From a business perspective, 1976 turned out to be a particularly good year for the Apple label to cease operations. Given that disco and punk were shaping up to be the sound of the late-seventies, it is unlikely that Apple – had it continued – would have been able to keep up with the changing musical tastes of the decade. By ceasing to operate as a record label, Apple was spared from becoming a decrepit, inconsequential relic of the sixties and it would not be relegated to coasting on the past glories and increasingly hard-to-market talents of middle-aged musicians who had once been members of the greatest rock group the world had ever seen.

Of course, the decision to shut down Apple as a record label had been made long before 1976. Paul McCartney had already signed a new solo deal with EMI and Capitol Records in 1975 and George Harrison had signed his new label, Dark Horse, to A&M Records the same year. With McCartney and Harrison signed to other labels, only John Lennon and Ringo Starr were free to continue on Apple should either of them have elected to keep Apple operating as a label.

But John Lennon had no intention to sign with any label after the expiration of The Beatles' Capitol/EMI contract in 1976. Withdrawing from the music business to raise his new son, Sean, Lennon would not record again until 1980. As for Ringo Starr, even though he had been fairly successful with his 1974 album "Goodnight Vienna", his subsequent records would prove to be a commercial liability to both Atlantic and Polydor to whom he signed after his Apple deal had expired.

The mid-seventies were a difficult time for the musical careers of the ex-Beatles. George Harrison continued to possess some of the commercial lustre he had experienced in the early seventies, although sales of his 1976 album "33 and 1/3" would be far more modest than any of his previous releases. Harrison's new label, Dark Horse, was also experiencing significant troubles. The main act on the label, Splinter, had been unable to follow-up the minor success of their debut single, *Costafine Town*. Worse still, in the space of three years, none of the albums released by Dark Horse artists – including the American rock band Jiva, the R&B band Stairsteps, former Wings guitarist Henry McCulloch, Ravi Shankar, or Attitudes (a band featuring session men Jim Keltner, David Foster and Danny Kootch) managed to crack the top 100. Harrison would allow the label to limp on for another year before finally letting go of all the Dark Horse artists (other than himself) in 1977.

Ringo Starr's Ring'O Records label would fare even worse than Dark Horse. During the three years that the company existed, Ring'O would issue an odd collection of records that ranged from an album of recording engineer David Hentschel interpreting the entire "Ringo" album on synthesizer, to a reissue of John Tavener's Apple album "The Whale". The only artist of merit to sign to Ring'O was Graham Bonnet who – while never scoring a hit for Ring'O – went on to join Rainbow and have several solo hits in the eighties. Starr eventually gave up on the label and shut it down in December 1978, explaining to journalist John Blake that, "If you don't sell records then it costs you money. You have to look at it straight and say, 'What's going on?' and you either turn it around or you do as I did yet again [and say] that it is time for it to end."

Paul McCartney was the only former Beatle who seemed to have kept pace with the music scene of the seventies. Whether undertaking a massive tour of American stadiums, or serving up catchy disco-pop hits like *Silly Love Songs*, McCartney seemed to have retained his Beatles-era ability to give the public exactly what they wanted. As a result, his career thrived as his former partners struggled to come to terms with the changing musical tastes of the seventies. McCartney also proved to be far more adept as a businessman than his former colleagues. After disassociating himself from Apple in 1969, McCartney pursued his interest in music publishing and started building an impressive catalogue of music copyrights. His publishing company, MPL, is now among the largest and most successful independent music publishing companies in the world.

Unlike McCartney, many of the Apple people found it difficult to fully make the transition from the sixties to the new decade. Erstwhile Apple executive Mal Evans was one such person, and by the mid-seventies, he was becoming increasingly lost without Apple or The Beatles in his life. Since 1963, Evans had served The Beatles on what amounted to a 24-hour a day, seven days a week basis. After The Beatles split in 1970, Evans had kept busy helping out at the recording sessions of Lennon, Harrison and Starr, as well as assisting with various projects at Apple. But as Apple wound up operations and there was little work to be had at what was left of the company, Evans relocated to Los Angeles where he hoped to find work as a record producer.

In Los Angeles, Evans had been involved in an unsuccessful attempt to produce a solo album by The Who's Keith Moon. Relieved of his production duties by Moon's label, MCA, Evans spent the final months of 1975 working on demo tapes for a group called Natural Gas, a new band formed by former Badfinger guitarist Joey Molland. Reunited with Molland for the first time since 1970 and finding the band receptive to his production ideas, Evans was in good spirits and he was – by all accounts – looking forward to starting work on Natural Gas's debut album on 5 January 1976.

During the demo sessions he produced for Natural Gas, Evans seemed to be the same old "Mal" that Joey Molland had known in 1970, yet many of Evans' friends from this period claim that he often seemed depressed. Evans' troubled emotional state finally caught up with him on the night of 4 January 1976, when officers of the Los Angeles Police Department were summoned to a rented duplex at 8122 West 4th Street that the 40 year-old Evans shared with his girlfriend, Fran Hughes, and her young child from a previous relationship. Evans had allegedly been drinking heavily, and in an alcohol-fuelled stupor, had been wandering around the apartment, yelling and waving an air rifle. Frightened by Evans' erratic behavior, Hughes called the police to request help. When the officers arrived at the scene, they broke down the door, saw Evans standing in the middle of the room holding a gun, and they fired – instantly ending the life of Mal Evans in a hail of bullets.

Harry Nilsson – who received a call from Fran Hughes within hours of the shooting – later told *Record Collector* journalist Ken Sharp that he had to go down to the L.A. jail to get Hughes out of jail (she was supposedly being "held" as a material witness) while his wife and another friend went to clean the apartment. The cleaning job was presumably not done to the satisfaction of the owner of the building, who later presented Hughes with a bill to cover the cost of cleaning the carpet in the room. Hughes promptly sent the bill to Apple. Peter Brown claims that Neil Aspinall refused to pay.

The ex-Beatles were stunned and reportedly very shaken by Evans' death, although that didn't stop John Lennon from making a final joke at the expense of his old friend. After learning that Evans' cremated remains had been lost in the mail while being shipped back to England, Lennon is alleged to have suggested that Mal had probably ended up in the dead letter office. Harry Nilsson later confirmed this was exactly what had happened.

As Nilsson related to Ken Sharp, it was his idea to cremate Evans, as it would cost less for his family to ship his remains back to England. Nilsson then sent Evans' ashes to Apple, only to receive a call from Neil Aspinall a few days later, telling him that Evans' distraught mother and wife had come to Apple to collect Mal's ashes but that the ashes had never arrived. A trace was hastily put on the package and the ashes eventually turned up at an airport, where – according to Nilsson – they had actually been found in the dead letter office.

The death of Mal Evans was only one of several links to Apple's past that were severed during 1976. In October, Apple finally sold its former headquarters at 3 Savile Row. Due to the poor condition of the building after Apple's attempted "renovations", the once stately townhouse would remain empty for the next five years. Ringo Starr paid final tribute to the Apple era when he put a photo of the graffiti-scrawled door of the abandoned Savile Row building on the back cover of his 1976 album, "Rotogravure".

Given that the ex-Beatles were no longer contractually tied together, many of their former associates were surprised when the group did not formally dissolve Apple in 1976. It appears that even though the individual ex-Beatles were no longer forced to pool all of their earnings into one central company, they grudgingly realized that Apple could actually serve a vital purpose of looking after their shared business interests. Despite Paul McCartney having spent a good deal of time and money in the early seventies trying to completely extract himself from Apple, as the tensions associated with The Beatles break-up began to subside it became apparent that a single organization was in a much better position to look after The Beatles' legacy than four individual companies.

Accordingly, from 1977 onwards, Apple – which was now little more than Neil Aspinall, a small accounts office headed by long time Apple accountant Brian Cappociama, and a battery of lawyers on both sides of the Atlantic – reconfigured itself to be the sole caretaker of The Beatles image and to represent The Beatles in ongoing lawsuits with Capitol/EMI, Allen Klein and any other party that they deemed to be a threat to The Beatles' legacy. "There was a lot going on," claimed Aspinall in an interview with *Mojo* magazine. "First of all, when I started running Apple again there was still the internal lawsuits between Paul and the other three. The second thing that had to be done was Allen Klein. That lawsuit with him had to be dealt with. After that, I was looking at various contractual commitments. Trying to sort out the legalities of what was going on with our record company, that took from '78 to '89. Sorting out what happened with *Yellow Submarine*. What happened to those 39 cartoons that had been made? What was the deal? There was a lot of stuff. So the hiatus period was really pulling as many strings together as you could, so we had an idea what was going on. A lot of it was establishing what you owned and what you didn't own."

One thing that Apple was certain that they didn't own was the royalties that they had been holding on behalf of Badfinger since 1974. Three years after agreeing to temporarily hold on to Badfinger's royalties until the group could get their managerial difficulties sorted out, Apple was becoming uncomfortable with holding on to this increasingly large sum of money. In 1977, Apple went to court to have the money turned over to a court-appointed receiver. The court complied with Apple's request and from then on, Apple paid Badfinger's publishing royalties directly into a court supervised account and would do so until Badfinger managed to reach an agreement on how to divide the royalties in September 1985.

Sadly, the agreement on how to divide the Apple royalties would come too late for Badfinger's Tom Evans, who hanged himself on 19 November 1983. Evans, who seemed to have never fully recovered from the shock of Pete Ham's suicide in 1975, had allegedly been despondent over career setbacks and frustrated by not being able to get his share of the Apple royalties.

Apple also spent many hours in court trying to resolve their dispute with Allen Klein. In October 1977, Apple finally settled with Klein, paying the former Beatles manager $4.5 million to settle his claim, which had been whittled down from the original $63 million that Klein had originally claimed he was owed for the work he did on behalf of Apple. But Klein's good fortune was bittersweet at best. In April 1977, the United States Internal Revenue Service had indicted Allen Klein on tax evasion charges. Working with information provided by former Apple/Abkco promotion man Pete Bennett – who himself had been indicted on 6 December 1976 – the Internal Revenue Service found that Klein was guilty of selling close to a quarter of a million dollars worth of records by The Beatles and several unnamed Apple artists without disclosing the sales to the United States tax authorities.

For a three-year period between 1970 and 1972, Klein had apparently instructed Capitol Records to send promotional copies of Apple albums directly to Abkco, requesting the albums not to be marked as promotional goods. Klein then had one of his Abkco employees sell the albums to record stores and distributors in the New York area as new product. Since Klein had received the records at manufacturing cost, he made a considerable amount of money from selling the records at wholesale prices to record stores. In the course of their investigation into Klein's business dealings, the Internal Revenue Service concluded that through the illegal sale of promotional records, Klein had earned $118,22.43 in 1970, $55,045.80 in 1971 and $42,974.38 in 1972.

In addition to falling foul of United States tax laws, Klein had also deprived Apple of sales of approximately 84,000 albums. Had these records been sold through legitimate means, they would have certainly helped secure stronger chart performances for the albums. While Klein's actions had deprived Apple Records of more than a quarter of a million dollars in potential revenue, Apple received no compensation from Klein as part of the court action, other than the satisfaction of knowing that Klein was to spend several months in jail as part of his sentence. Though sentenced in 1978, Klein would not serve his jail term until 1980.

After settling with Klein, the company appeared to drift into an extended period of limited activity. Aspinall kept himself busy sorting out the details of ancient contracts and endless legal disputes, yet he also had enough time on his hands to enable him to attempt to launch a second career in artist management. Working with John Gilbert – the former manager of the English rock band, Family – Aspinall set up a management company called G&A Productions in 1977.

The company's principle artist was Charlie Ainley, a competent though somewhat undistinguished vocalist who had enjoyed minor notoriety during the brief "pub rock" craze that swept through London in 1974 and 1975. Aspinall used his decade-old business relationship with Nat Weiss to secure Ainley a contract with Weiss' Nemperor Records label and two of Ainley's albums were eventually issued on Nemperor. From a commercial perspective, neither album did particularly well and Aspinall soon gave up pursuing a career in artist management and returned to devoting his full attention to Apple.

11
Apple In The Eighties

By the early eighties, there were few traces of Apple left to be found – it had been effectively transformed into what was little more than a holding company. Even the old Apple building had changed beyond recognition. When the new owners of 3 Savile Row took over the building, it was so close to collapsing that it was necessary to gut the entire inside of the building and assemble a new interior. On a nostalgic visit back to 3 Savile Row in the early eighties, Derek Taylor had a look around the newly remodelled building and was saddened to find that the building's once grand interior bore almost no resemblance to how it had looked during the Apple years.

Since divesting itself of Apple Records and the studio operation, Apple had evolved into an anonymous office, handling contractual matters, initiating lawsuits with increasing efficiency, and doing whatever it could to keep out of the limelight. Due to a decreased workload, by 1980 Apple had been pared down to Aspinall and approximately three staff members. Few visitors – including the company's owners – ventured into Apple's second floor office on St. James Street.

One unexpected but very welcome visitor to the office was Derek Taylor, who spent the afternoon of 11 December 1980 ensconced in the office with Aspinall, talking about the past and fielding the many phone calls that were being made to the usually quiet Apple office. On this cold, sunny day, it was like 1969 all over again, with Taylor and Aspinall discussing The Beatles and attending to Apple business, except this time John Lennon was dead and the two old friends were trying to make sense of Lennon's murder in New York City the previous evening. And for a brief moment later that day, Taylor was once again asked to serve as Apple's press officer, advising George Harrison on the wording and tone of Harrison's press statement about Lennon's death.

Apart from the profound personal loss experienced by the three surviving Beatles, Lennon's death would dramatically change the make-up of Apple. It could not have been long before the three remaining Beatles realized that Yoko Ono was now an equal partner in Apple Corps. Considering the tension and ill-will that had existed between the three Beatles and Ono in the sixties, becoming business partners with her would certainly be a challenge. But Ono's elevation to partner status did not turn out to be as dramatic as it could have been, given that Ono had represented Lennon on Apple business ever since he had elected to stay at home and raise the couple's son, Sean. In fact, Ono had proved to be an astute businessperson and she was generally (if perhaps grudgingly) regarded as an asset to the Apple board.

Ono's assumption of partner status at Apple seemed to have had little impact on Apple's day-to-day activities. After Lennon's death, Aspinall and Apple's lawyers resumed their vigilant watch over The Beatles' empire and continued to work towards reaching a settlement with Capitol and EMI. Curiously, one of Apple's most significant legal matters of 1981 had nothing to do with Capitol Records or even The Beatles, but rather with the Apple name itself.

In the early eighties, it had come to Apple's attention that an American computer company in California had been trading under the name "Apple Computers" for several years. Once Apple became aware of the existence of Apple Computers, Apple's lawyers took immediate action to protect the trademark that Apple had held since 1968. A settlement was quickly reached, where Apple Computers paid Apple an estimated several million dollars (the terms of the agreement were never publicly disclosed) and agreed not to use the Apple name to manufacture computers capable of making music. In exchange, they would be allowed to share the "Apple" name.

With the Apple name safely secured, little was then heard from Apple until 1983, when the company left the St. James Street office they had occupied since 1975 to move to new offices at 48 Charles Street. Like the St. James Street office, Apple's new location on Charles Street was a far cry from the elegant office at Savile Row.

Former Apple artist Pat Savant of The Sundown Playboys remembers visiting Apple in the early eighties. "The first time I visited England was in June of 1983 and I went to Apple Records when they had this small insignificant office on Charles Street. I talked to Neil Aspinall's secretary, Chris. I just wanted to talk to Neil, that's all. I went back three or four times and she kept saying that he was out and the last time she said that he was on vacation. I guess I shouldn't have been as forward, but I said, 'Before you can go on vacation you should work first,' and she got a big laugh out of that. I never was able to make contact with him."

Although Aspinall probably was on holiday when Savant visited the new Apple office in 1983, he would spend a significant time away from the Apple office after reportedly suffering a heart attack in December 1983. While Aspinall ultimately recovered to the extent that he could resume his duties as head of Apple, his heart attack was a further striking reminder to Aspinall and the three remaining Beatles that they were no longer invincible young men.

Once recovered, Aspinall generally kept a low profile and little was heard from Apple for the next few years. It was during this time that several members of Apple's management team from the sixties began formulating an ambitious plan to re-launch the Apple Records label. Former Apple Records head Ron Kass had long felt that Apple could have and should have been a viable record label, had it not been for Allen Klein. Perhaps in an attempt to reclaim past glories, or maybe simply just to give Apple Records the chance he felt it deserved, he contacted former members of Apple's 1968-69 management team in early 1986 to discuss the possibility of a re-launch.

Ken Mansfield remembers: "Ron Kass called me in Nashville where I was living at the time and told me that he had just got back from London and asked, 'If we put Apple back together, would you come back?' We'd had some conversations in London about putting Apple together. We wouldn't reconstruct the label, but we'd re-do Apple with the original people. He said what he wanted to do was to not have The Beatles fund it, but rather fund it through someone else. I had a friend, Ted Solomon, who was a big financier and he committed ten million dollars to the venture. So Ron, Ted and I went to London and met Neil Aspinall and Tony Bramwell and Kass had already talked to Ringo and George about it. He thought it could happen as long as The Beatles didn't have to dip into their own pockets again. Ron had even made the concession that Apple's home office could be in Nashville Tennessee, because I had had my fill of New York and L.A. When we got back from London we all had specific tasks we had to do," recalls Mansfield, "but I suddenly couldn't get a hold of Ron Kass. While we were in London, we had noticed that Ron Kass seemed unwell. When he got back to the States, he went to the doctor, found out he had colon cancer and died six months later." With the death of Ron Kass, the idea of re-launching Apple seemed to slip quietly by the wayside for the next several years.

Having spent most of the eighties in relative obscurity, Apple suddenly found itself back in the headlines in February 1989 when they were once again lined up in court against the now-giant Apple Computers, arguing that Apple Computers had violated the terms of its 1981 agreement with Apple. In less than a decade since the original trademark sharing agreement was forged between the two Apples, Apple Computer's simple desktop computers had evolved into powerful machines that could be used to create sophisticated music via their midi capabilities. Apple's case against Apple Computers – which has since become somewhat of a benchmark case for trademark law – would require significant legal and business resources from Apple. Fortunately for Apple, just as they were launching their lawsuit against

Apple Computers, they finally managed to reach an out-of-court settlement in their long-standing dispute with Capitol Records.

The settlement – which paved the way for the original Beatles albums to finally be issued on CD – granted Apple complete creative control over The Beatles' catalogue. Capitol would also be required to add the Apple logo to all of The Beatles' albums, as well as the reissued 1970-1975 solo albums by John Lennon, George Harrison and Ringo Starr. Finally, Capitol also agreed to a comprehensive reissue program of the non-Beatles' catalogue of Apple albums. Unlike Ron Kass' fanciful vision of re-launching the Apple label by re-issuing the back catalogue and signing new artists to Apple, the Capitol agreement would focus solely on reissuing the original Apple albums that had been out of print for more than a decade.

The resolution of the Capitol suit set the stage for a new burst of activity from Apple. Perhaps in anticipation, Apple moved their offices from the Charles Street location to new offices at 6 Stratton Street.

12
The Nineties And Beyond : Apple's Back

While no "new" Apple products came out in 1990, it was a busy year for Apple as the company worked on several new projects that were scheduled for 1991. In preparation for the impending reissue series of original Apple albums, Apple began searching through their tape and photo archives to find unreleased photos and music to be utilized for the reissue series, while engineers at Abbey Road began dusting off and re-mixing tapes of albums that had been sitting on Apple's shelves since the early seventies. Aspinall even brought Derek Taylor back to Apple to create a press kit for the reissue series and to write the liner notes for the reissued version of George Harrison's "Wonderwall" album. Apple appeared to be fully committed to developing a high quality reissue series, and as Taylor optimistically noted in an interview that came with the press kit he created, "It's about progress and a little bit of respect for the past... no money spared on it... just make a good job on it. And it will sell!"

The reissue series was finally launched in September 1991, when Apple Records issued its first "new" product since 1974. The inaugural release was a four-song vinyl and CD single (released only in Britain) that featured a track each by Badfinger, Mary Hopkin, Billy Preston and Jackie Lomax.

At the same time, the company also reactivated Apple Films to develop and produce a documentary film about The Beatles' first visit to America in February 1964. Completed in early 1991, the first new Apple Films project since 1974 was a video called *The Beatles First US Visit*.

In addition to reviving Apple Films, Apple also set up an entirely new subsidiary company called Apple Productions for the sole purpose of producing a definitive video history of The Beatles. The project – which was ultimately dubbed "Anthology" – was essentially an update of the *Long And Winding Road* film that Neil Aspinall had originally compiled in 1970 and 1971. Since there was little free space at Apple's Stratton Street office, Apple Productions set up shop in a run-down residential neighbourhood of London and soon employed eleven people, including producer "Chips" Chipperfield, director Geoff Wonfor and writer Bob Smeaton.

1991 proved to be not only a very busy year for Apple, but also a highly lucrative year for the company on the legal front. On 11

October, Apple's London attorney, Gordon Pollock, announced to a high court judge that, after 116 days in court, Apple Music had reached an "amicable" out-of-court settlement with Apple Computers. While the terms were once again secret, it is generally thought that Apple Computers agreed to pay Apple Music somewhere between 29 and 30 million dollars for the right to continue to use the Apple name on their computers.

Apple appeared to be on a roll, and a month after the resolution of the Apple Computers trademark action, Apple Records reissued five long out-of-print Apple albums on CD. (All of the reissues would also be released on vinyl and cassette.) The November 1991 releases included Billy Preston's "That's The Way God Planned It", Jackie Lomax's "Is This What You Want", Badfinger's "Magic Christian Music", Mary Hopkin's "Postcard" and James Taylor's self-titled Apple album.

While there were certainly a few thousand people around the world who were delighted to finally get Jackie Lomax's 1969 album on CD, there were a few questions raised about the timing and motivation behind Apple's decision to reissue the original Apple albums. Although it has never been officially confirmed, it has been suggested that Apple reissued the Apple Records catalogue primarily to prove ongoing international usage of the famous Apple logo and trademark as part of their dispute with Apple computers. Capitol's limited promotion of the Apple reissue series – which consisted of a single poster proclaiming "Apple's Back!" and a handful of Apple tracks being featured on a Capitol Records sampler – certainly does lend some support to this theory.

The Apple reissue campaign would continue throughout 1993, culminating with the long awaited release of Badfinger's "Straight Up" album on CD. Later that same year, Badfinger would add hundreds of thousands of dollars to the Apple coffers once again when red-hot pop vocalist Mariah Carey's internationally successful remake of *Without You* became one of the biggest selling records of the decade. Although profits from the song were now shared with Warner Brothers Music Publishing – the company that Apple had assigned to administer the Apple Music Publishing catalogue – Apple earned an enormous sum of money from Carey's hit rendition of the 1970 Badfinger song.

Having essentially re-entered the record business via the reissue series of the non-Beatles Apple albums, Apple soon started to give serious consideration to issuing new albums of previously unreleased Beatles recordings. Granted full creative control of The Beatles' EMI recordings as a condition of the 1989 settlement of their suit against

Capitol, Apple was now free to develop albums comprised of archive Beatles material. While all four ex-Beatles had long maintained that there was little music of merit that remained unreleased, Apple would prove them wrong by releasing no less than four albums of previously unreleased Beatles music between 1994 and 1997. The first album of unreleased Beatles recordings (discounting "Live At The Hollywood Bowl" which had been issued by EMI in 1977) was a two-disc set entitled "Beatles At The Beeb". The album comprised various Beatles performances that had been taped for BBC Radio between 1962 and 1966 featuring The Beatles performing many songs that had never been officially released by the group. Issued in November 1994, "Beatles At The Beeb" quickly sold over three million copies in America and nine million copies worldwide.

In the midst of coordinating several different record projects and overseeing the completion of *Anthology*, Apple somehow also managed to find the time to move into new offices. The new Apple building – an impressive four-storey townhouse at 27 Ovington Square – is the largest office that Apple has occupied since 1975 and it is also home to George Harrison's Harrisongs music publishing company.

Keeping true to a tradition that was established when Apple left Savile Row in 1972, Apple strives to draw as little attention as possible to their office. The only indication of Apple's presence in Ovington Square is a hand-lettered note over the front doorbell that says "Apple". The interior of the building, however, is an entirely different matter.

Writer Robert Sandall, who was given an audience with Neil Aspinall (though curiously not allowed to tape the conversation) for a 1996 profile on Apple in the English *Arena* magazine, suggested that Apple's new office reflected the company's re-emergence as a music and entertainment company. "Concert posters line a foyer wall that leads into the office, with its two storey wall of gold and platinum records and its reception area dominated by Richard Avedon's 1968 psychedelic portraits... The odd thing about the place, though, is the noise. There isn't any.

"Aside from the discreet chirruping of phones, Apple feels almost deserted. Apple today is a reluctant employer. On the two days a week that he's in the office, Derek Taylor spreads his papers over the table in the ground floor boardroom. There is a small phone-answering, photocopying, coffee making secretariat which includes Ringo's son Jason."

Sandall's article was one of the first published accounts of life at Apple since the early seventies, and several similar interviews soon followed. Given Aspinall's celebrated reclusive nature, the music press were perplexed by the sudden accessibility of Neil Aspinall and Apple. But as soon as journalists sat down to speak with Aspinall in his second floor office in the Ovington Square building, it was clear that Apple had big plans for 1995 and that the company was willing to do whatever was necessary to gear up the publicity machine.

Apple's first project for the year was the release of the long-awaited greatest hits album by Badfinger, the first "new" album to be issued by Apple Records in almost two decades. The album was issued in May 1995 and became Apple's best selling non-Beatles release since the reissue of Badfinger's "Straight Up". Along with the Badfinger collection, Apple also released an updated version of "Those Were The Days" – a collection of Mary Hopkin singles that had originally been released in 1972. While "Those Were The Days" was released in the UK at the same time as the Badfinger album, for reasons unknown Apple and Capitol did not issue Hopkin's album in the United States.

To promote the albums in the UK, Apple bought ads in several British music magazines that showed the covers of both albums under a cryptic headline that could have be lifted straight from the original Apple advertisements of the late sixties. The ad copy – almost certainly written by Derek Taylor – simply stated: "The stars are so big, the earth is so small, stay as you are." Whether or not this ad stimulated sales of the Badfinger or Mary Hopkin albums is open to debate, yet its appearance represented a welcome, albeit small, return to form for Apple.

The release of the Badfinger and Mary Hopkin CDs, however, was insignificant when compared to Apple's big project for 1995: *Anthology* – the definitive film history of The Beatles that Apple Productions had been working on since 1991. The first stage of the *Anthology* project would be the international release of the film, which would be broadcast over several nights as a "mini-series". Although Apple had originally envisaged *Anthology* as a home video, they wisely changed their mind and elected to sell the worldwide broadcast rights for the series.

In America, the ABC television network bought the rights for nearly $20 million, while in England, ITV outbid the BBC with an offer of almost £5 million. And to the surprise of many television industry insiders who thought that the series could not generate enough interest and capture the amount of viewers needed to justify such an outlay, ABC announced that almost all of the advertising time for *Anthology* had sold within days of being offered.

Starting on the evening of Sunday 19 November, *Anthology* was broadcast for over three nights and it touched off a mini wave of Beatlemania. Reacquainting old fans with the group and introducing the band to a new generation of music buyers, *Anthology* was an unequivocal creative and marketing triumph. Featuring pristine versions of rarely seen films and promo clips, *Anthology* was indeed the definitive history of The Beatles. The only real criticism of the film was that it tended to gloss over the more difficult periods of the group's career, instead offering a fairly sanitized version of The Beatles story.

Due to the tendency of *Anthology* to gloss over anything that made Yoko Ono or the three surviving Beatles uncomfortable (as the owners of Apple, they had final say over what made it into the finished product and what remained on the cutting room floor), the story of Apple was downplayed in the film. The Apple era was represented by a brief montage of filmed performances by The Iveys, James Taylor, Jackie Lomax, Badfinger and Mary Hopkin, followed by some perfunctory remarks by Aspinall and the ex-Beatles. Many former Apple employees were surprised at how easily Apple was dismissed in *Anthology*. After viewing the film, former Apple Records President Jack Oliver remarked: "It was a real downer. I felt let down by the *Anthology* video. I liked the first one, it was quite good, but when they got to the Apple years, basically they skipped most of it. I was sort of depressed when it was over... I never felt that when I was there. It never felt as depressing as they depicted. A lot of people say how bad it was, but it wasn't that bad. I think it was pretty crazy, but it wasn't overly crazy. Everybody was having a good time working and you weren't supposed to have a good time working. We sort of invented having a good time and having a job at the same time."

Fortunately for fans, while The Beatles may have elected to keep certain elements of the group's history "off limits", they were less inhibited about sharing their music. As a result of The Beatles' decision to fully open the vaults, *Anthology* featured a bounty of rare music that ranged from The Beatles' 1958 recording of Buddy Holly's *That'll Be The Day*, to *What's The New Mary Jane*, a meandering, drug-inspired "song" from 1968 that Lennon had recorded with the assistance of George Harrison, Yoko Ono and Mal Evans.

As was expected, a critical component of the *Anthology* campaign would be the corresponding "Anthology" albums that would accompany the film. The project ultimately spawned three albums worth of previously unreleased tracks, alternative versions and a host of live recordings. On 21 November, Capitol/Apple released the first two-CD set in the "Anthology" series. It entered the American charts at number 1 and stayed there for three weeks – a very impressive feat for an album by a group that had split up over 25 years ago.

The entire Anthology campaign was a critical and commercial triumph and by late 1995 and into 1996, The Beatles were once again on the covers of countless magazines, were regularly featured on television and were even back on top 40 radio. In January 1996, Apple Records released the "new" Beatles single *Free As A Bird* (which featured the three surviving Beatles playing along to one of John Lennon's unreleased demos from 1977) and it quickly became a substantial hit in both Britain and the United States. In addition to being the first "new" Beatles single to be released since 1970, *Free as A Bird* was significant in that it was the first Beatles single to be actually owned by the members of the group.

While all of The Beatles records and solo efforts by the individual ex-Beatles that were issued between 1968 and 1976 may have appeared with an Apple label, the actual recordings were, and still are, fully owned by Capitol and EMI. But since Lennon was no longer under contract to EMI when he wrote *Free As A Bird* in 1977 and given that both Harrison and Starr were without record contracts in 1996, ownership of the song was retained by the Lennon Estate, Harrison, Starr and Paul McCartney. It made perfect sense for The Beatles to license the rights to *Free As A Bird* to Capitol and EMI via Apple Records. Paul McCartney was still under contract to Capitol, but one key element of the deal that he signed with the label in 1975 was that he was to retain ownership of all his recordings, which he then licenses back to Capitol and EMI.

As previously noted, the *Anthology* project was a marketing triumph. Looking to augment the extensive distribution of the record, television and home video components of *Anthology*, Apple also ventured into merchandising by launching a mail-order clothing line, called Apple Organics. Operated in conjunction with EMI Merchandising, Apple Organics offered a collection of Beatles hats, backpacks and several shirts with an Apple logo. All of the products offered were manufactured from environmentally friendly organic fibres and order forms for the products were included in every "Anthology" album.

The final stage of the campaign was launched on 5 September 1996, when Apple released the *Anthology* video set, which consisted of eight videos packaged together in a custom sleeve. Despite the fact that many consumers had taped the *Anthology* series at home, it quickly became one of the best-selling home videos of the year.

So by 1997 – close to thirty years since The Beatles launched the company – Apple was once again active and thriving. Like its four owners, Apple had travelled a long and winding road since its inception. However, even at this late date, a number of familiar faces from the old days could still be found at the Apple office. Neil Aspinall was still in charge of the entire Apple organization, and Apple's loyal accountant, Brian Cappociama, was a fixture in the accounts department. Even Derek Taylor was back at Apple, coming into London from his Surrey home once a week to work on a number of different projects. As Taylor explained to *Request* magazine in 1997, the new Apple, "certainly isn't the philanthropic organization it was in the late sixties, but in some surreal way it does quite resemble the sixties again..." with The Beatles, "all back together again, making decisions in the same room."

Sadly, just as the activity at Apple was reaching fever pitch with the *Anthology* campaign, Derek Taylor was hospitalized for cancer surgery in March 1996. While Taylor made a modest recovery and was able to contribute to the ongoing publicity campaign, he relapsed in early 1997 and died on 7 September 1997.

In some ways, Taylor's death appeared to mark the end of Apple's brief rebirth. For many former Apple employees and Beatles fans, Derek Taylor encapsulated the true spirit of Apple. His wit, intense sincerity and warmth seemed to touch everyone who met him, and more than any other Apple employee, Taylor was a true champion of the Apple dream. In the press handout that accompanied the first wave of reissued Apple albums, Taylor wrote: "...and in a wonderful loop of time suspended, the Apple singles and albums are newly out and about and we find ourselves again approving the same artwork and liner notes and worrying anew in case we aren't honouring our old pledges to give everyone their best shot... so, really, these are the days."

Since Taylor's passing, "these are the days" seems to have relapsed into "those were the days". Apple has since suspended the reissue schedule of the Apple catalogue and many of the reissued Apple titles are once again out of print. With Taylor no longer Apple's spokesperson, little more than product now emerges from Apple's Ovington Square office. Paul McCartney's longtime publicist Geoff Baker is now usually quoted as "Apple spokesman," but the genial, somewhat anonymous Baker has little of the style and panache that made Derek Taylor such an ideal Apple spokesperson.

The Beatles music, however, remains as powerful as ever. When Apple and EMI issued "1" (a collection of The Beatles' number 1 singles) in 2000, the album topped the charts around the world and became one of the best selling albums of the year.

So what remains of Apple? Following the November 2001 death of

George Harrison, Apple is poised to enter yet another period of transition. Even before his death, Harrison appeared to be distancing himself from Apple. When Harrison's "All Things Must Pass" album was reissued in early 2001, the Apple logo and "Produced by George Harrison and Phil Spector for Apple Records" credit that had adorned the original album and CD reissue were strangely absent from the new packaging, replaced by a mysterious logo for "GN Records".

Only time will tell what role Apple will play in the future plans of the surviving Beatles. Until then, it will presumably be business as usual, despite the significant changes that have taken place in recent years. More than three decades since Apple burst out of the summer of love and onto the world's stage, two of the company's original owners are dead, and the Apple offices are quiet and no longer filled with young, enthusiastic employees working for the most famous young men in the world. There is no more talk of changing the system, finding new talent or getting Apple artists on *Top of the Pops*. Indeed, the only goal of Apple's small staff is to make sure that The Beatles' legacy is handled with some degree of dignity, and to earn the two surviving Beatles and the Lennon and Harrison estates their rightful rewards.

And that is exactly what Neil Aspinall will do until the day he dies – probably still behind his desk at Apple.

Apple UK Discography:

UK Singles

Aug	1968:	Apple 1 - Not Issued
Aug	1968:	The Beatles - Hey Jude/Revolution - R 5722
Aug	1968:	Mary Hopkin - Those Were the Days/Turn Turn Turn - Apple 2
Sep	1968:	Jackie Lomax - Sour Milk Sea/The Eagle Laughs At You - Apple 3
Sep	1968:	Black Dyke Mills Band - Thingumybob/ Yellow Submarine - Apple 4
Nov	1968:	The Iveys - Maybe Tomorrow/And Her Daddy's A Millionaire - Apple 5
Jan	1969:	Trash - Road To Nowhere/Illusions - Apple 6
Jan	1969:	Brute Force - The King Of Fuh/Nobody Knows - Apple 8
Mar	1969:	Apple 9 - Not Issued
Mar	1969:	Mary Hopkin - Goodbye/Sparrow - Apple 10
Apr	1969:	The Beatles with Billy Preston - Get Back/ Don't Let Me Down - R 5777
Apr	1969:	Jackie Lomax - New Day/I Fall Inside Your Eyes - Apple 11
May	1969:	The Beatles - The Ballad Of John & Yoko/ Old Brown Shoe - R 5786
June	1969:	Billy Preston - That's The Way God Planned It/ What About You - Apple 12
July	1969:	Plastic Ono Band - Give Peace A Chance/Remember - Apple 13
July	1969:	The Iveys - Dear Angie/No Escaping Your Love Apple 14 (Europe & Japan only)
July	1969:	Various - Wall's Ice Cream - Promotional EP (contains tracks by James Taylor, Jackie Lomax, The Iveys & Mary Hopkin) - CT 1
Aug	1969:	Radha Krishna Temple - Hare Krishna Mantra/ Prayer To The Spiritual Masters - Apple 15
Aug	1969:	Mary Hopkin - Que Sera Sera/ Fields Of St. Etienne - Apple 16
Oct	1969:	Trash - Golden Slumbers - Carry That Weight/ Trashcan - Apple 17
Oct	1969:	Hot Chocolate Band - Give Peace a Chance/ Living Without Tomorrow - Apple 18
Oct	1969:	Billy Preston - Everything's Alright/ I Want To Thank You - Apple 19

Oct 1969:   Plastic Ono Band - Cold Turkey/Don't Worry Kyoko -
            Apples 1001
Oct 1969:   The Beatles - Something/Come Together - R 5814
Dec 1969:   Badfinger - Come And Get It/Rock Of Ages - Apple 20
Dec 1969:   Plastic Ono Band - You Know My Name
            (Look Up The Number)/What's The New Mary Jane -
            Apples 1002 (Not issued)
Jan 1970:   Billy Preston - All That I've Got/As I Get Older -
            Apple 21
Jan 1970:   Mary Hopkin - Temma Harbour/Lontano Dagli Occhi
            - Apple 22
Feb 1970:   Jackie Lomax - How The Web Was Woven/
            Thumbin' A Ride - Apple 23
Feb 1970:   Doris Troy - Ain't That Cute/Vaya Con Dios - Apple 24
Feb 1970:   Lennon/Ono/Plastic Ono Band - Instant Karma/
            Who Has Seen The Wind? - Apples 1003
Mar 1970:   Radha Krishna Temple - Govinda/Govinda Jai Jai -
            Apple 25
Mar 1970:   The Beatles - Let It Be/You Know My Name
            (Look Up The Number) - R 5833
Mar 1970:   Mary Hopkin - Knock Knock, Who's There?/
            I'm Going To Fall In Love Again - Apple 26
Summer 1970: Apple 27 - Not Issued
Aug 1970:   Doris Troy - Jacob's Ladder/Get Back - Apple 28
Summer 1970: Billy Preston - My Sweet Lord/
            Long As I Got My Baby - Apple 29 (Not Issued)
Oct 1970:   Mary Hopkin - Think About Your Children/Heritage -
            Apple 30
Nov 1970:   Badfinger - No Matter What/Better Days - Apple 31
Nov 1970:   James Taylor - Carolina On My Mind/
            Something's Wrong - Apple 32
Jan 1971:   George Harrison - My Sweet Lord/What Is Life? -
            R 5884
Feb 1971:   Paul McCartney - Another Day/
            Oh Woman, Oh Why? - R 5889
Mar 1971:   John Lennon/Plastic Ono Band -
            Power To The People/Open Your Box - R 5892
Apr 1971:   Ringo Starr - It Don't Come Easy/Early 1970 - R 5898
Apr 1971:   Ronnie Spector - Try Some, Buy Some/
            Tandoori Chicken - Apple 33
Spring 1971: Badfinger - Name Of The Game/Suitcase -
            Apple 35 (Not Issued)

June 1971:	Mary Hopkin - Let My Name Be Sorrow/
	Kew Gardens - Apple 34
July 1971:	Bill Elliot & Elastic Oz Band - God Save Us/
	Do the Oz - Apple 36
July 1971:	George Harrison - Bangla Desh/Deep Blue - R5912
July 1971:	Paul & Linda McCartney - Back Seat Of My Car/
	Heart Of The Country - R 5914
Aug 1971:	Ravi Shankar - Joi Bangla/Oh Bhaugowan/
	Raga Mishra And Chorus - Jhinjhoti - Apple 37
Oct 1971:	Yoko Ono - Mrs. Lennon/Midsummer In New York -
	Apple 38
Dec 1971:	Mary Hopkin - Water, Paper And Clay/Jefferson -
	Apple 39
Jan 1972:	Badfinger - Day After Day/Sweet Tuesday Morning -
	Apple 40
Jan 1972:	Yoko Ono - Mind Train/Listen, The Snow Is Falling -
	Apple 41
Spring 1972:	Badfinger - Baby Blue/Flying - Apple 43 (Not Issued)
Feb 1972:	Wings - Give Ireland Back To The Irish/(version) -
	R 5936
Mar 1972:	Ringo Starr - Back Off Boogaloo/Blindman - R 5944
Mar 1972:	Wings - Mary Had A Little Lamb/
	Little Woman Love - R 5949
June 1972:	Chris Hodge - We're On Our Way/Supersoul -
	Apple 43
Nov 1972:	Sundown Playboys - Saturday Night Special/
	Valse De Soleil Coucher - Apple 44
Nov 1972:	John & Yoko - Happy Xmas (War Is Over) /
	Listen, The Snow Is Falling - R 5970
Dec 1972:	Wings - Hi, Hi, Hi/C Moon - R 5973
Dec 1972:	Elephant's Memory - Power Boogie/
	Liberation Special - Apple 45
Mar 1973:	Lon and Derrek Van Eaton - Warm Woman/
	More Than Words - Apple 46
Mar 1973:	Paul McCartney - My Love/The Mess - R 5985
May 1973:	Yoko Ono - Death Of Samantha/Yang Yang - Apple 47
May 1973:	George Harrison - Give Me Love/Miss O'Dell -
	R 5988
June 1973:	Wings - Live And Let Die/I Lie Around - R 5987
Oct 1973:	Ringo Starr - Photograph/Down And Out - R 5992
Oct 1973:	Paul McCartney/Wings - Helen Wheels/
	Country Dreamer - R 5993

Nov 1973:   Yoko Ono - Run Run Run/Men Men Men - Apple 48
Nov 1973:   John Lennon - Mind Games/Meat City - R 5994
Feb   1974:   Ringo Starr - You're Sixteen/Devil Woman - R 5995
Feb   1974:   Paul McCartney/Wings - Jet/Let Me Roll It - R 5996
Mar 1974:   Badfinger - Apple of My Eye/Blind Owl - Apple 49
June 1974:   Paul McCartney/Wings - Band On The Run/
              Zoo Gang - R 5997
Oct   1974:   John Lennon - Whatever Gets You Thru' The
              Night/Beef Jerky - R 5998
Oct   1974:   Paul McCartney/Wings - Junior's Farm/Sally G -
              R 5999
Nov 1974:   Ringo Starr - Only You/Call me - R 6000
Dec 1974:   George Harrison - Ding Dong, Ding Dong/
              I Don't Care Anymore - R 6002
Jan   1975:   John Lennon - No. 9 Dream/What You Got - R 6003
Feb   1975:   Ringo Starr - Snookeroo/Oo-Wee - R 6004
Feb   1975:   George Harrison - Dark Horse/Hari's On Tour - R 6001
Apr   1975:   John Lennon - Stand By Me/Move Over Mrs. L -
              R 6005
Sep   1975:   George Harrison - You/World Of Stone - R 6007
Oct   1975:   John Lennon - Imagine/Working Class Hero - R 6009
Jan   1976:   Ringo Starr - Oh My My/No No Song - R 6011
Feb   1976:   George Harrison - This Guitar/Maya Love - R 6012

UK LPs
Nov 1968:   George Harrison - Wonderwall Music - (S)APCOR1
Nov 1968:   The Beatles - The Beatles (White album) -
              PCS7067/8 PMC7067/8
Nov 1968:   John Lennon and Yoko Ono - Unfinished Music No. 1,
              Two Virgins - (S)APCOR2
Dec 1968:   James Taylor - James Taylor - (S)APCOR3
Dec 1968:   Modern Jazz Quartet - Under The Jasmine Tree -
              (S)APCOR4
Jan   1969:   The Beatles - Yellow Submarine - PCS7070 PMC7070
Feb   1969:   Mary Hopkin - Postcard - (S)APCOR5
Mar 1969:   Jackie Lomax - Is This What You Want - (S)APCOR6
May 1969:   John Lennon and Yoko Ono - Unfinished Music No 2,
              Life With The Lions - ZAPPLE01
May 1969:   George Harrison - Electronic Sound - ZAPPLE02
May 1969:   Delaney and Bonnie - Delaney and Bonnie -
              SAPCOR7 (Apple copies were pressed without album
              covers – but this record was withdrawn and later
              issued on Elektra as "Accept No Substitute")

July	1969:	The Iveys - Maybe Tomorrow - SAPCOR8 (UK Copies probably never pressed, but the LP received limited distribution in Europe (Germany and Italy) and Japan)
Aug	1969:	Billy Preston - That's the Way God Planned It - SAPCOR9
Sep	1969:	The Beatles - Abbey Road - PCS7088
Oct	1969:	Modern Jazz Quartet - Space - SAPCOR10
Nov	1969:	John Lennon and Yoko Ono - The Wedding Album - SAPCOR11
Dec	1969:	Plastic Ono Band - Live Peace In Toronto 1969 - CORE2001
Jan	1970:	Badfinger - Magic Christian Music - SAPCOR12
Mar	1970:	Ringo Starr - Sentimental Journey - PCS7101
Apr	1970:	Paul McCartney - McCartney - PCS7102
May	1970:	The Beatles - Let It Be (boxed set with book) - PXS1
Sep	1970:	Doris Troy - Doris Troy - SAPCOR13
Sep	1970:	Billy Preston - Encouraging Words - SAPCOR14
Sep	1970:	John Tavener - The Whale - SAPCOR15
Sep	1970:	Ringo Starr - Beaucoups Of Blues - PAS10002
Nov	1970:	The Beatles - Let It Be (standard issue, no book) - PCS7096
Nov	1970:	Badfinger - No Dice - SAPCOR16
Nov	1970:	George Harrison - All Things Must Pass - STCH639
Dec	1970:	John Lennon - John Lennon/Plastic Ono Band - PCS7124
Dec	1970:	Yoko Ono - Yoko Ono/Plastic Ono Band - SAPCOR17
Dec	1970:	The Beatles - From Then To You (fan club only release of collected Christmas messages) - LYN2154
May	1971:	Radha Krishna Temple - Radha Krishna Temple - SAPCOR18
May	1971:	Paul and Linda McCartney - Ram - PAS10003
July	1971:	John Tavener - Celtic Requiem - SAPCOR20
Oct	1971:	Mary Hopkin - Earth Song/Ocean Song - SAPCOR21
Oct	1971:	John Lennon - Imagine - PAS10004
Dec	1971:	Yoko Ono - Fly - SAPTU101/2
Dec	1971:	Wings - Wild Life - PCS7142
Jan	1972:	Various Artists - The Concert For Bangla Desh - STCX3385
Feb	1972:	Badfinger - Straight Up - SAPCOR19
Sep	1972:	John Lennon/Yoko Ono - Sometime In New York City - PCSP716

Nov	1972:	Elephant's Memory - Elephant's Memory - SAPCOR22
Nov	1972:	Mary Hopkin - Those Were The Days - SAPCOR23
Dec	1972:	Various Artists - Phil Spector's Christmas Album - APCOR24
Feb	1973:	Lon and Derrek Van Eaton - Brother - SAPCOR25
Feb	1973:	Yoko Ono - Approximately Infinite Universe - SAPDO1001
Apr	1973:	Ravi Shankar - In Concert 1972 - SAPDO1002
Apr	1973:	The Beatles - 1962-1966 (red album) - PCSP717
Apr	1973:	The Beatles - 1967-1970 (blue album) - PCSP718
May	1973:	Paul McCartney and Wings - Red Rose Speedway - PCTC251
June	1973:	George Harrison - Living In The Material World - PAS10006
Nov	1973:	Ringo Starr - Ringo - PCTC252
Nov	1973:	John Lennon - Mind Games - PCS7165
Nov	1973:	Yoko Ono - Feeling The Space - SAPCOR26
Dec	1973:	Paul McCartney & Wings - Band On The Run - PAS10007
Mar	1974:	Badfinger - Ass - SAPCOR27
Oct	1974:	John Lennon - Walls And Bridges – PCS253
Nov	1974:	Ringo Starr - Goodnight Vienna - PCS7168
Dec	1974:	George Harrison - Dark Horse - PAS10008
Feb	1975:	John Lennon - Rock 'N' Roll - PCS7169
Oct	1975:	George Harrison - Extra Texture (Read All About It) - PAS10009
Oct	1975:	John Lennon - Shaved Fish (Collectable Lennon) - PCS7173
Dec	1975:	Ringo Starr - Blast From Your Past - PCS7170
Mar	1995:	Badfinger - The Best Of Badfinger - SAPCOR28

Apple US Discography:

US Singles

Aug	1968:	The Beatles - Hey Jude/Revolution - 2276
Aug	1968:	Black Dyke Mills Band - Thingumybob/ Yellow Submarine - Apple 1800
Aug	1968:	Mary Hopkin - Those Were The Days/Turn Turn Turn - 1801
Aug	1968:	Jackie Lomax - Sour Milk Sea/ The Eagle Laughs At You - 1802
Jan	1969:	Iveys - Maybe Tomorrow/ And Her Daddy's A Millionaire - 1803
Mar	1969:	Trash - Road To Nowhere/Illusions - 1804
Mar	1969:	James Taylor - Carolina In My Mind/Taking It In - 1805
Apr	1969:	Mary Hopkin - Goodbye/Sparrow - Apple 1806
May	1969:	The Beatles - Get Back/Don't Let Me Down - 2490
Jun	1969:	Jackie Lomax - New Day/Thumbin' A Ride - 1807
Jun	1969:	Beatles - The Ballad Of John & Yoko/ Old Brown Shoe - 2351
July	1969:	Billy Preston - That's The Way God Planned It/ What About You - 1808
July	1969:	Plastic Ono Band - Give Peace A Chance/Remember - 1809
Aug	1969:	Radha Krishna Temple - Hare Krishna Mantra/ Prayer To The Spiritual Masters - 1810
Oct	1969:	Trash - Golden Slumbers - Carry That Weight/Trash - 1811
Oct	1969:	Hot Chocolate - Give Peace A Chance/ Living Without Tomorrow - 1812
Oct	1969:	Plastic Ono Band - Cold Turkey/Don't Worry Kyoko - 1813
Oct	1969:	Billy Preston - Everything's Alright/ I Want To Thank You - 1814
Oct	1969:	The Beatles - Something/Come Together - 2654
Jan	1970:	Badfinger - Come And Get It/Rock Of Ages - 1815
Jan	1970:	Mary Hopkin - Temma Harbour/ Lontano Dagli Occhi - 1816
Feb	1970:	Billy Preston - All That I've Got/As I Get Older - 1817
Feb	1970:	Lennon/Ono/Plastic Ono Band - Instant Karma/ Who Has Seen The Wind? - 1818
Mar	1970:	Jackie Lomax - How The Web Was Woven/ I Fall Inside Your Eyes - 1819

Mar 1970: Doris Troy - Ain't That Cute/Vaya Con Dios - 1820

Mar 1970: Radha Krishna Temple - Govinda/Govinda Jai Jai - 1821

Mar 1970: The Beatles - Let It Be/You Know My Name (Look Up The Number) - 2764

Jun 1970: Mary Hopkin - Que Sera, Sera/Fields Of St. Etienne – 1823

Sep 1970: Ringo Starr - Beaucoups Of Blues/Coochy-Coo - 2969

Sep 1970: Doris Troy - Jacob's Ladder/Get Back - 1824

Oct 1970: Badfinger - No Matter What/ Carry On Till Tomorrow - 1822

Oct 1970: Mary Hopkin - Think About Your Children/Heritage - 1825

Nov 1970: George Harrison - My Sweet Lord/Isn't It A Pity - 2995

Dec 1970: Billy Preston - My Sweet Lord/Little Girl - 1826

Dec 1970: John Lennon - Mother/Why? - 1827

Feb 1971: George Harrison - What Is Life?/Apple Scruffs - 1828

Feb 1971: Paul McCartney - Another Day/ Oh Woman, Oh Why? - 1829

Mar 1971: John Lennon/Plastic Ono Band - Power To The People/Touch Me- 1830

Apr 1971: Ringo Starr - It Don't Come Easy/Early 1970 - 1831

Apr 1971: Ronnie Spector - Try Some, Buy Some/ Tandoori Chicken – 1832

Jun 1971: Jackie Lomax - Sour Milk Sea/ I Fall Inside Your Eyes - 1834

July 1971: Bill Elliot & Elastic Oz Band - God Save Us/ Do The Oz - 1835

July 1971: George Harrison - Bangla Desh/Deep Blue - 1836

Sep 1971: Paul & Linda McCartney - Uncle Albert, Admiral Halsey/Too Many People - 1837

Aug 1971: Ravi Shankar - Joi Bangla/Oh Bhaugowan/ Raga Mishra-Jhinjhoti - 1838

Sep 1971: Yoko Ono - Mrs. Lennon/Midsummer In New York - 1839

Oct 1971: John Lennon - Imagine/It's So Hard - 1840

Nov 1971: Badfinger - Day After Day/Sweet Tuesday Morning - 1841

Dec 1971: John Lennon/Yoko Ono - Happy Xmas (War Is Over)/Listen, The Snow Is Falling - 1842

Dec 1971: Mary Hopkin - Water, Paper And Clay/ Streets Of London - 1843

Mar	1972:	Badfinger - Baby Blue/Flying - 1844
Mar	1972:	Lon and Derrek Van Eaton - Sweet Music/ Song Of Songs -1845
Feb	1972:	Wings - Give Ireland Back To The Irish/(version) - 1847
Mar	1972:	Ringo Starr - Back Off Boogaloo/Blindman - 1849
Apr	1972:	John Lennon/Yoko Ono - Woman Is The Nigger Of The World/ Sisters O' Sisters - 1848
Apr	1972:	Wings - Mary Had A Little Lamb/ Little Woman Love - 1851
May	1972:	Chris Hodge - We're On Our Way/Supersoul - 1850
Sep	1972:	Sundown Playboys - Saturday Night Special/ Valse De Soleil Coucher - 1852
Nov	1972:	Yoko Ono - Now Or Never/Move On Fast - 1853
Nov	1972:	Elephant's Memory - Liberation Special/ Power Boogie - 1854
Nov	1972:	Mary Hopkin - Knock Knock Who's There?/ International - 1855
Dec	1972:	Wings - Hi, Hi, Hi/C Moon - 1857
Jan	1973:	Chris Hodge - Goodbye Sweet Lorraine/ Contact Love - 1858
Feb	1973:	Yoko Ono - Death Of Samantha/Yang Yang - 1859
Apr 1973:		Paul McCartney - My Love/The Mess - 1861
May	1973:	George Harrison - Give Me Love/Miss O'Dell - 1862
Apr 1973:		Wings - Live And Let Die/I Lie Around - 1863
Sep	1973:	Ringo Starr - Photograph/Down And Out - 1865
Sep	1973:	Yoko Ono - Woman Power/Men Men Men - 1867
Oct	1973:	John Lennon - Mind Games/Meat City - 1868
Nov	1973:	Paul McCartney/Wings - Helen Wheels/ Country Dreamer - 1869
Dec	1973:	Badfinger - Apple Of My Eye/Blind Owl - 1864
Dec	1973:	Ringo Starr - You're Sixteen/Devil Woman - 1870
Jan	1974:	Paul McCartney/Wings - Jet/Let Me Roll It - 1871
Feb	1974:	Ringo Starr - Oh My My/Step Lightly - 1872
Apr 1974:		Paul McCartney/Wings - Band On the Run/ Nineteen Hundred Eighty Five - 1873
Sep	1974:	John Lennon - Whatever Gets You Thru' The Night/ Beef Jerky - 1874
Nov	1974:	Paul McCartncy/Wings - Junior's Farm/Sally G - 1875
Nov	1974:	Ringo Starr - Only You/Call Me - 1876
Nov	1974:	George Harrison - Dark Horse/ I Don't Care Anymore - 1877

Dec 1974: John Lennon - No. 9 Dream/What You Got - 1878
Dec 1974: George Harrison - Ding Dong, Ding Dong/
Hari's On Tour - 1879
Jan 1975: Ringo Starr - No No Song/Snookeroo - 1880
Mar 1975: John Lennon - Stand By Me/Move Over Mrs. L - 1881
Jun 1975: Goodnight Vienna/Oo-Wee - 1882
Sep 1975: George Harrison - You/World Of Stone - 1884
Dec 1975: George Harrison - This Guitar/Maya Love - 1885

US LPs
Nov 1968: The Beatles - The Beatles (White album) - SWBO 101
Nov 1968: John Lennon and Yoko Ono - Unfinished Music No. 1,
Two Virgins - T 5001
Dec 1968: George Harrison - Wonderwall Music - ST 3350
Jan 1969: The Beatles - Yellow Submarine - SW 153
Feb 1969: James Taylor - James Taylor - SKAO 3352
Feb 1969: Modern Jazz Quartet - Under The Jasmine Tree -
ST 3353
Mar 1969: Mary Hopkin - Postcard - SW 3351
May 1969: Jackie Lomax - Is This What You Want - ST 3354
May 1969: John Lennon and Yoko Ono - Unfinished Music No 2,
Life With The Lions - SW 3357
May 1969: George Harrison - Electronic Sound - ST 3358
July 1969: The Iveys - Maybe Tomorrow - ST 3355 (Not Issued)
Sep 1969: Billy Preston - That's The Way God Planned It -
ST 3359
Oct 1969: The Beatles - Abbey Road - SW 383
Nov 1969: Modern Jazz Quartet - Space - STAO 3360
Oct 1969: John Lennon and Yoko Ono - The Wedding Album -
SMAX 3361
Dec 1969: Plastic Ono Band - Live Peace In Toronto 1969 -
SW 3362
Feb 1970: The Beatles - Beatles Again - SO 385
Feb 1970: Badfinger - Magic Christian Music - ST 3364
Apr 1970: Paul McCartney - McCartney - SMAS 3363
Apr 1970: Ringo Starr - Sentimental journey - SW 3365
May 1970: The Beatles - Let It Be - AR 34001
Sep 1970: Ringo Starr - Beaucoups Of Blues - SMAS 3368
Nov 1970: Badfinger - No Dice - ST 3367
Nov 1970: John Tavener - The Whale - SMAS 3369
Nov 1970: Billy Preston - Encouraging Words - ST 3370
Nov 1970: Doris Troy - Doris Troy - ST 3371

Nov 1970:   George Harrison - All Things Must Pass - STCH 639
Dec 1970:   John Lennon - John Lennon/Plastic Ono Band -
              SW 3372
Dec 1970:   Yoko Ono - Yoko Ono/Plastic Ono Band - SW 3373
Dec 1970:   The Beatles - From Then To You (fan club only
              release of collected Christmas messages) – SBC 100
May 1971:   Paul and Linda McCartney - Ram - SMAS 3375
May 1971:   Radha Krishna Temple - Radha Krishna Temple -
              SKAO 3376
Sep 1971:   Soundtrack - "Come Together" - SW 3377
Sep 1971:   John Lennon - Imagine - SW 3379
Nov 1971:   Mary Hopkin - Earth Song/Ocean Song - SMAS 3381
Dec 1971:   Yoko Ono - Fly - SVBB 3380
Dec 1971:   Soundtrack - "Raga" - SWAO 3384
Dec 1971:   Various Artists - The Concert For Bangla Desh -
              STCX3385
Dec 1971:   Wings - Wild Life - SW 3386
Dec 1971:   Badfinger - Straight Up - SW 3387
Dec 1971:   Soundtrack - "El Topo" - SWAO 3388
Apr 1972:   David Peel - The Pope Smokes Dope - SW 3391
Jun 1972:   John Lennon/Yoko Ono -
              Sometime In New York City - SVBB 3392
Sep 1972:   Elephant's Memory - Elephant's Memory -
              SMAS 3389
Sep 1972:   Lon and Derrek Van Eaton - Brother - SMAS 3390
Sep 1972:   Mary Hopkin - Those Were The Days - SW 3395
Dec 1972:   Various Artists - Phil Spector's Christmas Album -
              SW 3400
Jan 1973:   Ravi Shankar - In Concert 1972 - SVBB 3396
Jan 1973:   Yoko Ono - Approximately Infinite Universe -
              SVBB 3399
Apr 1973:   The Beatles - 1962-1966 (red album) - SKBO 3403
Apr 1973:   The Beatles - 1967-1970 (blue album) - SKBO 3404
Apr 1973:   Paul McCartney and Wings - Red Rose Speedway -
              SMAL 3409
May 1973:   George Harrison - Living In The Material World -
              SMAS 3410
Nov 1973:   Badfinger - Ass - SW 3411
Nov 1973:   Yoko Ono - Feeling The Space - SW 3412
Nov 1973:   Ringo Starr - Ringo - SWAL 3413
Nov 1973:   John Lennon - Mind Games - SW 3414
Dec 1973:   Paul McCartney & Wings - Band On The Run -

		SO 3415
Sep	1974:	John Lennon - Walls And Bridges - SW 3416
Nov	1974:	Ringo Starr - Goodnight Vienna - SW 3417
Dec	1974:	George Harrison - Dark Horse - SMAS 3418
Feb	1975:	John Lennon - Rock 'N' Roll - SK 3419
Sep	1975:	George Harrison - Extra Texture (Read All About It) - SW 3420
Oct	1975:	John Lennon - Shaved Fish (Collectable Lennon) - SW 3421
Nov	1975:	Ringo Starr - Blast From Your Past - SW 3422
Mar	1995:	Badfinger - Best Of - 8301292

Additional Resources

If you are a former Apple artist, employee or scruff, I would be very interested in hearing your thoughts on this book and would like to include your story in future editions. Please email me directly at: applebook2002@aol.com.

If you enjoyed this book and are interested in finding out more about Apple and the artists who recorded for Apple Records, there are many web sites and publications that will be of interest.

Apple:

Ken Mansfield has written a wonderful book about his time as Manager of Apple (and his life after Apple) called "The Beatles, The Bible and Bodega Bay." To learn more about his book, please visit:

www.fabwhitebook.com

Applelog is the definitive discography and price guide for US and Canadian Apple Records releases and promotional items. The Applelog series also includes publications that focus on Apple Studios and Apple press advertisements. For more information, please visit:

http://infoweb.magi.com/~design1/Applelog1.html

Badfinger:

If anyone can be considered a Badfinger expert, it's Dan Matovina. His meticulously researched book, "Without You," is a must-read for any fan of rock music, let alone those with an interest in Badfinger, The Beatles or Apple. While supplies last, the latest edition of the book comes with a limited edition CD of unissued Badfinger and Iveys recordings. To learn more about "Without You" and for updates on the forthcoming 4-CD "Anthology" of previously unreleased Iveys' demos and live tracks, please visit:

www.mindspring.com/~crimson3 or www.badfinger-iveys.com

You can also cmail Dan directly at: crimson3@mindspring.com

Badfinger/Iveys drummer Mike Gibbins has an excellent website at www.mikegibbins.com that features a history of The Iveys, a gallery of never before seen Iveys and Badfinger photos and more. You can also purchase Mike's solo albums and rare Badfinger recordings on the site.

For a peerless online library of recording session data, record release info, vintage concert listings, news and more for Badfinger, The Iveys and Dark Horse artists Splinter, visit Tom Brennan's "Badfinger Library" at:

http://home.earthlink.net/~tomjbr/Tom/BadfingerIveys/Badfinger.html

Mary Hopkin:

The New Mary Hopkin Friendly Society (named after the original Mary Hopkin fan club) is the premier Mary Hopkin web site on the internet. For updates on the latest activities of Mary Hopkin, a comprehensive history and discography, and much more, visit:

http://homepage.ntlworld.com/pat.richmonds/newmhfs.htm

Jackie Lomax:

To learn more about the remarkable four-decade career of Jackie Lomax (including details on his new 2001 album), be sure to visit:

www.jackielomax.com

Record Companies:

For superb reissues of albums by some of the groups mentioned in this book, including John's Children (the band led by Apple Publishing's John Hewlett), Misunderstood (featuring Apple Publishing writer Tony Hill) and Tony Rivers and The Castaways (who evolved into Grapefruit), be sure to visit RPM Records at:

http://www.rpmrecords.co.uk

Acknowledgements

This book could not have been written if not for the generosity of time and spirit of the following individuals who graciously agreed to share their Apple memories, photos and memorabilia. Special thanks must be given to Bill Oakes, who convinced me that this project could be done, and George Peckham, for his hospitality and genuine enthusiasm for Apple, life and music. Many thanks also go to (in alphabetical order): Peter Asher, John Barham, John Beland, Peter Bennett, Tony Bramwell, Dan Bridgeman, Peter Brown, Mrs. Daphne Brown, Terry Doran, Rick Frank, Stephen Friedland, Mike Gibbins, Tom Hanley, John Hewlett, Chris Hodge, Tony King, Kosh, John Lewis, Jackie Lomax, Ken Mansfield, Guy Masson, Joe Molland, Charlie Nuccio, Jack Oliver, Nigel Oliver, May Pang, David Peel, John Perry, Pat Savant, Tom & Joy Smith, Al Steckler, Geoff Swettenham, Doris Troy, Lon and Constance Van Eaton, Derrek Van Eaton.

I am also greatly indebted to the staff of Cherry Red Publishing, especially Iain McNay, who took on this project and was dedicated to creating a truly exceptional book, Paul Widger for his expert advice and editing and Jim Phelan and Sarah Reed for their help with the cover, graphics, layout and photo editing. I would also like to thank Dan Matovina, for his help with contacts, proof-reading and photos, and for helping inspire this project with his superb Badfinger book, "Without You," Pat Richmond, Matt Hurwitz, Kristopher Engelhardt (for contacts and encouragement), Nick Johnstone, Shane Arbogast, Sean Body at Helter Skelter Books, Neil Smithies, Keith James, Chris Charlesworth, Richard Younger, and Jeff Levy.

Thanks must also go to my parents, Johanna and Bob, for raising me in a home full of music and for purchasing my first Apple 45s (Badfinger's *Day After Day*, *No Matter What*, and Paul McCartney's *Helen Wheels*, if you must know, all packaged together for 79 cents!) so many years ago.

And finally, I thank my wife Margaret, for her encouragement, love, proof-reading and for allowing me to conduct interviews while we honeymooned in the UK! I truly could not have done this without you.

Photos from the personal collections of: Jack Oliver, Al Steckler, Pat Richmond, John Perry, Tony King, John Hewlett, George Peckham, Dan Matovina, Stephen Friedland, Guy Masson and Tom Smith.

Bibliography

Primary Book Sources

Badman, Keith *The Beatles Diary Volume 2: After The Break-Up, 1970-2001* (Omnibus UK 2000)

Beatles *The Anthology* (Chronicle Books US 2000)

Brown, Peter *The Love You Make: An Insider's Story Of The Beatles.* (McGraw Hill U.S. 1983)

Castleman, Harry and Podrazik, Walter *All Together Now: The First Complete Beatles Discography, 1961-1975* (Ann Arbor: Pierian Press U.S. 1976)

Clayson, Alan *Ringo Starr: Straight Man Or Joker?* (Sidgwick and Jackson U.K. 1991)

Coleman, Ray *Lennon* (McGraw Hill U.S. 1984)

DiLello, Richard *The Longest Cocktail Party* (Playboy Publishing U.S. 1972)

Engelhardt, Kristofer *Beatles Undercover* (Collector's Guide Publishing Canada 1998)

Fletcher, Tony *Moon: The Life And Death Of A Rock Legend* (Harper Entertainment U.S. 2000)

Giuliano, Geoffrey *Dark Horse: The Private Life Of George Harrison* (Plume Publishing U.S. 1991)

Haydon, Geoffrey *John Tavener: Glimpses Of Paradise* (Victor Gollancz UK 1995)

Jackson, Tim *Virgin King* (Harper Collins UK 1995)

Levy, Jeff *Apple – Log IV: A Guide For The U.S. & Canadian Apple Records Collector* (MonhunProd Media Group Canada 1990)

Bibliography

Lewisohn, Mark *The Complete Beatles Chronicle* (Harmony Books U.S. 1992)

Mansfield, Ken *The Beatles, The Bible, And Bodega Bay* (Broadman & Holman U.S. 2000)

Matovina, Dan *Without You: The Tragic Story Of Badfinger* (Frances Glover Books U.S. 1997)

McCabe, Peter and Schoenfeld, Robert *Apple To The Core* (Pocket Books U.S.1972)

Miles, Barry *Many Years From Now* (Henry Holt and Company U.S. 1997)

Neaverson, Bob *The Beatles Movie*s (Cassell U.K. 1997)

Norman, Phillip *Shout* (Simon and Schuster U.S. 1981)

Pang, May *Loving John* (Warner Books U.S. 1983)

Schaffner, Nicholas *The Beatles Forever* (McGraw Hill U.S. 1978)

Shotten, Pete *John Lennon: In My Life* (Stein and Day Publishers U.S. 1983)

Taylor, Derek *As Time Goes By* (Pierian Press U.S. 1983)

Taylor, Derek *Fifty Years Adrift* (Genesis U.K. 1985)

Wilkie, Jim *Blue Suede Brogans: Scenes From The Secret Life Of Scottish Rock Music* (Mainstream Publishing UK 1991)

Zimmer, Dave *Crosby, Stills & Nash: The Authorized Biography* (St. Martins Press U.S. 1984)

Primary Magazine Sources

Alterman, Loraine "The Ballad Of Todd Rundgren" *Melody Maker* March 25, 1972

Charlesworth, Chris "Whatever Happened To Sweet Little Mary." *Melody Maker* June 26, 1971

Dallas, Karl "The Real Mary" *Melody Maker* January 22, 1972

Davis, Andy "Apple Records Beyond The Beatles." *Record Collector*

DeYoung, Bill "She's A Joan Baez Type, But We'll Soon Alter That." *Goldmine* April 14, 1995

Doggett, Peter "Apple Records: The Beatles Great Experiment." *Record Collector*, August 1988

Du Noyer, Paul "Just Out Of Shot" *Mojo* October 1996

Fong-Torres, Ben "That's The Way He Planned It." *Rolling Stone* September 15, 1971

Greenfield, Bob "Jackie Lomax Is Leaving London" *Rolling Stone* November 26, 1970

Hennessey, Mike "Apple Plans To Invade U.S." *Billboard* January 11, 1969

Hodenfield, Jan "Ethel? It's Me, Yeah Doreen" *Rolling Stone* June 11, 1970

Hopkins, Jerry "James Taylor On Apple: The Same Old Craperoo" *Rolling Stone* August 23, 1969

Hurwitz, Matt "Meet The Real Percy Thrillington" *Good Day Sunshine*

Irwin, Colin "Harrison's Dark Horses" *Melody Maker* August 1974

Bibliography

Johnson, John "Death And Taxes: An Interview With Badfinger's Joey Mollard" *DISCoveries* February 1991

King, Bill "*Beatlefan*" – Various issues

Miles, Barry "My Blue Period" *Mojo* November 1995

Moseley, Willie "Golden Apple Days." *Vintage Guitar* 1996

Newcomb, Peter and La Franco, Robert "All You Need Is Love And Royalties" *Forbes* September 25, 1995

Norman, Phillip "The Circus Has Left Town But We Still Own The Site." Unknown Publication

"Our staff" "The Beatles: You Never Give Me Your Money" *Rolling Stone* November 15, 1969

Pearson, Stan "Paul's Shout Up At Shipley" *Melody Maker* July 13, 1968

Schwartz, Francie "Memories Of An Apple Girl" *Rolling Stone* November 15, 1969

Simmons, Sylvie "The Fall And Rise Of Apple" *Request* 1996

Skiera, Peter "Listening To Lomax" *Good Day Sunshine*

Tiegel, Elliot "Beatles Apple Firm Picking US Core Of Staffers, Artist Roster" *Billboard* June 11, 1968

Vetter, Craig "Playboy Interview: Allen Klein" *Playboy* 1971

Walsh, Alan "Has Apple Gone Sour?" *Melody Maker* November 1968

Watts, Michael "Preston Power" *Melody Maker* February 5, 1972

Watts, Michael "Ringo" *Melody Maker* July 24, 1971

Welch, Chris "Why Grapefruit Squeezed Out Of Apple" *Melody Maker* November 30, 1968

Wells, David "Fire" *Record Collector* January 1999

White, Adam and Mulligan, Brian "A Dead Apple In London; Apple's Staff Gets Pared" *Billboard* May 10, 1975

Williams, Richard "Doris Troy And The Marriage Of Music." *Melody Maker* March 7, 1970

Wilson, Tony "George, The A&R Man With A New Discovery." *Melody Maker* September 1968

Bibliography

Sleeve Notes

Davis, Andy. Mary Hopkin: "Those Were The Days" (Apple/EMI) 1992

Davis, Andy. John Tavener: "Celtic Requiem" (Apple/EMI) 1993

Davis, Andy. John Tavener: "The Whale" (Apple/EMI) 1992

Doggett, Peter. Billy Preston: "Encouraging Words" (Apple/EMI) 1993

Kolanjian, Steve. Jackie Lomax: "Is This What You Want" (Apple/EMI) 1991

Kolanjian, Steve. James Taylor: "James Taylor" (Apple/EMI) 1991

Taylor, Derek. George Harrison: "Wonderwall" (Apple/EMI) 1992

Taylor, Derek. Mary Hopkin: "Earth Song/Ocean Song" (Apple/EMI) 1992

Taylor, Derek. Radha Krsna Temple: "The Radha Krsna Temple" London (Apple/EMI) 1993

Index

Index

Index

Index

Also available from

CHERRY RED BOOKS

Indie Hits 1980-1989
The Complete UK Independent Charts (Singles & Albums)

Compiled by Barry Lazell

Indie Hits is the first and only complete guide to the first decade of Britain's
Independent records chart, and to the acts, the music and the labels which made up
the Indie scene of the 1980s.

Paper covers, 314 pages, £14.99 in UK

Cor Baby, That's Really Me!
(New Millennium Hardback Edition)

John Otway

It is the story of a man who …
*   has never repaid a record company advance in his life
*   once put on a benefit concert for his record company after they had cancelled his contract
*   signed himself to the mighty Warner Bros label simply by pressing his own records with
    the WB logo
*   broke up with Paula Yates telling her it was the last chance she would get to go out with
    a rock star

Hardback, 192 pages and 16 pages of photographs, £11.99 in UK

All the Young Dudes
Mott the Hoople and Ian Hunter The Biography

Campbell Devine

Devoid of borrowed information and re-cycled press clippings, this official biography
contains new, sensational and humorous inside stories, controversial quotes and an
array of private and previously unpublished views from the band, embellished with
comprehensive appendices including discographies and session listings.

Paper covers, 448 pages and 16 pages of photographs, £14.99 in UK

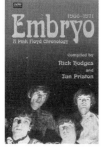

Embryo
A Pink Floyd Chronology 1966 – 1971

Nick Hodges & Ian Priston

'Embryo: A Pink Floyd Chronology' is the most fully comprehensive and in-depth study
of the early work of the Pink Floyd that has been compiled to date.

Paper covers, 302 pages and photographs throughout, £14.99 in UK

www.cherryred.co.uk

Also available from

CHERRY RED BOOKS

In Cold Blood
Johnny Thunders

Nina Antonia

Nina Antonia's book is a detailed, inside look at the life of Thunders, right through his career from his early pre-Heartbreakers days to his tragic death in 1991.

The book comes with a 10 track CD.

Paper covers, 270 pages and photographs throughout, £14.99 in UK

Songs In The Key Of Z
The Curious Universe of Outsider Music

Irwin Chusid

This book profiles dozens of outsider musicians, both prominent and obscure, and presents their strange life stories along with photographs, interviews, cartoons and discographies.

Paper covers, 311 pages, fully illustrated, £11.99 in UK

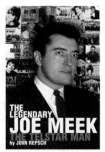

The Legendary Joe Meek
The Telstar Man

John Repsch

JOE MEEK was a mystery. He was Britain's first independent pop record producer and one of the most important figures in that fabulous decade of Sixties music.

Paper covers, 350 pages plus photographs £14.99 in UK

Random Precision
Recording The Music Of Syd Barrett 1965 – 1974

David Parker

The author David Parker was co-editor of the respected Syd Barrett fanzine 'Chapter 24', and has spent four years researching and writing this book, which is based principally on information obtained from the official archives at EMI Records and Abbey Road Studios.

Paper covers, 320 pages, photographs throughout, £14.99 in UK

www.cherryred.co.uk

Also available from

CHERRY RED BOOKS

Rockdetector
A-Z of BLACK METAL

Garry Sharpe-Young

For over a decade Black Metal has spawned legions of bands making up a truly global rebellion. For the first time ever this ultimate authority documents detailed biographies, line-ups and full discographies with track listings of over 2,000 groups.

Paper covers, 416 pages, £14.99 in UK

Rockdetector
A-Z of DEATH METAL

Garry Sharpe-Young

Reviled and revered in equal measure since its inception over a decade ago, the phenomenon known as Death Metal has pushed Hard Rock music to the very edge of acceptability and way beyond.

Paper covers, 366 pages, £14.99 in UK

www.cherryred.co.uk

CHERRY RED BOOKS

We are always looking for interesting books to publish.
They can be either new manuscripts or re-issues of deleted books.
If you have any good ideas then please
get in touch with us.

CHERRY RED BOOKS
a division of Cherry Red Records Ltd.
Unit 17, Elysium Gate West,
126-128 New King's Road
London sw6 4LZ

E-mail: iain@cherryred.co.uk
Web: www.cherryred.co.uk